Y0-BUM-867

Huntington Library Publications

James Claypoole's Letter Book
London and Philadelphia
1681-1684

EDITED BY MARION BALDERSTON

THE HUNTINGTON LIBRARY
SAN MARINO, CALIFORNIA
1967

COPYRIGHT 1967 HENRY E. HUNTINGTON LIBRARY AND ART GALLERY
Library of Congress Catalog Card Number 66-25063
Printed in the United States of America
by Anderson, Ritchie & Simon
Designed by Ward Ritchie

For Jean

Contents

[vii]

Introduction

CLAYPOOLE COAT OF ARMS.

Introduction

FOR THREE YEARS, from May 1681 to April 1684, the London merchant James Claypoole had his letters, about one thousand of them, copied into a large book, now in the possession of the Historical Society of Pennsylvania in Philadelphia. It might be expected that such a letter book would be a dry record of prices, exports and imports, credits and debits, interesting only to economic historians and statisticians.

Claypoole, however, was a friendly, garrulous man who found it hard to write a short formal note. Combined with strictly business affairs are details about his family and his fellow Quakers in London and Philadelphia, all faithfully copied. It is a romantic story, or rather it is three stories, for in addition to chronicling the daily life and trials of a seventeenth-century merchant, the letter book gives details of the trade with the West Indies and tells about the founding of the colony of Pennsylvania, in which he had an important part. As no man can write a thousand letters without giving away a great deal about himself, it is appropriate that James should emerge as the hero —although not always very heroic—of this tale.

James Claypoole was a younger son of a Northamptonshire family which rose from obscurity to the upper middle class in the 1540's, purchased Northborough Manor (called Norborough) and other lands in the northeast tip of that county, acquired a coat of arms, a handsome tomb in their own private chapel, and other amenities considered necessary to the good life in that period.[1]

[1]John Bridges, *The History and Antiquities of Northamptonshire* (Oxford, 1791), II, 529; *The Victoria History of the County of Northampton*, II (London, 1906), 508-509; Rebecca Graaf, *The Claypoole Family* (Philadelphia, 1893).

Here James was born in 1634, one of fourteen children, eight boys and six girls, and was brought up in the rough luxury of the seventeenth century.[2] The yeomen Claypooles were rising in the world; James's grandfather Adam had married into the family of the great Lord Burghley of Elizabeth's time, and his father, John, married the daughter of a wealthy London merchant. Young Claypooles went to the university and then to study law at Gray's Inn. When James was twelve, his oldest brother, John, carried the family to near nobility by marrying Elizabeth, Oliver Cromwell's favorite daughter. She was seventeen.

After a brief period at Norborough, the young couple followed her father, living in the royal palaces Cromwell had annexed. John was addressed as "Lord Claypoole" and Elizabeth as "Princess." The other brothers benefited: Wingfield was captain, later colonel, of horse in Cromwell's army; Edward, a captain of foot; and Graveley, a cornet, the lad who carried the colors. Robert became a merchant; Norton and Benjamin, small boys, were either at home or at school.

As the fifth son, James had no share in the family properties and apparently no taste for a military career. He was sent, perhaps around 1650 when he was sixteen, to be apprenticed to a merchant in Bremen. He learned the language sufficiently well so that in later life his letters to Hamburg and Bremen were written in German. In England his family continued to accumulate honors. His father was knighted and given important posts by Cromwell; his brother John became one of the lords of the bedchamber—for by this time there was very little difference between Cromwell's household and the royal court—then ranger of Whittlebury Forest, then master of the horse. All these offices entitled him to take a leading part in court ceremonies, always richly dressed. Though never actually ennobled, he sat in the House of Lords. It was wonderful while it lasted.

Meantime James had completed his apprenticeship, and in 1658 in Bremen he was married to Helen, or Helena, Mercer by a Calvinist minister. Shortly after this he returned to London and set up in business for himself. Possibly this was because Cromwell had adopted a more lenient policy toward dissenters, and James was now thinking independently about religion; more probably it was because his

[2]In order of birth: Mary, John, Elizabeth, Robert, Wingfield, Graveley, Dorothy, Frances, James, Edward, two Marthas (one died very young), Norton, and Benjamin.

brother Robert, a merchant, had just died and there was a business to inherit. As he wrote later, he settled in Nicholas Lane, within the City, and there his first child, John, was born at the end of 1658.[3]

He never benefited from his family's brief importance. His brother John's wife died in August of that year and John's father-in-law, the Protector, in September. James may have gone to the strange midnight ceremony when Elizabeth Cromwell Claypoole was buried among royalty in the Henry VII chapel of Westminster Abbey.[4] He may have watched Cromwell's elaborate funeral procession a few weeks later and the last ceremonial appearance of his brother John, who walked before the coffin, leading the riderless horse.

He took no part in the shifting politics of the time but applied himself to building up his business. His brothers made their peace with the Royalists. John went back to Norborough with his son Cromwell Claypoole and several members of the Protector's family, and in one year he was in debt.

James moved shortly to Mincing Lane, and his next child, Mary, was born there in 1660. Finally he settled in Scots Yard, where his third child, Helen or Eleanor, was born in 1662, and there he remained until he left London for Philadelphia twenty-one years later.

He described Scots Yard in many of his letters as being "by London Stone." At that time, London Stone stood on the south side of Cannon Street, where some Roman had placed it, probably to mark the center of Londinium, and there it had remained through all those centuries. It had always been a famous landmark; ancient maps marked their towns as being so many miles from London Stone. It survived the Great Fire of 1666, and James continued to use it as a means of directing people to his home.[5] Visitors to James's house turned off Cannon Street, walked downhill along Bush Lane, and turned sharply right into Scots Yard, where, according to his letters,

[3]Claypoole's own account, *Pennsylvania Magazine of History and Biography*, XIV (1890), 86-87.

[4]See R. W. Ramsey, "Elizabeth Claypole," *English Historical Review*, VII (1892), 37-47; see also the articles on John Claypoole and Elizabeth Claypoole in the *Dictionary of National Biography*. Her funeral is said to have cost only £26; this is not in the Registers of Westminster Abbey, but in the Westminster Muniment, No. 6368.

[5]Built into the wall of St. Swithin's Church, across Cannon Street from its original spot, when the Railway Station was built in the nineteenth century. London Stone was taken away after St. Swithin's was destroyed by bombs and is now built into the Bank of China, which replaced the church.

his was the second house from the corner. Ogilby and Morgan's map of London in 1677 shows a small open square there.[6]

The brothers adjusted in different ways to life without a powerful patron. Edward entered Gray's Inn to study law[7] but gave it up and went to Barbados, where he married a rich widow, managed a plantation, and exported sugar to James to sell. Norton, being "in straits," joined him for a time but went on to New York and finally settled near New Castle, now Delaware, on land bought with money borrowed from James.[8] Graveley and Wingfield were in the country, presumably in or near Norborough; Graveley made and sometimes exported cider.

The restless John had some notion of being a physician and was admitted as an "Extra-Licentiate" at the College of Physicians in 1676,[9] but he never qualified as a doctor. He mended his fortunes temporarily by marrying a wealthy widow, by whom he had a daughter, but his temper was so bad that she left him after five years, complaining that he had run through her dowry of £10,000. He became a second-rate journalist.[10]

Shortly after settling in London, James and Helena joined the Friends. This was certainly before 1661, for in September of that year they attended the Quaker marriage of a Robert Dunton to Ann James, and after that their names appeared frequently on other Quaker wedding certificates.[11] They went to the Bull and Mouth Meeting, where by the 1670's James was an important member. He and Helena were present at William Penn's wedding in 1672.[12]

His fourth child, the religious son James, was born in Scots Yard in 1664, and a daughter, Priscilla, two years after that. They had survived the plague of the year before, but when the new baby was a few months old, the Great Fire of 1666 swept over London. The flames reached Scots Yard at midnight on Sunday, September 2, hav-

[6]Bush Lane runs off Cannon Street, on the east side of the big railway station, and Scots Yard is a right-hand turning. There is still a small open space there.

[7]Joseph Foster, *The Register of Admissions to Gray's Inn, 1521-1889* (London, 1889), p. 283.

[8]*Our Early Emigrant Ancestors: The Original Lists of Persons . . . to the American Plantations*, ed. J. Camden Hotten (New York, 1880), pp. 356, 461, 468.

[9]William Munk, *The Roll of the Royal College of Physicians of London* (London, 1878), I, 388.

[10]*Calendar of State Papers, Domestic, 1680-81*, pp. 466, 468, 477. See also ibid., *1683-84*, p. 53.

[11]Non Parochial Records, now in Public Record Office, Chancery Lane, London.

[12]Ibid. On that occasion Mrs. Claypoole signed her name Helenn.

ing started about one o'clock that morning.[13] In the incredible con-
fusion of that day, James managed to remove his family to the safety
of Horselydown, now part of Bermondsey, on the other side of the
Thames. There the short-lived first Nathaniel was born.

The Claypooles were back again in a rebuilt Scots Yard in time for
the birth (1669) of Josiah, who died the next year at Kingston. After
him came Samuel, 1671, the second Nathaniel, 1672, George in 1674,
the first Joseph who was born and died in 1676, and the second
Joseph a year later. An Elizabeth was born in 1678 but lived only a
few days, and between Nathaniel and George there was a stillborn
son.[14]

In spite of the two catastrophes of plague and fire, James's business
prospered. He had correspondents in Amsterdam, Hamburg, Bremen, Lisbon, Bordeaux, and Ireland, as well as the West Indies. He
had a country home which he described as a "small" place for his
children, where he often went for weekends. From his letters we can
locate this farm as being near Richmond, not far from the Thames.

Scots Yard is the setting in which we find James when the letter
book begins, and it is easy to imagine what it was like. Before the last
war, the City part of London had many such small squares; one at
least, Wardrobe Court, survives today. The houses, after the postfire
fashion, were brick, three to four stories high, with large windows
filled in with oblong panes of glass set in lead, sometimes with quite
large panes framed in wood. There was almost certainly a tree or
two in the center of the small square, for Londoners always managed
to grow trees and flowers in even the tiniest spaces, as they do today.

James was obviously proud of his home, and he entertained in it
the most important Quakers of the time. George Fox stayed with
him; George Whitehead and William Penn were frequent visitors,
while he and Helena more than once traveled to stay with the Penns
at Warminghurst in Sussex. His house was also his office, after the
manner of the time, and he managed his considerable business with
the help of his seventeen-year-old son James and an indentured ap-
prentice, Edward Haistwell.[15] Haistwell had recently signed for

[13]Walter George Bell, *The Great Fire of London in 1666* (London, [1920]).

[14]*PMHB*, XIV, 86-87. Samuel died when he was only ten years old.

[15]Edward Haistwell belonged to a Westmorland family. He traveled with Fox
through England, Holland, and Germany, leading an interesting but strenuous life,
for he became ill in Germany. Perhaps that was why he left Fox and signed with
Claypoole, becoming, in the language of the day, his "servant."

seven years' service with Claypoole, having spent two years traveling with George Fox as amanuensis and companion, keeping what has become known as the Haistwell Diary.

The oldest son, John, is never named as taking any active part in the business, though it is plain from the letters that Claypoole expected all his family to help. John had recently returned from Barbados[16] and from Ireland, where he had got into some mischief, not explained in the letters, and he was sent off to Pennsylvania in the spring of 1682 as an assistant to Thomas Holme, the surveyor general.

James took little interest in the life of his busy, overcrowded city and rarely mentioned anything outside his business or his religious interests. His was the world of the moderately prosperous merchant, concerned with getting "minks" and "catts" from Hudson Bay, sugar from the West Indies, linen and beer from Germany, and wine from Bordeaux, while he acted as banker, bookkeeper, adviser, and errand boy to his foreign correspondents. His weekdays were spent between his Scots Yard house, the docks and Customs House, and the Exchange.

To reach the Exchange, Claypoole would walk up Bush Lane, cross Cannon Street, go along St. Swithin's Lane to Lombard Street, where the goldsmiths had their banking business, and through the narrow Pope's Head Alley to Cornhill. In this new building merchants met to exchange news and gossip, and captains sought goods for their ships. Other times James went down Bush Lane toward the river and along Thames Street to the Customs House. Here all outgoing or incoming merchandise was examined and duty paid before it could be loaded on to the ships or sent to the warehouse. Claypoole's route can be followed today.

The complications of seventeenth-century trade would appall a modern merchant. It could be six months before a letter was answered from abroad; duplicates of letters were sent in two or three different ships to avoid the perils of shipwreck, pirates, and enemies, and a fourth copy was written into the letter book. Trade abroad was made possible by bills of exchange, "a small piece of paper of some two fingers broad," as a contemporary writer put it, which "of his high nature doth carry with it a command" and so avoided sending specie from country to country.[17] This was before the founding of

16Hotten, p. 356. John returned in the *Patience* in 1678.
17*Lex Mercatoria* (London, 1686), p. 270.

the Bank of England, so that the bills were drawn by one merchant on another, and each man's credit was determined by talk on the merchants' meeting place, the Royal Exchange.

An English trader had to figure his own illogical system of pounds, shillings, and pence, into an equally illogical system of crowns, sols, ducats, milreis, etc. In the *Lex Mercatoria*, the seventeenth-century merchant's vade mecum, a simple example of how to do this was given:

> If you have a *Bill of Exchange* sent you from *France*, the money to be received in *London*, . . . To know how much you must receive here in Sterling Money, you must first bring your French crowns into Pence Sterling, at the price or rate set down in your Bill, and then bring your Pence into Pounds, and you will have your desire: As for Example, If your Bill be drawn to pay 250 Crowns at 56¼ *d. per* Crown, first multiply the 250 Crowns by 56¼ *d.*, and it will make 14000 Pence, whereunto add for the ¼ 62½ Pence (because 62½ is the ¼ part of 250) and it will make 14062½ *d.* Sterling, and divide the 14062 by 240 *d.* (because 240 *d.* makes a Pound Sterling) and it will produce 58 Pounds Sterling, and there will remain 142 Pence, which divide by 12 *d.* and it will make 11 Shillings, and there will remain 10 *d.* then add the ½ *d.* remaining of your multiplication, and it will be together £58:11:10½.[18]

Weights and measures at home and abroad were equally complicated. A "wey" of cheese, for instance, in the county of Suffolk was 256 lbs., across the border in Essex, 336 lbs. Cotton was sold by the goad, linen by the yard, wool by the pound—and a pound of silk was 24 ounces. A hundredweight was usually 112 lbs. but sometimes 100; a chalder of coal had one weight at Newcastle and quite another at London, ad infinitum. England was still on the Julian calendar, other countries had changed to the Gregorian, and the new year in England began on March 25.

Besides learning these things, the merchant had to know at least one foreign language and to make frequent trips abroad to discover the needs of his European or Colonial markets. How well the English did in these matters is shown by the rapid expansion of world trade from one small island.

Claypoole was a "factor" and middleman and as such came in for abuse from both foreign and local merchants when anything went

[18]"Advice concerning Bills of Exchange," by John Marius, from the third part of the *Lex Mercatoria* (London, 1684), p. 37.

wrong, as happened frequently. His horse and cart fell into the Thames, taking with them bales of linen; these had to be renovated and sold cheaply, to the annoyance of the original exporter, who held Claypoole responsible. No one else was concerned that the cartman nearly drowned, "and the horse," James wrote, "is not yet well recovered." Moths infested the furs, and sailors stole valuable ginger root or cut into bales of material. Customs House officers had to be judiciously bribed, and the silver "pieces of 8" from the West Indies came packed for safety in barrels of fish, which made his house smell so his friends would not come to it.

On Sundays—"First Days" in the Friends' language—he went with his family to the Bull and Mouth Meeting, which stood where the General Post Office now is, and, while that was being rebuilt after the Great Fire, to Devonshire House Meeting in Bishopsgate Without. When the authorities locked the Quakers out of these houses, they held their meetings standing quietly in the street. The first Meeting for Sufferings (1676) to help those who were poor or in prison, to rescue those captured by the Turks, was organized in the Claypoole house, with James taking an active part, as were weekday meetings to keep in touch with other Quaker groups. Claypoole also belonged to the small but supremely important Six Weeks Meeting.[19]

James rarely mentioned a successful deal but complained frequently of the money he was losing. At the same time he had to explain why he lived in such worldly comfort. He would go to great trouble to collect a debt for a friend or to arbitrate a dispute. A large part of the early letters is concerned with his pathetic and often humorous attempts to settle difficulties between the Rogers brothers in Ireland and the slippery Sir Thomas Clutterbuck. If a merchant tried to pay Claypoole and could not, he never sent him to the debtors' prison; but if the man tried to cheat him, he cheerfully sent the bailiffs after him.

He scolded his correspondents if they spent an extra sixpence to add a second page to a letter but forgot the high cost of postage when he sandwiched a lengthy sermon between notes on bills of exchange and the difficulties of selling sugar at a good price. If he was annoyed with the other man, he would tell him so in strong and un-

[19]*The Friends' Library,* XI (1847), 431-433; *Friends' Miscellany,* ed. Isaac Comly, I (1834), 45-46.

Quakerlike language, extending his lecture over several pages. He was very often annoyed.

This was James in 1681—a man with a comfortable home and a large family, respected by his friends and his Meeting, deeply religious, and more than a little short-tempered. He was forty-seven when the letter book began, and he suffered from "the stone."

In August of that year he went to Tunbridge Wells to drink the medicinal waters. They did not help him, but two years later he was cured, and by George Fox. This is the cure that Fox described in detail in his *Short Journal*. It was in March 1683. James and Helena had traveled to Warminghurst in Sussex with Fox to visit Penn's wife, Gulielma, who had recently had a baby and was still very ill. The journey must have been extremely uncomfortable though they took two days over it, the roads being so bad that once they had to go ten miles out of their way to get round an impassable bit; and no doubt James suffered severely. As Fox described the cure, Claypoole

Could neither Lye nor Stand he was in such extreamity of ye Stone yt he Cryed out like a woman in travell and I went to him & Spoke to him and was moved to Lay my hand upon him & desired ye Lord to rebuke his Informity and as I Laid my hands upon him the Lords power went through him & his wife had faith & was sensible [emotionally conscious] of ye thing & he presently fell of a Sleep & presently after his Stone came from him like dirte & soe then he was presently well, formerly he used to lye a month or 2 weeks of the Stone, as he said, but ye Lords power in his time soon gave him ease yt he came ye next day 25 miles in a Coach with me. . . .[20]

Coincidence? Perhaps. But Fox had the magnetism that every great leader must possess, and Claypoole was only one of hundreds to find healing in his touch or his presence. It is odd, however, that James did not mention this miracle in a long letter that he sent to Penn in Philadelphia a few days later. But referring to the visit he wrote, "I believe I shall never forget it."

Two years before this, in 1681, and not very long after the letter book began, James was thinking of buying land in Pennsylvania. He would not, however, commit himself until he was sure that Lord Baltimore's claims could not jeopardize the deal. Cautiously he thought of sharing 5,000 acres with his Irish friend, Samuel Claridge.

[20]*The Short Journal and Itinerary Journals of George Fox*, ed. Norman Penney (Cambridge, Eng., 1925), p. 78.

Claridge held off, but James, in October 1681, with growing enthusiasm for the colony bought an entire block of 5,000 for himself.

He became more and more involved in the plans for the colony. He sent out Penn's pamphlets with information about Pennsylvania; he was appointed treasurer of the Free Society of Traders in Pennsylvania, though secretly he had hoped to be elected at least deputy president. Before long he resolved to sell everything he owned in England, including his well-established business, and to take his family to the new country. This was no easy decision for a middle-aged man.

To make the change as comfortable as possible, Claypoole sent servants ahead to Pennsylvania to build a house, with a good cellar to store his wines, and to buy livestock, plant a garden, and set out an orchard. He wrote long letters to his brother Edward in Barbados and to Norton near New Castle, asking what life was like out there and what supplies he should take. He looked about for a good-sized ship, saw that private cabins were built for his family, and made sure that they would not be too crowded.

His letters go into all these details. He wrote praising a new ship, the *Concord*, as one of the best and biggest—it was, he said, 500 tons. Its captain, William Jeffries, was a splendid shipmaster; the men taking over his business were among the most important merchants in London. But the sailing of the *Concord* was delayed more than four months, and another ship took Francis Daniel Pastorius and some of the *Concord*'s passengers. Claypoole then secured thirty-three people from Germany to go with them, but their arrival was delayed and they very nearly missed the ship. Another anxiety was added: James could not collect a lot of his debts. He was threatened with imprisonment by his own brother Wingfield, to whom he owed a small sum, while John, who owed him £300, refused even to see him. Two of his children came down with smallpox. No wonder he wrote his brother Edward that he was feeling ill when they finally sailed in July 1683.

With his wife, seven children, and five servants he reached Philadelphia in October. The voyage had gone well, except that by this time he had come to hate the captain he had formerly praised. The town of Philadelphia was less than a year old, consisting of only a few hastily built houses among the trees and some caves dug into the river bank. But it was full of his friends, including William Penn.

The home about whose building he had written so carefully was a disappointment. The people he had sent ahead had followed his orders literally—too literally. The building was the size he had suggested and there was the cellar he wanted. He had not said anything about a fireplace, so there was no fireplace—with winter on the way! But he managed to add a kitchen with a chimney and double fireplace, so they did not freeze, though in one letter James complained that his hands were too cold to write.

Later he built a large and comfortable home. John Watson, in his *Annals of Philadelphia and Pennsylvania*,[21] has left a description of it, based on a conversation early in the nineteenth century with one of James's descendants. The house was on the north side of Walnut Street between Front and Second. It was double-fronted with four windows across, front and back, the panes set in lead frames. In time it became the Rattlesnake Inn, and it must have been large to accommodate the family and the servants. Claypoole's descendants shared the common romantic illusion, firmly believing that the family had started their new life in a cave by the river.

James was pleased with his town lot, which ran more than one hundred feet along the Delaware River bank, back to Second Street, and down to a swamp by Dock Creek, which could, he wrote, be dug out and made into a snug harbor for ships. From the merchant's point of view, it was an ideal location. He described it at once to Edward, letters now taking only a few weeks instead of two or three months, and he urged him to join them in the new city. Land, he wrote, had doubled in value and the price was going higher. His brother Norton, who had settled farther down the Delaware, might come and join them. A thousand people had arrived within six weeks, he wrote; this was probably a conservative estimate, as the names of ten ships arriving during that period can be found in Pennsylvania records.[22]

From the beginning Claypoole had little leisure. He complained that his work as treasurer of the Free Society of Traders, in spite of

[21]Philadelphia, 1844, I, 558.

[22]The ships within that period were: *Bristol Comfort*, Sept. 28 (*PMHB*, VIII [1884], 333); *Endeavour*, Sept. 29 (ibid., IX [1885], 226); *Concord*, Oct. 6 (ibid., VIII, 331); *Lyon*, Oct. 14 (ibid., VIII, 334-335); *Unicorn*, Oct. 31 (ibid., VIII, 334); *Providence*, Nov. 10 (ibid., IX, 227); *Morning Star*, Nov. 14 (ibid., IX, 233); *Friendship*, Nov. (ibid., IX, 229); *Jeffrey*, Nov. (ibid., IX, 228). The *Bristol Factor* came at this time but is not recorded; the port book P.R.O. E 190/1146/1 shows it loading July 6 to Aug. 1 for Pennsylvania.

its £100-a-year salary, took too much of his time. He had planned to bring over about £700 worth of goods to start his Philadelphia business, but this cannot be traced in the London Port Books, at least not in 1683. It is probable he had very little money then, for he wrote Edward he was ashamed at leaving England without paying all his bills; in fact he had borrowed money from friends. He did, however, send immediately from Philadelphia some luxury items for Edward to sell, such as eighteen beaver hats.

Before the end of the letter book he was writing enthusiastically about the Society's whaling endeavor, and he was sending over to London skins and silver bullion from a ship that had sunk somewhere south in the Delaware.

Claypoole had much besides business to keep him busy. In February 1684 he acted as interpreter for Penn and Margaret Matson in Pennsylvania's one witchcraft trial; Claypoole's German and Margaret's Swedish were apparently similar enough for them to understand each other.[23] In February, too, he refused Christopher Taylor's offer to make him deputy registrar and in a somewhat tactless reply said he would take over the entire office.[24] In May he was to help raise £300 for public aid; by August he was serving with Robert Turner on the Board of Property. He refused a judgeship in September 1685 on the grounds of ill health[25] but was commissioned justice of the peace that November, to take office in February.[26]

That year, 1686, he served in the Assembly and in July, on the death of Christopher Taylor, petitioned for the office of registrar-general. He was made a judge of the Provincial Court in August and by November was confirmed in the coveted office of registrar. The next spring he was elected to the Provincial Council itself.[27] He had been "chairman" of the Court of Quarter Sessions, and he had many tasks for the Meeting as well.[28]

Having been an important man among the London Friends, he found it natural to assume a leading role in Quaker Philadelphia. His

---

[23]*Colonial Records of Pennsylvania*, I (Philadelphia, 1852), 95.

[24]Claypoole's letter of Feb. 12, 1684.

[25]*Colonial Records*, I, 112, 119, 153.

[26]Ibid., 156, 162, 167.

[27]Ibid., 168, 185, 187, 195, 196.

[28]Court of Quarter Sessions . . . of Philadelphia, Philadelphia County Court Records, 1685-1686, MS, Historical Society of Pennsylvania.

certificate from the Bull and Mouth Meeting was unusually long and almost eulogistic: "Our dear and ancient Friends, James Claypoole and Helena his wife . . . [the seven children accompanying them were then named] have walked with us, in the love and fellowship of the gospel, for many years past . . . [they] have freely given up themselves according to the gift of God." It begged the Friends in the New World to "receive them in the same love and tenderness, in which they parted from us."[29]

So Claypoole was loved by his Meeting, and, although not a religious leader like William Penn, he was certainly considered a "public Friend." Perhaps he was moved to address the Meeting in long, rambling speeches, not unlike those he sometimes wrote to his correspondents. That he was a valuable member can be seen from his letters. Joseph Besse spoke of him as "valiant" and a leader.[30] But there is nothing to show that he ever languished in jail, as so many Friends did. He was no martyr.

George Fox recognized him as a "public Friend," for in May 1686 he addressed a letter to Claypoole and others "that use to minister." The letter suggested that they should go, two and two together, to New England, Virginia, Carolina, etc., "to declare the truth unto the People, and turn their minds to the light of Christ."[31] The letter was certainly received by the end of the summer, but Claypoole did not send it on until January, with apologies for his tardiness, when he appointed a February date to consider it. It was not the action of a religious enthusiast, nor is there anything to show that he ever went far afield to spread the Word.

James was not a scholar, yet he was a good friend of such intellectuals as the mystic, Baron Franciscus Mercurius van Helmont, Robert Barclay and George Keith, and the versatile William Penn. He contributed to at least two of Penn's pamphlets and was in consultation with him and with George Fox about the writing of others. He was one of the small group who signed Penn's Frame of Govern-

[29]*Friends' Miscellany*, I, 45-46.

[30]Joseph Besse, *A Collection of the Sufferings of the People Called Quakers* (London, 1753), I, 452, 484. Besse gives only one incident, wrongly dated. He wrote that on April 8, 1682, Friends, being locked out of Meeting, stood worshiping in the street and that Claypoole was arrested and sent to jail for seventeen days. James reported the affair as May 1683 and wrote that he "had like to have been [almost] sent to Newgate."

[31]*PMHB*, XXIX (1905), 105-107.

ment.[32] He was probably the practical man of business that every church and every Meeting needs, and he was always a generous subscriber to every needy cause.[33]

Certainly his brothers John and Norton knew this generosity. John had borrowed £300, possibly part of £1,000 needed to release him from the Tower after some political indiscretion; he was suspected of friendliness to the king's enemies.[34] Norton, some years before the letter book began, had borrowed money to go to the New World. No sooner had James landed at Philadelphia than Norton asked for still more money to pay for a thousand-acre plantation he had bought that summer near New Castle.

Neither brother repaid him. James had given up John as hopeless some time before, knowing he was living in poverty in the Temple with a mistress. There was, however, some chance that Norton might clear his debt, as Penn, either at James's request or out of friendship for him, had given him a post, worth, so Claypoole wrote to Haistwell, £50 a year. Norton was not even grateful, for he supported Lord Baltimore's claim against Penn on the question of the southern counties, now the state of Delaware. "For N[orton] Claypole," Penn wrote in 1684, "I wave his unhandsome carriage to me if conscience were in ye matter. I should for give him, but he yt eats ye bread of others might have held his tongue in my title to Sussex [County]."[35]

James suffered family and business losses more or less philosophically, but he fumed for years over losing part of the £30 he had advanced to print Samuel Fisher's collected works, and he spent much valuable time and expensive postage trying to sell the surplus copies he had been given. He was a kindly man, but his attitude toward slavery was not different from that of his century; the black man was only a kind of superior animal. He wrote Edward—the 11th, 8th month, 1682—to send him two strong Negro slaves to fell trees and do other hard work. Later he wrote that he had been told that "men without women will not do well," so he ordered instead a man and a

<hr>

[32]Facsimiles of the signatures are in *Memorial History of the City of Philadelphia,* ed. John Russell Young, I (New York, 1895), 20.

[33]Money to redeem captured Friends was sent Claypoole from outlying Meetings.
[34]*Cal. S.P., Dom., 1680-81,* pp. 439, 477.
[35]Penn to William Clark, *Pennsylvania Archives,* 2nd Ser., VII (1891), 6.

woman. He knew, of course, Penn's law, which stated that all slaves automatically became free at the end of fourteen years.[36]

It is unfortunate that the happy relationship between James and his fellow Quakers in London did not extend to his business associates. He damned John Bawden, who lived next to him in Scots Yard, as a "rogue" in May 1682 but praised him extravagantly a year later when Bawden was to take over the Claypoole business, only to damn him again after James had settled in Philadelphia.

He quarreled intermittently with the Rogers brothers in Ireland, although these were fellow Quakers, but the behavior of Sir Thomas Clutterbuck was enough to break up any friendship. He quarreled bitterly with William Rogers of Bristol, but Rogers was a "backslider" and had written a pamphlet against George Fox and his teachings. This quarrel James tried to patch up, Rogers being a useful correspondent in the West Country. He spoiled it when they were on the point of being friends again, by arguing over a few shillings for some bottles of cider. He also quarreled with the Chares in Hamburg over another petty matter. It would appear that James was always right, and he called on heaven to witness that he was—but then we have only his side of the story. He praised William Jeffries, master of the *Concord,* when he wanted to fill that ship but after two months at sea with him said he would not travel with him again for £1,000.

One of the best things about James was his genuine devotion to William Penn. "Truly I value thy love," he once wrote to him. "It is part of my best treasure and I prize it beyond all outward things." It was a friendship Penn returned, for, busy as he was when he first came to his colony, he took time to write Claypoole on December 29, 1682. Other friends with far fewer responsibilities did not take the trouble; his son John did not even send a verbal message.

Claypoole's trust in Penn's judgment was complete, although he was Penn's senior by ten years. Penn was, he wrote, "as fit a man as any is in Europe to plant a colony," and after that brief initial doubt about the power of Lord Baltimore to spoil Penn's grant, he was an enthusiast for the new country. He was sure that if Penn would go with him to see the recalcitrant Clutterbuck, that artful dodger could be made to pay his debt.

---

[36]It was the German Friends who, in 1688, condemned the whole system of slavery, sending their paper of condemnation from the Germantown Meeting. Eventually Friends were forbidden to own slaves.

Penn's respect for Claypoole is shown by the fact that he chose him to be treasurer of the Free Society of Traders in Pennsylvania, though there were other Quaker merchants in London who were richer and more important. It was not Claypoole's fault that the Society was a failure; it had had bad luck from the beginning of its operations in the New World. James could not take up his duties in Philadelphia until his arrival in the late fall of 1683; his deputy meantime was a Quaker friend, Ralph Withers.

Possibly Withers should not have allowed the colonists to buy on credit the supplies the Society sent in, but it is difficult to see what else he could have done. When Claypoole took charge, he found it impossible to collect the money already owing, nor was he offered payment in kind. This was not surprising since there was almost no money in the form of cash in the colony, and it would be years before the farms would yield much surplus in the way of stock or grain. Foreseeing this, Penn had asked permission to mint small coins,[37] but the lords of the Treasury refused, and the £300 worth of halfpennies and farthings brought over in the *Unicorn* from Bristol[38] in the fall of 1682 was not enough to help. Lack of coin continued to hamper the colony until well into the next century.

There had been, then, a year of mismanagement before Claypoole took over. He tried hard to pull the Society out of the red, as we can tell from his letters to his clerk Haistwell in London. But when he wrote he would not have taken it over for many times his £100-a-year salary had he known the work, it was in a mood of temporary depression. At least it gave son James an immediate post as the local secretary.

The Society's affairs did not improve, though it owned a sawmill, a gristmill, glassworks, and the whaling rights in the Delaware Bay. Presently the investors in London began to ask why they were not receiving dividends, and where the books were so they could see for themselves. Penn wrote from England to have the books sent over.

The Society, and James, were attacked by Samuel Carpenter, one of Philadelphia's richest merchants, in 1685. He carried his case from a lower court to the Provincial Council itself. Claypoole's claim that he had appealed to England was denied, Carpenter saying no money

[37]*Cal. S.P., Dom., 1682*, p. 348 (S.P. Dom., Entry Book 55, p. 204).

[38]*The Loyal Impartial Mercury*, No. 34, London, Oct. 3-6, 1682. It also said forty Quaker families were sailing on the ship.

had been put up, as the law required.[39] The next year, 1686, a more serious suit was brought up by the Society's former president, Nicholas More, and another rich merchant, Benjamin Chambers. According to a letter James Harrison wrote to Penn, this involved "several hundred pounds."[40]

Mails were so slow that Penn was not able to answer this until January 28, 1687, when he wrote Harrison, "I am in my spirit secreetly dissatisfyed with J. Clayp. conduct, he is but low, & came far & seeks preferment[,] has writ to A[lexander] P[arker,] G[eorge] W[hitehead,] G[eorge] F[ox] to speak to me; & if he be not prefrd to all the rest, I know who will be out of all patience, . . . he has a secret slye spirit . . . inclinable to be to inferiors insolent, to superiors creeping [cringing] his numerous family & sometimes hott house are some small Apology . . . he is the man of all the Province that next G. J. [Griffith Jones?] is least well spoken of. I desire that thou [James Harrison] & J[ohn] Simcock would deal plainly with him as to his behaviour. . . ."[41]

This is one of the strongest letters of criticism Penn ever wrote, but he had no doubt been hearing other comments about James's conduct. The colonists seemed to run to Penn with all their worries and complaints.

The year 1686 had been a bad one for James. In September he was "presented" before the Grand Jury, being at that time justice of the peace and chairman of the Court of Quarter Sessions, and was accused of "menacing and abusing ye jurors in the trial of John Moon."

Young John Moon had been convicted of seducing his servant. The girl, Martha Wilkins, had been fined £10, which Moon promised to pay. The court had him put up £100 security for the care of the child and ordered him to marry Martha before the child was born. It is a pity that James had to "menace" the jury to obtain what now seems a humane and sensible verdict.

The same month James was accused of "endeavouring by an indirect way to prepossess Judge Moore in a Case yt was to be tryed before him in the Provincial Court, being by us lookt upon to be of a

[39]*Colonial Records*, I, 146-147.

[40]Pemberton Papers, Etting Collection, MS, HSP. Harrison to Penn, 3rd, 8th month, 1686.

[41]Penn MSS, Domestic and Miscellaneous Letters, HSP. J. Francis Fisher in copying the letters misread "creeping" and wrote it "weeping."

[19]

dangerous Consequence." Also, he was under suspicion when Patrick Robinson was to "administer upon the estate of benj. Eccorod, for giving ill Counsell and assuming more power to himself yn ye law alloweth of."[42]

As is the way with Quakers, the rebuke having been administered, the Provincial Council gave James the coveted post of registrar-general in November to show there were no hard feelings. It may have annoyed him to know he was fourth choice, Christopher Taylor and his successor, William Frampton, having died and William Southersby and Robert Turner having refused the office.[43]

Meantime, more reports of trouble in his colony reached Penn, not only about Claypoole, but about the Free Society of Traders. In February 1687 he wrote to Thomas Lloyd in Philadelphia:

This quarrel about ye Society has made your great guns heard hither. I blame nothing, not ye Society here to be sure, but I could wish Dr. Moore and P[atrick] R[obinson] could have been softened, and yt J. Cl. had been more composed, thou sayest well of James. I close [agree] with thy Judgement his faults arise of meaness rather than evil, but yt may be a mighty Politicall vice yt is not a moral one . . . he is fitt in capacity for business if he were fitt in temper, he is very Jealous and too Implacable . . . too apt to underwork [undermine] others, but not wth me, for I know him entirely. I voluntarily putt him in Christopher Taylor's place. . . .[44]

This is less severe than it sounds, owing to the quite different value of many of the words in that century. Also, Penn's standards of behavior were those of a saint, and Claypoole had been brought up in a school where bribery in one form or another was not considered dishonest. He could not have dealt with the customs people without it.

Certainly the good opinion of Claypoole prevailed; he was elected to the Provincial Council and took his seat in March 1687. Nor had Penn ceased to like and respect him, for on that same February 1 he sent another letter to Lloyd, but addressed also to Robert Turner, Nicholas More, James Claypoole, and John Eccle (also spelled

[42]Court of Quarter Sessions . . . of Philadelphia, 1685-1686; *Colonial Records*, I, 189. Also see Samuel W. Pennypacker, *Pennsylvania Colonial Cases* (Philadelphia, 1892), pp. 88-89.

[43]*Colonial Records*, I, 195. But Sussex Co. appointed Norton Claypoole.

[44]Quoted on p. 8 in the catalog of the sale of the Proud Papers, Philadelphia, May 3, 1903. Penn referred to Nicholas More and Patrick Robinson.

Eckley, Eckles), giving them, with three to act as quorum, practically unlimited powers to act for him in Pennsylvania "as if I myself were there present." He could not have shown his faith in Claypoole's honesty or ability more plainly.

The ship (carrying this letter) was ready to sail, Penn added, so allowing for the extra time needed for the long trip by the southern winter route, the letter should have reached James by June. He was to be one of five men, often one of three, to govern Pennsylvania! It was the pinnacle of his career, and it takes no imagination to know that he was pleased and proud. Unfortunately, he was not well that summer, though he attended most of the council's meetings. The council adjourned from mid-May until mid-August, and when it reconvened, Claypoole was dead (August 6).

In 1675 a very important meeting had been held in London, at which time Claypoole helped draft rules of conduct for the Friends in both civil and religious life. These were copied and sent to all Meetings everywhere. The rule "Concerning Trading" said that none should "trade beyond their ability nor stretch beyond their compass & that they use few words in dealings. . . ."[45] It is most fortunate for us that James was never able to follow the last part of this rule.

James's will[46] showed that he had many possessions; his estate was valued at £481 10s 3d. To his wife Helena, who survived him by only a year, he left, among other things, his "largest and least" silver tankards; the largest, with the Claypoole coat of arms, was apparently the one later given to William Penn and his second wife, Hannah. The coats of arms of the two men were similar; the Claypoole one was three "hurts," or balls, and a chevron, the whole surmounted by a crest of a fleur-de-lis, banded by a ducal coronet.[47]

His son John, always a problem, held the post of sheriff of Philadelphia for many years but was finally dismissed for "lameness and misbehaveour." Part of his unpopularity was perhaps because he let

[45]*The First Minute Book of the Gainsborough Monthly Meeting of the Society of Friends, 1669-1719*, ed. Harold W. Brace, Publications of the Lincoln Record Society, Vol. XXXVIII (Hereford, 1948), I, 43.

[46]A photostat of Claypoole's will is in the Pennsylvania Genealogical Society, Philadelphia. A condensation of it, with a list of many debtors to the estate, was published in the *Pennsylvania Genealogical Magazine*, I (1898), 60-61.

[47]Benjamin, James Claypoole's youngest brother, in 1706 wrote his nephew George in Philadelphia, describing the coat of arms. See *PMHB*, X (1886), 354; also ibid., XIII (1889), 250.

the pirates out of prison to walk about the streets on hot summer days.[48] In his father's will he was left only five shillings and some money due him in the "great ledger." But his wife Mary was left the furniture previously loaned them, and his son was given £5.[49]

Claypoole's daughters inherited silver and valuable parcels of land. Helen married William Bethell and went to Barbados to live; Priscilla, Dr. John Crappe; and Mary, Francis Cooke, a young man supposed to have come over with them in the *Concord*. Joseph and Nathaniel, having followed Keith in the tragic "separation" of the 1690's, eventually, with some of George's family, joined Christ Church.

Nathaniel's grandson John married Betsy Ross, the flag maker. Joseph's son by his second marriage was James Claypoole, Philadelphia's first native-born artist, whose daughter Mary married into the famous Peale family of artists. James's wife's name is not known. Early records and tax lists show that John and James lived side by side on what had been their father's river lot.[50] Some of this valuable land belonged to the elder Claypoole's brother Edward, who never came to Philadelphia but sold his share of the property in 1693.[51] It would seem from this that he had loaned James money at one time.

Claypoole's son George married three times. The third wife, Deborah, survived her husband and five children, who died of smallpox within one week. She died in 1785 at the age of ninety-three, more than a century after her husband had come to Philadelphia. Then it had been a cluster of small, temporary houses in the wilderness; now it was about to become the capital of a young, free, and vigorous nation.[52]

[48]*Colonial Records*, I, 531, 562.

[49]See n. 46.

[50]The "Blackwell Rent Roll, 1689," by Hannah Roach, is in *PGM*, XXIII (1963), 68-94. The 1693 Tax List also shows John and James Claypoole. There were, however, two Jameses in that generation, Norton's son being then a grown man.

[51]Edward sent a letter of attorney to Patrick Robinson in 1693 to sell his half of his deceased brother James's lot on the river. But his name, as owner, got into the Tax List. *Pennsylvania Archives*, 2nd Ser., XIX (1890), 103; also *Philadelphia Deed Book*, E-2-5/155, for June 2, 1691.

[52]Joseph and Nathaniel are in the long list of those who left the strict Quaker faith; see "Deaths of Persons Not Friends," in William Wade Hinshaw, *Encyclopedia of American Quaker Genealogy*, II (Ann Arbor, 1938), 442. It would seem that James also defected, as a Mary, daughter of James, and Rebecca, wife of James, are listed in the Christ Church records as buried in 1746 and 1749 (*PMHB*, II [1878], 222).

The letter book came into the possession of James Claypoole's granddaughter Mary, who was the daughter of John and Mary Claypoole and who married John Bringhurst. The note on the introductory page of the book in error makes Mary the daughter of James, and it puts under the name James the birth and death dates of James, the writer of the letters. In 1852 a descendant, Deborah Bringhurst, gave the letter book to the Historical Society of Pennsylvania, and in 1885 they published a few extracts from it relating to Pennsylvania. The volume contains about four hundred fifty closely written pages.

Some of the letters were copied by James Claypoole himself and others by his son James in the easy, almost modern hand he had learned at Christopher Taylor's school near London. Many were copied by the indentured clerk Edward Haistwell in the very ornate script of the period. There are, however, several unidentifiable hands. These probably belonged to John, at that time living at home and without an occupation, and to some of James's daughters. It was customary then for the family to help in the business, and James once wrote that his wife and daughters could manage his affairs under his supervision.

Toward the end of his time in London, Claypoole took on a new clerk who was not a Quaker, for he headed his letters with the date, and "March," "June," etc. Otherwise all letters were headed in the Quaker fashion, with numerals for months, instead of their pagan-inspired names. As the year began on March 25, all letters from the beginning of January—the eleventh month—to that time were double-dated; February 1682, for instance, would be the 12th month, 1681/82.

Claypoole used certain symbols to identify the merchants with whom he was dealing. His own mark was some form of JC. The merchants' marks and those for crowns and milreis, while not reproduced in the letters, are illustrated below.

CROWN   MILREIS   MERCHANTS' MARKS

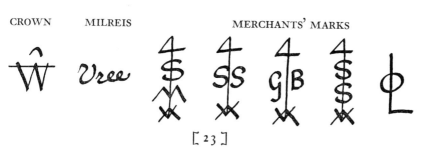

It seems pointless to follow the vagaries of spelling of at least half a dozen people who wrote in a period when the rule—if it could be called that—was to spell each word approximately as that person heard it pronounced and who used symbols and abbreviations, whenever possible, to shorten their work. Probably to save paper, the letters written into the book were copied without paragraphing. Punctuation was as erratic as the spelling. For ease in reading, spelling has been largely modernized, paragraphing has been introduced, and punctuation has been changed. As phonetics seemed to be the rule for spelling proper names, these also have been made uniform with the spelling most frequently found in port books, the letter book itself, and the 1667 directory of London merchants or the spelling found in the *Dictionary of National Biography*. Names heading the letters have been spelled out; these rarely followed the original form of address but were often only a notation to show to whom the letter had been sent.

The letters that have not been selected were those containing only information about bills of exchange or repetitions of Claypoole's grievances with some of his correspondents. Relevant information about the people mentioned has been bracketed in the letters and, when it seemed important, a summary of omitted letters or contemporary events inserted between them, so that these three important years in the life of James Claypoole and of Pennsylvania can be read as a running story.

I should like to express my thanks to Mr. Nicholas Wainwright and the Historical Society of Pennsylvania for permission to use the letter book; to the Board of Trustees of the Huntington Library and to its director, Dr. John E. Pomfret; to Dr. Frederick Tolles of Swarthmore College; and to Mrs. Nancy C. Moll and Mrs. Anne W. Kimber of the Huntington Library editorial staff.

MARION BALDERSTON

San Marino, California
January 1966

James Claypoole's Letter Book

Samuell Carridge

London the 18, 2 mon: 1682

Joseph Grove

London the 19, 2 mon: 1682

Reproduced from James Claypoole's Letter Book

London, the 6th, 3rd mo., 1681

WILLIAM CHARE AND GEORGE MITLEY

. . . When any furs are at our market, shall endeavor to get good otters, minks, and sables alone, but if they be extraordinary dear shall not buy. I take notice our bears [skins] are sold; here is none at present. That bale I had of R[ichard] G[awthorn] I let him have them again, and he has sold them to another.

As for Ball [James and sometimes Joseph, masters of the *Hope*] and his crew swearing they delivered all the ginger they received, signifies little, for a thief will swear he did not steal. Let us have your certificate of what you received from aboard his ship, and we shall try to deal with him here. But I must know whether there were any wanting [missing] of the 27 bags of J C old mark [Claypoole's identifying mark, painted on all his shipments] No. 1 to 27.

However, it is not to be understood that a factor is to run the hazard of the seamen's honesty and other casualties, to make good to his principal weight and measure. What I recover you shall have ½, but you must not expect more.

As for the 2 bags wanting, I do not doubt of allowance for them [to] the full, but the want of weight is a thing more disputable, and I know not how to fix it on the seller, because we took the weight [our]selves of every draught at the scale, which I have now by me,

As for the sale of it, I would not have you be hasty of it, for it [the ginger] is a rising commodity here. They say the black is worth 20s and the white 36s if it be good. . . .

Edmund Holt lives at the [Golden] Key in Lombard Street and says he wrote to you. Here is one [bill?] to Christian Pitch; I wish I had not undertook that business, Van Baselar being such a proud huffing fellow. I observe you have accepted Aurend Brummer's bills for 750 Rich [Rix] dollars [roughly four to five shillings each] for my account, which is well. I suppose he will not have occasion to draw above 100 Rich dollars more. . . .

London, the 6th, 3rd mo., 1681

CHRISTIAN PITCH

This day I received thine by James Crop [master of the *Biscay Merchant*]. Indeed I am troubled that in all this time I cannot give thee an account of thy business with [Van] Baselar. But I assure thee it is not my fault, for I have long since given him some of the accounts to examine, upon his pretense that he would make up the difference with me alone. So I have followed him, I think, every week, sometimes three or four in one week, to know when we should discourse the matter, and he has put me off hitherto that he has not leisure. And this afternoon I sent my man to his house to tell him that I might come to him in an hour, but he said it was post day, etc.

I intend to try him again tomorrow or beginning of next week, and then if he and I cannot agree, to give it up to our arbitrators. For thee I conclude to have Theodore Jacobson and Samuel Richardson, and then I shall write thee farther.

Pitch traded between Hamburg and the West Indies; Jacobson was a London merchant living near the Steelyard, Thames Street. There were several merchants named Richardson at that time in the City; a Samuel Richardson, a wealthy man then living in Jamaica, may have been the one Claypoole meant. This Samuel later came to Philadelphia.

Several short letters were copied by Haistwell now and apparently written by him as well. The next, also by Haistwell, to a merchant at Appledore, Devon, introduced Miles Forster, who later became prominent in New Jersey history.

London, the 10th, 3rd mo., 1681

RICHARD HOLCOMBE of Appledore

In answer to thine of the 3rd ditto about the bill of £250 drawn per Miles Forster, his brother Luke would not accept it, and, Miles being disappointed about the sale of his ship and other matters, after he had been a while at London, absented himself and is not able, as he pretends, to give any security or satisfaction at present. But his mother says when the ship is sold, she hopes they shall, amongst them, raise enough to pay the creditors. . . .

Two other worries were building up for Claypoole. In a letter copied this same day to William Rogers, merchant in Bristol and brother of the big Irish traders, Francis and George, he complained that he was not only out of cash for Rogers' account but must soon pay out another £500.

The following letter, to George Rogers at Cork, introduces the famous Clutterbuck, who was to cost James months of anxiety and eventually lose him the Rogers brothers' friendship.

London, the 10th, 3rd mo., 1681

GEORGE ROGERS

. . . I shall give you some account of Sir T[homas] C[lutterbuck], I hope, in a week or two. . . . I sold all the sugar at 22½ s per cwt., the buyer to pay customs and officers' fees. . . . The cotton will yield 8d per lb., and if it be good will yield 8¼ d per lb. or ½ d more possibly if it be very good. There is some damage in the cotton, so I have appointed two skillful men to pack it and mend it tomorrow. . . . My son [John] would have his things sent that he left there, but I am loath to trouble thee about them. . . .

Nine days later, the reason for Claypoole's recent neglect of his affairs, and his comparatively short letters, came out.

London, the 19th, 3rd mo., 1681

ROBERT DIMSDALE

I writ to thee the 5th [the day before the letter book began], which I hope came to hand. I had then and some time since great hopes of my wife's recovery, but within this week she has grown worse and worse with a violent looseness that constantly follows her, that she is brought very weak and hath neither appetite nor digestion, and sometimes burning hot and other times very cold, and now and then straining to vomit, so that we are doubtful of her recovery. She has taken all the cordial within a spoonful or two, but the drops and the mixed cordial she will not endure. We cannot give her anything now but jelly of hartshorn, and ivoury, but what will disturb her. All other things that has any nourishment in them, if it be but chicken broth, or barley broth, disturbs her, and she is very dry. But her chiefest drink is sage posset, and sometimes cardus posset.

I hope we shall see thee in town in a few days. If not, I desire thee write to me, and if thou knowest of anything may be proper for my wife, let us have it. With my love.

Dimsdale, a physician, went to New Jersey shortly after this and settled near Burlington but did not stay. Posset was a curdled milk drink; sage, belonging to the mint family, would not disturb an upset digestion. Cardus was a variety of thistle; its supposed virtue was that it made people sweat. Hartshorn was a kind of calves-foot jelly and "ivoury," probably darnell, an herb or weed with stupefying qualities, from the old French "ivraie." In spite of treatments, Mrs. Claypoole recovered.

London, the 19th, 3rd mo., 1681

SIR THOMAS CLUTTERBUCK

I suppose it is not unknown to thee that I have taken several unpleasant journeys to Greenwich to speak with thee, some in the dead of winter, other times in wind and rain, and never had the kindness offered me as to be asked to come into thy house, besides sending my servant often, and still [all this] proved ineffectual. And I am still reflected on by my correspondents [the Rogerses of Cork], as I told thee formerly, as if I were too easily overruled by thee and neglected their concerns; insomuch as they threaten, I must bear part of the damage they sustain by thee, which they account to be above £150. And it is come to that I must either suffer a reference [refer the dispute to two other merchants] in the case between me and them, or lose their correspondence. So if thou hast any respect for me, let me know when and where I may speak with thee in 14 days at the farthest, either at London if it may be, or else if it cannot be, otherwise I will come to thy house at Blakesware, though I can be ill spared from my business at present.

But there is a necessity for it; I must speak with thee one way or other. So if I have not an answer from thee, nor know where I may see thee, I must go [to] thy house and stay two or three days or more till I can speak with thee.

I have something to propose to end the difference between you, which I do believe thou canst not reasonably deny, and thereby I may prevent farther charge and trouble to us all. And this might have been done ½ year ago much more to their advantage than now, but thou hast made it of late so difficult to speak with thee that I think a man might have easier access to any nobleman in England, I may say to the king himself, than to thee. . . .

There were three Clutterbucks in London, all merchants, in the 1677 directory. Sir Thomas lived with "Mr. Clouterbock" in Threadneedle Street at that time. He must have been a man of some learning and culture, as he was a Fellow of the Royal Society.

London, the 19th, 3rd mo., 1681

JOHN CURLIS

I was lately enquiring of Henry Stout how I might send a letter to Sir T[homas] Clutterbuck, and he told me he would undertake thou shouldst do it for me, so I desire thee to give it into his own hand by the first opportunity, either at his house or at Hertford. But give it not to any other for him, for then I shall never know whether he had it or not. And press him for an answer, which send to me in London, and for any charge thou art at, when I see thee I will pay thee, and for the trouble, requite thee some way or other. I have left my seal on the letter, but thou may open it and read it and show it to Henry Stout if he be there, and wet the underside of the wafer and it will seem to be well sealed.

WILLIAM CHARE AND GEORGE MITLEY

. . . I have been myself with Theophilus Smith and used all the means to persuade him to pay the bond, or part of it, but could not prevail, he being in straits. And I should be loath, if it were my own money, to use severity with him, for I believe he is honest but not able. I offered to take black cloth, but he said he had none. Then I would have taken any sort in part, but he was not willing, his shop being but meanly furnished.

I did sometimes threaten him with giving the bond to an attorney, but he entreated me not to do it, till I had a farther answer from W[illiam] C[hare]. . . . I paid Markwerk the 23rd past, £7½ for W. C.['s] watch, and had sent it to Gravesend to go by the *Swallow*, but the ship was gone, so now I intend to send it by John Rawlings. I shipped in him yesterday for our partable [joint] account in 2 halves, bags of ginger 59, being [bearing] the Barbados mark, which comes to about £90, cost 35s per cwt., but are extraordinary good, especially 52 of them; 7 cost something less. May send invoice and bill of lading per next. . . .

The master of the Swallow *was Thomas Simpson; John Rawlings had the* Lark. *Both made regular trips to Hamburg. The mark Claypoole drew in his letter book was painted on his bags and other containers. He had several West Indies correspondents, his brother Edward being one of them. His chief imports were ginger root and sugar, but he exported a wide variety of goods.*

A long letter followed to Abel Ram in Cork, Ireland, lecturing him in a kind and fatherly way about keeping his accounts up to date, as several credits were missing. The Irish mail had apparently brought a needling letter from the Rogers brothers, and Claypoole started his reply to them with the usual complaints about the trouble of collecting money.

FRANCIS AND GEORGE ROGERS

. . . You reflect on me about Sir T[homas] C[lutterbuck] without a cause, for I have been very solicitous to please you in that matter, and my trouble has been such, I had rather given £20 I had never seen him. I lately wrote him a smart letter and sent it by a friend that was to give it into his own hand and send me an answer, wherein I proposed to him if he would not appoint time and place for me to speak with him, either in Hertfordshire or elsewhere, I would come to his house and stay there several days till I did find him. Whereof I expect an answer next week.

I assure you I have been diligent in the dispatch of your ship [the *Increase*, Maskolin Alcock, master], and with much ado got her cleared this morning at the Custom House. . . . The ship intends to be gone tomorrow morning and next day to clear at Gravesend. I send 2 barrels of excellent mum on board this night. The salmon will be very acceptable if it lies not too long by the way. . . .

Having loaded and cleared customs, all ships dropped down river and anchored off Gravesend for final clearance, out of the crowded river traffic around London Bridge—a long sail around the sharp bend of the Isle of Dogs but a short haul overland. It was a good place to take on passengers, mail, and last-minute items.

Mum, which Claypoole mentioned frequently, was a sweet beer, first made by Christian Mumme in Germany in 1492; it was still a popular drink. As a conciliatory gesture, the Rogerses had apparently offered to send over a freshly caught salmon, a great delicacy. One method of keeping it fresh was to wrap it in wet straw, as is sometimes done today.

The next letter went to Matthew Bridges of Londonderry, a new correspondent brought in by Richard Gay. Claypoole mentioned the Rogers brothers of Cork and Abel Ram and Samuel Claridge of Dublin as people who could recommend him as an able London representative. By the next letter, to a Rogers of another family, he acquired still another correspondent.

London, the 21st, 3rd mo., 1681

ROBERT ROGERS

. . . I sold lately a great parcel of Barbados sugar at 24*s* per cwt. on board, unseen, good or bad, and I judge Nevis sugars may yield 1 or 2*s* more as in goodness. They are greatly requested by the refiners, being a strong sort of sugar.

I have no correspondent at Liverpool, nor cannot recommend

thee to one till next post, but I am persuaded I shall be able to make thee as good a proceed [profit] here as can be made there. I do assure thee if thou wilt try and consign them [the goods] to me, I will use the best of my skill to spare charges and advance price. And then consider, this is no prison for any goods, which country towns are, for here is plenty and variety of chapmen....

Chapmen were retail dealers; Claypoole was importer and exporter. It is interesting that he classed Liverpool as a "country town"; it was, in fact, just beginning to expand into a great port. He did a little business later with a Liverpool merchant but never knew much about the place.

Short letters followed for the Irish mail: to the Quaker merchants Joseph Pike and Samuel Claridge; to Abel Ram; then one to Lisbon to Richard Gay, containing Claypoole's one small joke. Still annoyed with Van Baselar, he referred to him as "Van Jerusalem."

London, the 28th, 3rd mo., 1681

FRANCIS AND GEORGE ROGERS

... My letter that I advised of to Sir T. C. my friend has delivered him and I have received an answer from him, whereof underneath is a copy to verbatim. I intend if I am in health the next week or the week after at farther, to go to his house and speak with him.

I cannot but take notice of a prejudice in G[eorge] R[ogers'] mind against me, which has been these two or three years, which is manifested upon every slight occasion. John Hammond complains of me without occasion, and as for his business, I had rather another had it, for it is far more trouble than profit. . . . Here was many good Friends at my house this day, as R[obert] Lodge, who is our guest, and William Penn, J[ohn] Blaykling, T[homas] Briggs, J[ohn] Tiffin, A[lexander] Parker, T[homas] Ellwood, C[hristopher] Taylor, R[alph] Withers, and divers others whose love is to F[rancis] Rogers. [Somewhat pointedly he did not extend their love to George.]

My wife has been sick about five weeks, sometimes like to die, and that has made me keep [in the] house more than ordinary, or else I believe I had been with Sir T. C. before now. William Rogers went away this day for Bristol.

[34]

Claypoole's list includes almost all the leading English Friends, lacking only George Fox. Robert Lodge of Yorkshire was a butcher by trade, a traveling preacher, friend of Fox, prisoner and martyr.

William Penn had been granted his colony less than three months before and was busy with plans for it. John Blaykling, another Yorkshireman, was a traveling preacher and writer, often in prison. Thomas Briggs was from Bolton-le-Sands, Cheshire; he frequently traveled with Fox. Alexander Parker of Bowland, Yorkshire, was a wealthy man and one of the half-dozen most influential Friends. John Tiffin of Pardshaw, Cumberland, was one of Fox's "First Publishers of Truth."

Thomas Ellwood was a friend of the Peningtons and of Gulielma, later Penn's wife; he was also at one time secretary to John Milton; and it was he who, after he had read the manuscript of "Paradise Lost," suggested that Milton write "Paradise Regained."

Christopher Taylor was head of the Quaker boarding school to which young James Claypoole had gone; he came to Pennsylvania in 1682 and was registrar-general of the province. Ralph Withers, who preceded Claypoole to Pennsylvania, deputized for him in the management of the Free Society of Traders.

Claypoole sent a copy of the Yearly Meeting letter, addressed to Friends everywhere, to Jan Claus and Pieter Hendricks, factors, at Amsterdam. The writing of this important yearly epistle of spiritual advice and encouragement, from the center of Quakerism, would explain the meeting at Claypoole's home of so many eminent Friends.

On May 31 he wrote again, quite unnecessarily, to the Rogers brothers, but in a conciliatory mood. He was out of cash, he said, a not unusual complaint. If he received the Lisbon money, 1,100 milreis, and money for the sugar, ginger, and cotton, and if the freight were paid, their accounts would be even. "If you draw £50 more, you will be in my debt," he warned them, adding generously, "but you can draw £500 if you please." He had heard from Maskolin Alcock, master of the Increase, *that he was at anchor at Dover, so they would have their merchandise in a few weeks.*

So ended the month of May. On June 3 he wrote to Hans Christopher Mauks, or Macks, for he spelled it both ways, his correspondent in Hamburg. He could buy him that bale of Tripoli silk, he wrote, though many merchants would not sell, hoping for higher prices, some as high as 19s per pound. This was for raw silk, not the woven material. But he had got some of the best for 18½s, or, in modern terms, 18s 6d a pound; he would see it carefully packed, send it free of all charges on board, and consign it to William Chare at Hamburg.

He also wrote to Chare and George Mitley in Hamburg, recommending John Moore "as good as any single man of a company." John and

*Joseph Moore were partners who had bought 1,000 acres of Pennsyl-
vania land when Penn first offered it; they sold it later to the wealthy
butcher Richard Whitpaine. He wrote to William End in Cork, explaining why Miles Forster had not met his bills.*

*Meantime, there had been agitation over the publication of another
attack on the Quakers by the Bristol merchant William Rogers, brother
of Francis and George in Ireland. He was "A man of fixed and narrow
opinions," according to William C. Braithwaite, in* The Second Period of
Quakerism *(London, 1921), p. 304. Once a Quaker, he became the chief
supporter of John Story and John Wilkinson, whose objections to the
business management of the Society through Yearly and Quarterly Meetings had degenerated into bitter personal attacks on George Fox. Rogers
had added a sixth part to his pamphlet* The Christian Quaker Distinguished; *Richard Snead had replied with* An Exalted Diotrephes Repre-
hended—*Diotrephes being a man in the Third Epistle of John who tried
to dominate the church. Nineteen distinguished Friends in Bristol and
thirty-five in London signed this, including Claypoole. He was no doubt
brooding about this backslider when he began an ordinary business letter
to him.*

London, the 4th, 4th mo., 1681

WILLIAM ROGERS

... I am now about £200 out of cash for thy account ... but next
week will come in £73 4s 7d by the bill thou sent me on [James]
Prescott. [Details of various bills he had paid for Rogers followed.]
... As to thy pernicious book, I have read and heard more of it than
formerly, and I am sensible that it is a great offense and grief to the
people of the Lord. Many a tender lamb of Christ's flock hast thou
oppressed and burdened therewith, and it will return upon thee and
be a burden too heavy for thee to bear, unless thou dost in time (before it be too late) repent and humble thyself before the Lord and
bow to His righteous judgments, and condemn thy book throughout
the nation, and that spirit that has led thee to this prejudice and
enmity which gave it forth.

Oh, how thou hast reproached God's heritage and exposed the
blessed truth to the professors and profane. It may be easier for Hicks
and Faldo to find a place of repentance than for such as thee, that
have tasted of the power of an endless life and partook with us of the

[36]

supper of the Lord and, as I may say, dipped in the dish with the rest of the disciples, and [yet thou] has betrayed the just (like Judas) into the hands of sinners.

Thou are become a sect master and a sower of division, but thou nor thy party shall not proceed much farther, for the Lord has hedged up the way and His power is gone over you, and you are as the salt that has lost its savor, cast out and trodden under foot by men, and except you repent and return to that from whence you are fallen, even to the pure, patient, meek, tender spirit of Christ Jesus you can have no part nor portion with us in that inheritance and crown which God hath laid up for the righteous.

Thou mayst see how treacherous a spirit thou art governed by, to make such false pretenses and covers which, as a man, thou would scorn to do but that thou art infatuated and blinded with envy that it may be said thou art given up to believe a lie, and thy foolish heart is darkened by forsaking the wisdom which is from above, which is pure and peaceable and gentle, and easy to be entreated, and joining to the wisdom which is below, which is carnal, sensual, and devilish.

I can truly say I have travailed for thee many [a] time, with sighs and groans and tears, and at this time is my heart tender before the Lord, and my desires are that if possible thou mayst find a place of repentance. I have seen thy state in a vision some years since and have been warned of the Lord not to join with thee, nor [with] them that were given to strife, at a time when I had too much favor for you.

When thou wert in town last, my wife was very sick, and I did expect thou would come to see us. But that unruly spirit did so hurry thee that I believe thou hadst scarce time to sleep or eat.

Claypoole's genuinely hurt feelings over the behavior of an old friend came out in the last few lines, a mixture of sorrow and heavy irony. John Faldo was an independent preacher living at Barnet, north of London, and his fury was largely due to the fact that most of his congregation left him for the Friends. Thomas Hicks was a Baptist minister who wrote a pretended dialogue between a Quaker and a Christian; the Quaker of course was made out a fool. Penn answered both men, pamphlet for pamphlet. The attacks were stupid but did much harm, and Friends were still resentful.

Letters for the next several days, entirely about bills of exchange and business, went to James Freeman at Bristol, Quaker merchant and mariner, Thomas Cooke and William End in Ireland, and William Alloway of

Minehead in Somerset. He also wrote to Abel Ram in Dublin, recom-
mending Alloway as an honest merchant. In a letter to Aurend Brummer
(7th, 4th month) in Bremen he wrote, "Through want of rain our corn
is much risen [our grain is higher priced] in England," and he desired
Brummer to ship him at once ten lasts of rye (800 bushels) and ten of
wheat. The dry spell was soon over and the grain stayed in Germany in
storage for years.

The Irish mail took a letter, dated the 21st, to Francis and George
Rogers: "As to Sir T. Clutterbuck, I believe that business has been more
vexatious to me than to you, though you are the greatest losers. I intend
to go to him again shortly, but truly I doubt it will signify nothing. He
lives about 24 mile from hence."

To his new correspondent Robert Rogers he sent six gammons of
bacon and a barrel of capers, sour-spicy additions to a meal, that, along
with ginger, nutmeg, and pepper, were much in demand to dress up the
heavy diet of the time.

London, the 21st, 4th mo., 1681

WILLIAM CHARE AND GEORGE MITLEY

... The want of the ginger by [James] Ball is not so extraordinary
considering it lay aboard all winter, and a great many bags loosed in
the ship. . . . There is 2 New England ships expected every day, and
I have the promise of Glover and Gawthorn to have the refusal of
their furs. So hope may send you a considerable parcel of minks,
otters, sables, etc. I never contradicted yours sending bears and foxes
to Stockholm and Danzig but have left it to your discretion, and so I
do still. . . .

Claypoole wrote on June 23 to William Popple and Robert Stewart,
English agents in Bordeaux, saying he would send Popple his spectacles
shortly. He wrote Chare and Mitley again, chiefly about some barrels of
mum delivered to Lord Conway's cellar at his house in Whitehall. He
was charging £3 10s for the mum and three shillings for the carman.
From the personal interest Claypoole took in this small transaction, it
would seem that Lord Conway would be Edward, husband of Anne.
She was a writer, metaphysician, and friend of Franciscus Mercurius van
Helmont, who became a Quaker. Anne died in 1679 when her husband
was in Ireland, and so that he might see her once more, Van Helmont
had the body preserved in wine and put in a coffin with a glass lid.

To *Francis* and *George Rogers* he reported that *"many Barbados ships come in, that sugar is fallen,"* news which did not help their strained relations. He wrote *Brummer* to hurry over the rye and wheat and added oats, beans, and peas. He wrote *William Rogers,* assuring him that he was not his enemy but a friend who would rejoice to see him once more united in the Lord's truth. *Rogers* was less forgiving.

Claypoole wrote *Samuel Claridge* in July, and at the end of the letter he added a line that the *Earl of Shaftesbury* was sent to the Tower. *Shaftesbury* was leader in the plot to prevent a Catholic from succeeding to the throne of England; *Claypoole* may have known that his brother *John* was working with the earl.

He credited the *Rogers* brothers' account with £351 15s 5d on July 2, having converted *1,100* milreis at a new rate, and he added: *"Sir T. Clutterbuck sent his man to me this evening, with whom I had a deal of discourse, and he promises me that next week or the week after he will be in London and send for me to make up the account."*

On July 5 he wrote *Chare* and *Mitley* that he was sending that bale of silk and the invoice, £277 2s 8d . The rest of the letter was addressed to *George Mitley,* who had gone over back records of the company and had found several items he thought he could charge to *Claypoole,* such as commissions for selling beaver skins to *Russia* and warehouse rent for them before they were sent to *Moscow* and *Archangel.* This was business done in the time of *William Chare's* deceased brother, and *Claypoole* was indignant. He and *Chare* had done business since *1666* and there had never been a warehouse charge, he wrote. There was also mention of collecting money from the sale of cubebs—berries dried and used medicinally and sometimes smoked for bronchial trouble.

He wrote *Robert Rogers* that Lord [*William*] *Howard,* another antipapist, had been arrested, as well as *Shaftesbury.* They were *"close prisoners,"* and many more arrests were expected. There were *"witnesses that will swear they say incredible things,"* he wrote, referring to the men who hired themselves as *"witnesses"* for either side of a dispute. He added, *"but I hope the Lord will deliver us from the Pope and his instruments."*

Now *Claypoole* had a new enthusiasm—Pennsylvania.

London, the 12th, 5th mo., 1681

Samuel Claridge

 . . . I have begun my letter in too little a piece of paper, as to give thee my judgment of Pennsylvania, but, in short, I and many others wiser than I am do very much approve of it and do judge William Penn as fit a man as any is in Europe to plant a country. When he comes to town, I shall treat with him for 5,000 acres for thee. I know £100 is the purchase thereof, and if thou dost not conclude [soon] it may be too late, for we suppose in a few weeks he will be gone thither.

As we live in the truth which is pure where the inseparable union is, our love will flow to each other, and we shall be as epistles written in one another's hearts, in which love I salute thee and rest. . . .

Exchange for Dublin, 7 to 8%.

In a letter the same day to Francis and George Rogers he added a line that "William Penn is like to embark for his new country in a few weeks." But it was August of the following year before Penn sailed. Most of the small group of rich Dublin Quaker merchants bought land from Penn, but of Claypoole's Irish friends only Robert Turner came to Philadelphia.

To Ralph Weeks in Barbados he wrote, "Thy bill for £30 to Daniel Wharley I have paid." Wharley was prominent as a Quaker and a London merchant; he sent a large consignment of goods on the Welcome *(Robert Greenway, master) in 1682.*

Another Friend, Joseph Grove, had recently gone to the West Indies; Claypoole wrote him saying he had heard of his safe arrival there. The same mail took a letter to another Barbados Quaker, Walter Benthall, with whom he wanted to do more business. "I shall render you as good an account as any man," he wrote him, "but I suppose thou art so engaged to Thomas Hart." The sugar Benthall had sent him was badly stowed; hogsheads were broken and the contents spilled and lost. "Robert Scotting [master of the Katherine*] has done very unkindly by us both," he complained. The same mail carried a letter to his brother Edward at Barbados.*

London, the 13th, 5th mo., 1681

DEAR BROTHER EDWARD CLAYPOOLE

. . . I have sent thee 6 pair of spectacles of 3 sorts, cost 9*s*. If thou dost not like them, thou mayst sell them. Key rings none to be had but the mean sort of 2 or 3*d*, except for women. So I have only sent 2 for my sister [-in-law] and her eldest daughter, which I desire them to accept of; they are a fine sort; they are to unscrew on the top.

[40]

Here is also a ream of the best post paper, which will bear ink on both sides, cost 11s. Thy letter per John Hirst came from the post office and cost 3d; I never saw him nor heard of him. [Hirst had carried the letter from Barbados to London but put it in the post instead of delivering it personally.] The perspective glass cost 6s. My sister Norton [his brother Norton's wife] and her son James are to embark this month for New Jersey to my brother.

I hope thou wilt be mindful of Lewger to force him to a compliance, for I believe nothing less will. If Charles Sawyer corresponds with Thomas Tryon, I am content, for his business was always more troublesome than profitable. But I hope he will pay me the balance of account due to me, which is £5 3s 3d, which I have been indisbursed almost 1 year.

I shall be mindful to send thee some servants as soon as I can meet with any that are fit.

My son James has more mind to be abroad than at home, and thinks he shall do better with another than with me. He writes a good hand and has arithmetic very well, and I have proposed to him to be with thee as a writer, etc., to which let me have thy answer, and upon what terms I may send him. He will be 17 years old next month.

My sister Staples is lately dead in Ireland. All our relations else are well so far as I know.

With my love to thyself and my sister, I rest.

James's sister Elizabeth had married Dr. Alexander Staples and had gone to Ireland to live. Young James did not join his uncle but went with the family to Pennsylvania. As a lad of fifteen in the Quaker boarding school north of London, he had been caught up in a religious revival meeting conducted by a young Scotsman, Alexander Patterson. He wrote his parents at the time an emotional letter describing sleepless nights of tears and prayers until he had a final conviction that his soul was saved.

A week of business letters followed, among them one to Chare and Mitley about the stolen ginger, adding that the barrel of mum for "the Secretary" (Lord Conway) had been extraordinarily good. To the Rogers brothers on the 19th he reported sadly: "I wait still to hear from Sir T. C., but nobody comes, nor know I where to find him . . . I must go to his house in Hertfordshire when I hear he is gone thither. . . . Mum is counted a very wholesome nourishing drink by the doctors and other people here, especially for such as are in a consumption."

London, the 26th, 5th mo., 1681

SAMUEL CLARIDGE

. . . My servant sent thee . . . a paper that William Penn gave him about Pennsylvania; I would have had some discourse with him but that he was in such extraordinary haste to be gone towards Bristol that we could not have time. But he said he had writ to thee and would discourse me fully in a few days. There is great encouragement both as to the country and governor, who, I believe, will establish good laws as near as he can.

I have not time, else I would say more. However, for my own part, if I had a mind to buy land there, I would forbear till I saw that he was not interrupted by Baltimore in his taking possession. For this Baltimore is a great governor in Maryland, that borders upon Pennsylvania, and has received rent for some years past of the inhabitants thereof and it's like does so to this day by connivance. But keep this to thyself. When I have discoursed, W. P. may write more at large. . . .

Claridge had been ready, early in July, to buy land—see Claypoole's letter of the 12th to him. He took this present advice seriously, for it was some time before he bought.

Several business letters were copied next; one, to the Rogers brothers, had the inevitable bad news of Clutterbuck. "I hear nothing from Sir T. C. I believe he is with the court at Windsor."

London, the 26th, 5th mo., 1681

JOHN BRUMMER

I have not lately written to thee, and now I have little to advise of, but that I have taken up the 2 packs of linen out of *Vogelsang* [a ship making regular runs between London and Bremen, named for its captain] (and several drapers to see them) but they were both packs loose. I can find none that will give above 4d per ell. I hold it at 4¼d, so I would willingly have thy advice. Vale. Remember me to M. von Middock.

London, the 2nd, 6th mo., 1681

MICHAEL TAUNT of Flushing

. . . Matthew Bridges of Londonderry desire that the *Christiana* may not sail till about the end of this month, for that the butter will be very backward by reason of the dry weather, and if she arrives there too soon, will raise the market. [The ship was bound for Lisbon, with cargo for Richard Gay.] But I have no power to order, being another man's concern, only advise thee what he writes. But I desire thee advise me when she sails, that I may have time to insure according to R[ichard] Gay's order.

London, the 2nd, 6th mo., 1681

Aurend Brummer

... I take notice thou hast bought 10 last of rye for me at 34 R[ix] D[ollars] per last and 10 to 11 last of good wheat at 65 R. D. per last, which now lies at my charge and hazard, which I am content with, according to my order ... but it seems my order came too late for beans and peas and oats. I wish it had come too late also for the wheat and rye, for this wet weather has made both fall considerably. ... The 1st article [of an enclosed bill] I do not understand; it is 2 sheffell per last *aus dem Kornhouse*. [A scheffell was about one bushel.] If we must pay 5% for bring[ing] it out [of] the house, it will come very high. I must let it lie awhile there yet till I consider how to dispose of it, whether to bring it over or sell it there. In the interim I desire once in 3 or 4 week to hear what price it bears with you, that, if I can, I may sell it without loss. ...

Excuse my writing English, being weary, I remain.

Claypoole had written a month before, adding beans, peas, and oats to his previous order for grain and saying then that he was unskilled in the corn trade. It would also seem that he was unskilled in predicting English weather.

A further trouble was beginning.

London, the 2nd, 6th mo., 1681

William Chare and George Mitley

... I have also received yours [of the] 18th, came by post and cost 4s; those accounts might as well have come by sea. ... Here is a New England ship come and some furs will be entered tomorrow, and I hope I shall have the sight [of them] in a short time. There was a parcel lately by one Byfield [a merchant who lived at Hackney], that came from New York. . . . William Baker is concerned, and he told me this day that the minks cost him 4s per piece, raccoons about 2s. They would sell them again but they are now in huckster's hands and I perceive will be excessive dear, but intend to see them. I perceive we had better sold our bear skins at ½ price at Hamburg, than to have sent them at such chargeable freight to other places. . . . I believe Van Baselar is as bad as C[hristian] P[itch] thinks him to be, and I intend to arrest him next week at farthest. . . .

As to the other part of the letter which concerns William Chare alone, I have not time to answer it particularly at present, but this I do desire, that my account may not be burdened with that which does not belong to it, till I have time to make my objections and show the unreasonableness of his demands. I must search possibly several years' letters to find out to make it appear that T[homas] C[hare] did willingly omit warehouse room [charge]. And as to the commission of 1%, without question he never intended it, for he was no[t] careless in his accounts as to forget such articles year after year.

But it might have been well for me [if] he had placed those articles to account 7 years ago, for that would have been an inducement to have given off the trade, and have employed my money some other way to better advantage. . . . In the account of goods sent to Archangel you include what was sent in September '73, which is above £1,800 of that sum of £2,600 in that account. . . . I will examine things farther and write you again what is needful in these matters. . . .

If William C[hare] was here, I do not question but we should agree without arbitrators, so it may be deferred till he comes. However, it were very unequal for me to refer a difference to those that are your friends and intimates, which are strangers to me and I to them, and you present and I absent. . . .

Thomas Chare, member of the original firm, had recently died, and it would appear, from the contents of this and other letters, that Mitley was going back over years of old records to see what he could charge to present correspondents, in some cases going back as far as eight years. Used to the easy, friendly ways of the other Chare, Claypoole was naturally upset.

WILLIAM POPPLE AND ROBERT STEWART

... I have received by a bill from David Poole £145 6s 4d ... and I have given to D. Poole's friend your bill for 1,000 crowns. I did it with the advice of Charles Clare, the charges being inconsiderable, about 50s which he says he will run the hazard of. [The crown, for which Claypoole used a symbol, was usually quoted at 56½d.] ...

Thomas Farnborough has desired me to write to you that if you can afford to send 100 doz., or 50 doz., of good walnut planks to sell at 5d per foot, he will engage to take them at the measure [estimate] of an indifferent person chosen by us both. He is a fair chapman and a sure payment. ...

On the 9th he wrote a letter to his brother Norton, but it was not copied into the letter book. It was headed in the usual way, marked "sent by Captain" and a blank left to fill in the captain's name, "with whom his wife and boy went," which shows it was not a ship or a captain familiar to Claypoole. Little is known of Norton's early life. He had emigrated, probably in 1675 when his name appeared in the port books taking or sending a bundle of oddments for sale in Barbados, and three years later he left Barbados for New York. He settled near New Castle, now Delaware, and sent for his wife and son James. Claypoole tried to persuade Norton's wife to take the Thomas & Anne, *whose master, Thomas Arnold, he knew, then loading for New Jersey. But she had other ideas. The Quakers favored the* Thomas & Anne; *on this crossing it took such important Friends as William Biddle and Elias Farr. The next voyage its master, Arnold, captained the fast* Jeffrey, *chartered by the Free Society of Traders.*

Norton's wife must have sailed with Elisha Bennett, master of the Elizabeth & Mary, *bound for New York. From there she could have gone to Perth Amboy and Burlington, where Norton met her.*

DAVID POOLE

I received long since thine dated 20th past, directed to Thomas Claypoole, though my letters to thee were subscribed James. Thou hast done well at last in ordering me the bill of £145 6s 4d, but I wish it had been sooner, that the charge and trouble of law might have been prevented. I have delivered up the bill accepted by thee for 1,048 crowns, 39 s[ols] to thy friend with a receipt on it, but I expect the charges of law which will be about £3, and interest from the time due. So, on thy answer I shall send thee an account what it is. Also, Popple and Stewart write of a bill of £7 15s they sent thee in April '79. . . .

A letter to Robert Avery in Ireland followed, and in one to John Hodgson in Lancashire he wrote, "The bill thou sent me on John Nanfan for £100 in part [payment] of the £120 . . . is not 1d of it paid to this day, nor know [I] what to say to it, for he promises time after time but never performs." In the 1677 directory of London merchants, Nanfan's address is given as the Insurance Office.

London, the 9th, 6th mo., 1681

FRANCIS AND GEORGE ROGERS

. . . As I have said before, I know not how to speak with T[homas] C[lutterbuck], unless I go to his house, which I intend, as soon as I have an answer of my last letter that he is there, and has the writings with him; however, I intend to go in a little time.

My son [John] pretends he is highly wronged by you and Nathaniel Bullock, both formerly and now again, and had writ a letter to thee in his own justification. But it is so peremptory that I would not send it. He is yet at home and keeps in pretty much, but remains still in a depraved state [in the old sense of being demoralized]. . . .

Young John had gone out to Barbados; he returned in 1678 in the ship Patience, Thomas Hudson, master. At some period between then and the beginning of the letter book he stayed with the Rogers brothers and got into some mischief that caused him to leave so hurriedly that he came away without the bedding all ships' passengers carried at that time.

On the same day, the 9th, Claypoole wrote Samuel Claridge that William Penn was expected back from Bristol the end of the week and that he would then treat with Penn for the land Claridge wanted. Penn had gone to Bristol the 26th of the previous month and was to leave again for Bristol the 24th of the following month, September, to say good-bye to the first shipload of Friends for Pennsylvania.

[46]

WILLIAM CHARE AND GEORGE MITLEY

... [I have] 2 letters from Christian Pitch, one to me, the other for Van Baselar, delivered to him but no answer. . . . Irish otters are at 7*s* and cannot be afforded at 5*m* [marks?], for I see there is still some thrown out, and by them is more loss than is got by all the rest. For my part, I intend not to be further concerned in furs till there is more encouragement. But I will use my interest with all diligence to serve you.

The 2 New England ships are come and the goods on shore. I offered R[ichard] G[awthorn] by his invoice, before any of his goods could be seen, 4*s* per skin for his minks which were 915 and 2*s* for raccoons, 4*s* foxes and woodchucks [marmots], and for other sorts, as some few cats and otters, his own price, 12*s* and 5*s*, provided I might throw away the trash. But he would not close with me, and now I have seen them, I could not pick above 400 minks, and the raccoons rise badly, so have no mind to them. [Claypoole probably meant that the fur, when unpacked, had no spring or life in it.]

I bid 4*s* [per] skin for another parcel of 700 minks on same terms, and 2*s* raccoons. The truth is, furs are run up to such an extravagant rate by Hazelwood and Byfield that it is better to look on than buy at present. . . .

John Hazelwood lived at Goodman's Fields, according to the 1677 directory, and John Byfield at Hackney. Claypoole added a postscript to his letter, repeating a former joke. "I desire you to ask Cornelius van Jerusalem when you can see him if he has not order from Richard Gay of Lisbon to remit me money or accept my bills."

WILLIAM ALLOWAY

My last to thee was the 2nd ditto, since have thine of 9th, with bills of exchange for £469 16*s* 6*d*, for account of Robert Rogers, which are most accepted, only the £320 bills are left out. Enclosed I send thee Proctor & Sedgewick's bill for 600 crowns at 56½*d*, for which I have paid for thy account, £141 5*s*, which is all.

To Matthew Bridges at Londonderry, Claypoole wrote that he had obtained £500 insurance on the Christiana. *He repeated his request about knowing her sailing time. There was a brief formal note to William Rogers.*

London, the 15th, 6th mo., 1681

RICHARD GAY

... Thy advice to prevent drawing on thee according to the order of F[rancis] and G[eorge] Rogers came too late, as thou mayst see by my last. Herewith I send thee thy account of wines, by balance whereof is due to me, and carried to the debt of thy new account of wines, where I have carried the remainder also, being 16¼ pipes. They are all sound but one with a X [on the barrel], which is something pricked, but I think no worse than at first coming here.

'Tis really a perplexity to me that they will not sell, and that I have refused a better market than now I can have. I got a grand vintner to see them lately, but the most he would offer me was £20 per tun, at which rate they should never be sold if were mine. I am in hopes of getting a better price by £4 or £5 per pipe in a little time. They have lain hitherto without hooping, but now they must be all hooped but I think will not need racking again. ...

A pipe held 126 gallons, a tun 252, so the vintner's offer was not very good. To rack a wine was to draw the clear away from the lees. Claypoole continued the letter, reporting that he had asked for the insurance at 3½%, finally getting it at 4 guineas %, with nine men subscribing. His commission would be 50 shillings, and he thought the whole deal cheap, "considering the great hazard of Turks." He had written to Great Yarmouth and Amsterdam about money on Gay's notes but had received no answer, and he was about £1,000 out on his account.

It was obvious that Gay had mishandled things and was in financial trouble.

London, the 15th, 6th mo., 1681

DEAR BROTHER EDWARD CLAYPOOLE

... I intended by this opportunity of Emmanuel Hudson [meaning Thomas, now of the *Elizabeth Ann & Catherine*] to send thee account of the 6 hhds. sugar by [John] Young [of the *John's Goodwill*],

[48]

10 by [Thomas] Aubenny [*Experiment*] and 9 by [Benjamin] Clark [*Speedwell*]; they came all in good condition. But he [Hudson] comes no more to the Exchange [Here a sentence was apparently omitted by the copier, to the effect that Hudson's ship had sailed.] which is sooner than I expected by several days. But it's like I may get them finished tomorrow [for the Barbados mail] and send after him. This I thought good, however, to write that thou mightst be sure of some advice by him.

[John] Hull [*Orange Tree*] and [John] Harding [*Carolina*] are come with the 6 hhds. and 16 hhds., which shall enter in due time and dispose of as well as I can. I take notice that Colonel [Philip] Newton has informed thee that Robert Marriott has outsold me 4*s* per cwt. in the same sort of sugar. I have heard as if P. N[ewton] had a prejudice against people of our religion, and as to the man he then sold to [Marriott] he broke twice if not thrice, and I would not have trusted him [even] if he would have given me 6*s* per cwt. more than I sold for and possibly it might be some of the best of that sort. . . .

I think I know how to sell sugar as well as he or any man, and I doubt not but in the end my account shall render as well as his. I passed these last parcels [of sugar] all for brown at the Custom House, but it is a very difficult matter to get any lsts pass[ed] so. [Brown sugar paid less duty.]

I am glad thou didst not send the shoat now, corn is so dear, and now that Ben[jamin] Grove is dead [late master of the *Amity*] I would not have it sent, for I know of none will take care of it. [On the voyage from Barbados] Thou writes very kindly concerning thy intentions of consigning to me, and so I receive it, and shall endeavor with all care and diligence to promote thy interest, that my advantage may not be thy loss. I take notice thou art about to arrest Lewger, which I am very glad of, and wish it had been 1 year sooner, for I was always in the mind, since he first began to cheat me, that he was a very knave, and nothing but law would procure right from him.

My brother Norton's wife and her son James are gone away last week from Gravesend in a ship bound for New Jersey [Perth Amboy]. We all wish her a good voyage, etc., for indeed both her relations and ours were weary of her, and my brother is to be pitied that has such a yoke-fellow, and if he has not the art of taming a shrew, he is like to live a miserable life with her.

I take notice of several bills thou hast drawn on me for £260, which shall all be accepted and punctually paid; there is none presented yet but that of £50 to James Harding. . . . I and my wife with our 8 children are in good health. Our love to thee, thy wife and daughters. . . .

James disliked his brother Norton's wife so much he never used her name, which was Rachel. In America she had a son Jeremiah and a daughter Elizabeth. After Norton's death she married Nehemiah Field of Sussex County and had two sons by him, Nehemiah (1689) and William (1693).

London, the 16th, 6th mo., 1681

DEAR BROTHER EDWARD CLAYPOOLE

Yesterday I writ thee at large, and now having another opportunity of sending by Hudson, I have sent copy of thy account of sugars by Young, Clark, and Aubenny, which was done in haste and so not exact, the charges of the 9 hhds. being put in the place of the 10 hhds. This day I have accepted thy bill for £130 and another for £10. I have sent thee a large Cheshire cheese; I ordered it to be sewed in canvas and tarred to preserve it from the rats. . . .

London, the 16th, 6th mo., 1681

WILLIAM CHARE AND GEORGE MITLEY

. . . [Claypoole began with an account of the money he had paid out for them.] Furs are bought so exceeding dear that I know I should not possibly please you with buying, so have let all go to Byfield and Hazelwood. There is about 2,000 minks, but half is trash such as I think would not sell with you, and the like for raccoons, etc., and a man must take all sorts or none, there is such striving for them. . . .

London, the 17th, 6th mo., 1681

SIR THOMAS CLUTTERBUCK

I am still urged by Francis and George Rogers to speak with thee, but it is so difficult that I have sent thee their letter, dated the 29th

March last, which they desired me to deliver myself. It is about the ship, which now I believe is much impaired by lying [idle in dock]. Please to let me have thy answer and when and where I may come to speak with thee, that so there may be some end of this troublesome business. They urge me upon arbitration, to try if they can fasten upon me some per cent of the balance of account due by thee, which might be prevented if I might but speak with thee and give them a reasonable answer.

London, the 17th, 6th mo., 1681

JOHN CURLIS

I desire thee to deliver these 2 enclosed next market day to Sir Thomas Clutterbuck, but if he be at home and not at Hertford I desire thee to ride thither next morning, and I will pay for the horse hire and what more thou wilt. I should have delivered myself and have been contriving this half year to see him but could not. If he be gone to Bristol, as I heard, then send me the 2 letters again by some friend next week, to the Exchange. I think if Sir T. C. were to be found, thou wert best seal the letters one in another before thou deliver them.

London, the 18th, 6th mo., 1681

SIR ST. JOHN BRODERICK

I fully intended to see thee this day at Wandsworth, but finding my indisposition of gravel and stone increase, and some of my intimate friends going tomorrow morning to Tunbridge [Wells], I was by them and wife, for my health's safe [sake?], persuaded to go with them. I hope to be home again in 8 days or 10 at farthest, and then I doubt not but to serve thee to [thy] content in that bill for Cork, so for this omission I hope thou wilt excuse me.

For the next two weeks the correspondence was handled by Edward Haistwell, who usually prefaced his letters by saying modestly something

about his "master James Claypoole." The next letter, however, was prob-
ably dictated by James himself before he left.

London, the 18th, 6th mo., 1681

BERNHARD COUDERT

[Coudert lived at Nantes, France.] . . . Trade is now open, not-withstanding the prohibition, and French goods are as cheap and plentiful with us as ever they used to be, and wines daily imported, as Rhenish wine, the additional duty being off. But they are very low [in cost] unless they be choice wine.

Thomas Roberts has been a long time here, but I have never yet had an opportunity to see him; he has nothing as I can hear of for his creditors, but hides himself and is reported to be less concerned for reputation and honesty than he was formerly. He owes me about £60. . . .

Thomas was the son of George Fox's friend, the Quaker merchant Gerard Roberts, of Gracechurch Street. A short letter followed to Thomas Cooke on the 23rd. His New England and Barbados sugar had not sold yet; the ordinary sugar "as thine is," he added, "is very plentiful." All these are in Haistwell's handwriting, the originals probably signed; to one of these copies Haistwell signed his own name without thinking, then crossed out his signature with heavy lines.

To Claridge on the 30th, 6th month, he wrote he "went this morning to Redriff [Rotherhithe] to the house of Thomas Lurting and read thy letter to his wife, which did very much satisfy her, being exceeding sorrowful for her husband, and would gladly have him return and not go this voyage."

This brings in one of the most fascinating characters among the Quaker shipmasters of the period. Since his "convincement" Thomas Lurting had refused to carry guns and had managed, though completely unarmed, to escape from an attack by Turkish pirates. His ship, the Owner's Adventure, *had been chartered by some Irish immigrants to go to New Jersey; they sailed from Dublin September 19, 1681. Lurting's wife, Eleanor, had reason to feel anxious, as her husband was ill at the time. In fact, he became too ill in Dublin to make the trip, and his mate, John Dagger, took the ship across. Lurting returned to his wife.*

A letter of the 3rd, 7th month, to William Hodges and Nathaniel Body at Tetbury, Gloucestershire, said his master lived at Scots Yard, Bush

Lane, near London Stone in Cannon Street, "but you need only direct to him (Merchant in London), and it will come safe."

London, the 6th, 7th mo., 1681

ABEL RAM

... [I] have thine of the 9th July which Mortagh Dowling brought me last night about 8 of the clock and demanded £500 on his bills, which I paid him for thy account at 9½% and send thee here inclosed his bills payable to thyself for £547 10s drawn on the king's commissioners, and now I am above £400 out of cash for thee. I have been out of town for my health about 16 days, and now must post thy books before I can send thy account. . . . I desire thy permission for me to employ such correspondents as I think good for return of thy money out of country towns, and to have it sometimes sent by carrier. I will do my best for thee but not run hazards.

London, the 6th, 7th mo., 1681

SAMUEL CLARIDGE

... I desire thee to write 2 or 3 lines to the Earl of Londonderry about the bill of £65, how I have disbursed the money long since to a low exchange to accommodate his brother, and now cannot have his bill accepted. When that bill is paid, and the £199 bill by Row [Thomas Rowe?], then thou wilt be but £143 15s 7d out of cash for me, which I hope to remit thee next post. . . .

London, the 6th, 7th mo., 1681

WILLIAM END AND DANIEL SAVERY

... M[iles] F[orster] is in prison, as I heard this day, and now is confirmed to me by a letter from his mother, and I am told he intends to put himself in the [Court of the] King's Bench. At present he is

[53]

about getting a letter of license from his creditors. I shall enquire what prison he is in and enter an action against him in your name, which is all I can do at present. ... I am sorry to see you disposed with so much severity. I believe if one should serve a child of yours under M. F.'s circumstances, you would count him a very hard man.

London, the 6th, 7th mo., 1681

HENRY SMITH

... [The letter began with mention of some bills that had been accepted.] As for the neat's tongues, if they be new, are very acceptable here, and an easy matter to get them ashore without any damage to the master; for our custom house officers will not scruple a merchant to have 1 doz. tongues in open view. When I have deserved them, I will get my friend S. Claridge [to] send them for me.

Neat's tongues, the tongues of cattle, were a great delicacy at that time. They were apparently being offered Claypoole as a gift from his Irish correspondent.

London, the 9th, 7th mo., 1681

AUREND BRUMMER

... The invoice of the mum and the account current I shall examine, and if there be any error, advise of it, and I take notice of the charges of the corn [grain] which must lie by till farther order.

The mum is very dear, as 14¼ R[ix] D[ollars]. Those ... [here Claypoole drew the merchants' marks of the brewers he preferred, instead of naming them] this year were very good, but I leave it wholly to thy care and skill to send the best, and I doubt not on the score of our friendship thou wilt do for me as well as for any, so my order is before the winter to send me, if can come per first ship, if not, I will none till spring, 50 barrels. Presume thou wilt have order from others on same account and so take on a ship to load her. And against spring I would have 100 more. ... The 12 barrels resting I shall let be mingled and sell it with my old mum. Have yet above 100 barrels resting.

I sold the diaper [linen woven with a small geometric pattern] 14 days since to Benjamin Antrobus, to pay in 3 months; the 17 pieces at 14*s* [each] and the 9 pieces at 11*s*. . . .

London, the 9th, 7th mo., 1681

WILLIAM CHARE AND GEORGE MITLEY

 . . . [I] have now dead in sugar above £1,000, and it sells very badly. . . . I desire you tell Christian Pitch that Van Baselar does now promise to refer the difference, if he and I can attend it, which we are to try next week. So hope shall save the expense and trouble of law. . . .

Irish otters are above 8*s* per piece, so I buy none. Raccoons, 2*s*; foxes, 4; minks, 4*s*; otters, 12*s*. I hope all our old furs are disposed of and that I may, in a post or two, have an account. The sale of my ginger I refer to you, but white [ginger] is a rising commodity and black is not falling. . . .

The same day a letter went to John Brummer, advising him not to send more hempen hammels—a cheap cloth—but "white may do better." "Remember me very kindly to my relations at Cassel and Wanfried and to Mark von Middock," he added.

He wrote the next day to Thomas Cooke: "John Spread has sent me for thy account, per the Endeavour *[Francis Richardson, master], which is come beyond Dover, as per bill of lading received, 750 pieces of 8, which I shall dispose of as soon as they come to hand." He also said he had been out of town drinking Tunbridge waters for his health, and that ordinary sugar was hard to sell even at 19s and only excellent Jamaica would yield as much as 24s.*

London, the 10th, 7th mo., 1681

SAMUEL CLARIDGE

 . . . William Penn does not intend for Pennsylvania till next spring, and then 'tis like there will be many people ready to go from England, Scotland, and Ireland. He is offered great things, £6,000 for a monopoly in trade, which he refuses . . . but he designs to do things equally between all parties, and I believe truly does aim more at justice and righteousness and spreading of truth than at his own particular gain. I tried him about thy proposals to take £100 for

[55]

5,000 acres and abate the quitrent, which he refused, intending to do equally by all. If thou wilt be concerned the half of 5,000 acres, I will have the other half and make as good terms for thee as for myself. It may be I shall get him to take his money in Ireland.

I disbursed £30 long since towards the printing of Samuel Fisher's works, a good Friend, and an eminent book for the service of truth. I have above 30 books of my share left. I should take it very kindly if thou wouldst help me to dispose of some of them in Ireland. It is a large book, well bound in calves' leather, at 10s per book.

I am, with true love to thee and thy wife.

No quitrent to begin, by the purchasers of Pennsylvania, till above 3 years hence. Vale.

The Testimony of Truth Exalted was the title given to the large, folio-size book containing Fisher's writings, more than 900 pages, printed in 1679. Fisher was the son of a Northampton shopkeeper, had been a priest at Lydd, in Kent, then became a Baptist and finally a Quaker. He died, a prisoner for his faith, in 1665.

London, the 10th, 7th mo., 1681

FRANCIS AND GEORGE ROGERS

. . . [Claypoole began with an apology, having been at Tunbridge for his health.] I have considered your 3 sides [of the paper] about Sir T. C. You have a great deal of trouble, and I wish it had been in my power to have prevented it formerly. I had sent your letter formerly by an express as you ordered, but I concluded that would signify nothing, for he would [have] thrown it by and given me no answer. So I went myself with it, but his being from home and afterwards removing into Hertfordshire where I could not hear of him, did lose much time. And then when I went to his house there on purpose with your letter and all the papers and a blank bill of sale for the ship, he being the night before gone to Windsor was another disappointment; and if I had stayed at his house, or near it, eight days, there had been no certainty of speaking with him, for they said they knew not when he would return.

Now since, his man was at my house and said he was going to Bristol and would stay several weeks. I have taken care in Hertfordshire to have notice as soon as he returns home and then intend to go to his house. . . . William Penn is not to go to America till spring.

[56]

I cannot sell your 3 hhds. sugar, unless at a miserable price.... [Referring to former letters about his son] I am to believe John deserved most of what was reported of him, but I writ so to satisfy my wife and him. If you will send £200 or £300 worth of butter, or what else is proper to send for Bordeaux, and consign them to William Popple and Robert Stewart and order them to send the proceed thereof to me in graves, claret, and sangoon white wine, or some other sorts which they know to be vendable, I am willing to be concerned with you ⅓ part, and shall remit you the money upon your advice what it is....

F. Rogers, I desire thee to help to dispose of some of Samuel Fisher's works, an excellent book in folio and well bound in calves' leather, for 10s per piece. I advanced £30 long since towards the printing of it, and am about £25 still out of my money.

Obviously young John and his mother had both protested about the Rogerses' strictures, but Claypoole's letter defending his son was not copied into the letter book.

London, the 12th, of 7th mo., 1681

RICHARD GAY

... [The first part is about bills of exchange, some of them as large as £1,000, and about goods going on the *Christiana*.] Thy wines are yet unsold.... Those 6 pipes that I shipped out I am like to be a great loser by them, for they do not sell, so must be sent to another port. I believe there is not ½ pipe sold to this day. As for thine resting [they] are all sound but one, and now, seeing thou dost still desire me to make money of them, I am resolved to sell them for the most I can get, which I doubt will be but £10 per pipe.... I hear no farther from Van Jerusalem....

Claypoole's next letter was to Popple and Stewart in Bordeaux saying that when he next met with Charles Clare he would "advise with him no farther to do with D. Poole." They had been having trouble collecting money from Poole. Claypoole also said that Francis and George Rogers had proposed to him to exchange butter for wine—an odd statement since it was he who had made the proposal. But he added, "they are fair dealer and sufficient men."

[57]

FRANCIS AND GEORGE ROGERS

... [Claypoole was worried about Richard Gay, and he hoped all was well with him. He had insured £400 on the things shipped on the *Christiana*, and he hoped Gay had not launched out too far. His wine had not sold, and one man told him he could buy old wine for £8 a tun, or 2 pipes.] I did hear that report you mention of Sir T. C., that his wife was over charged [overburdened] with protested bills and was fain to come away from Leghorn privately ... but none darest report him failed, neither did I hear he was arrested, for it was judged he had a protection. I do not think he would have been so easily persuaded to have given up his ketch as you think, for he used to say you were greatly in his debt, and rail against you for [selling] stinking beef, and want of weight, which he did always allege far exceeded the balance of account demanded by you. I shall not give him over thus but be at him again when [he] comes from Bristol. ...

London, the 20th, 7th mo., 1681

THOMAS COOKE

... I shall be considerably out of cash for thee, for I cannot sell the sugar to any content. I aim to have 21s per cwt. for it and under I would not sell it if it were my own. I have a very likely chapman tomorrow or next day.

I have received up the pieces of 8, viz. 750, and sold them to a goldsmith, weight 641¼ ozs. at 5s 3½d per oz. Abating for freight and primage [an allowance by the shipper to the master and crew of a ship], is £167 18s carried to thy credit, and have sold thy beaver to R[ichard] Gawthorn, weight 179 lbs. at 7s 6d per lb., is £67 2s 6d. ...

Claypoole wrote End and Savery he believed they would get more if Miles Forster were released; imprisonment would give "sorrow and affliction to him and his relations, and make him the less capable to pay his debts. But do as you please. I will serve you so far as I can with a good conscience."

On the 23rd he wrote Chare & Mitley that the price of furs was still going up; he had had the refusal of 1,000 minks, but scarcely 500 of them were good. Beaver had fallen; otter was still good. He would remember a warning they had written him about Hans Christopher Mauks and his London factor, again referred to as "Van Jerusalem."

London, the 24th, 7th mo., 1681

Dear Brother Edward Claypoole

The aforegoing is copy of my two last by [Thomas] Hudson [master of the *Elizabeth Ann & Catherine*] by whom I sent account of 25 hhds. sugar, which was done in haste by my son James, and so was some parcels misplaced. But since, he has written it out fair, which I send thee enclosed. I also send thee account of the 22 hhds. sugar per Hull and Harding [masters of the *Orange Tree* and the *Carolina*]. . . . [Here follow a few more details of business deals and the error of young James, which, however, had been corrected and made right in the books.]

Now I am to answer thine of the 8th and 23rd, 5th month [July]. I desire thee to tell C[harles] Sawyer that what I received of [Benjamin] Clark and [Allan] Cock for damaged ginger was [only enough] to pay the charge of picking the dry from the wet and washing the molasses out and drying, and for bags, which, if I give him credit for, he must be debtor for the charges. . . .

I perceive Lewger is troublesome, but I hope thou wilt not give him over till thou hast made him pay. But I had rather it were in money than in sugar, for I doubt his sugar will be bad. . . .

I am sorry to see that the lawsuit with the executors is like to be so tedious, and as for removing it to London, I doubt that will be out of the frying pan into the fire . . . and for my brother Graveley to be solicitor, that cannot be expected, for his cider takes up all his time. I hope there will be no occasion [for a prolonged lawsuit], but if there be, doubtless we shall be both ready to do what we are capable therein. . . .

John's son, Cromwell Claypoole, had died three years before, leaving £50 to Graveley, to Norton, and probably to the other brothers as well. His father, as executor, refused to pay, as Claypoole explained later.

There were other vexations. Claypoole was having trouble with the landwaiters, customs officers who waited on the docks for the ships to come and examined the cargoes before unloading. They were "cross fellows," Claypoole said mildly. *There were different charges for brown sugar and white sugar, and with proper tipping white could sometimes be passed for brown. For some reason, possibly just because he was a Quaker, he was in disfavor with some of the customs officers, who seized some sugar and threatened to fine him £5. "But I intend not to give them 1d,"* he boasted hopefully.

London, the 24th, 7th mo., 1681

RALPH WEEKS

. . . The damage of the cotton was by rats, else it should have been paid for out of the freight. There was one bag so rummaged that one would have thought it had been repacked, it was so loose and hollow. . . .

I am willing to act for thee as formerly, for I love to deal with honest men, though their business be but small, and thou must use thy own freedom of sending little or much in a ship; I shall not be displeased. But whatever thou consigns to me hereafter, let it be by endorsement upon the bill of lading, and in the inside let it be to Ralph Weeks or his order, and let not the master know who is to receive them. For here are some shirking fellows that belong to the king's beam, as they call it, that lay claim to weighing of sugar and will have 16d per hhd. and 2s per butt for weighing, and 4d per bag ginger and 9d cotton, and they search the master's entry at [the] Custom House and then put men to trouble. I was fain to compound with them this week and give them 40s for nothing rather [than] go to law. But keep this private to thyself.

London, the 24th, 7th mo., 1681

JOSEPH GROVE

. . . I take note thou hast sold most of the linen for our account in ½, for near 40% advance, but little money received, and the wine sold but slowly, and therefore thou intended to send 8 hhds. bottles to Jamaica, with which I am well satisfied, and refer all to thy discretion. I hope they will sell at last. Better [to] take 18s per doz. than keep long. It was kindly done to send 4 hhds. [of sugar] by the *Amity*, but they came to a very bad market, 19s and 20s for indifferent parcels, and fine sugars may yield 25s.

[60]

We have not got all up yet but may in a few days. I intend next week to ship some osnaburgs [coarse linen cloth] and blue linen for our partable account, whether I sell the sugar or not. . . .

He included compliments about Grove's "care and kindness" in shipping goods and repeated his sad tale of the "shirking fellows" who had attached themselves to the "king's beam," the official scales. This claim to weigh incoming merchandise and charge for doing it seems to have been a temporary annoyance, as it was not mentioned again. But Claypoole gave Grove directions for marking parcels so they were not so obviously directed to himself, and again lamented that he had had to tip the dishonest rascals 40s. He may not have intended to pay them one penny, as he boasted, but they had him up before the lord mayor, and he changed his mind.

A line under these Barbados letters said they were "All sent by Strutt." The Strutts, James and John, were the Quaker brothers who took their Concord yearly to the West Indies and back.

London, the 24th, 7th mo., 1681

ARTHUR COTTON

. . . There is a ship going to Pennsylvania from Bristol, and William Penn is gone thither to take his leave of the Friends, and there is another ship going thither from hence, and may be ready in a fortnight. But William Penn goes not till spring. With mine and my wife's entire love to thee and thy wife and also to T[homas] Salthouse, I rest.

Arthur Cotton, an early convert to Quakerism, lived in Plymouth and later in Colchester. He was the husband of the more famous Priscilla Cotton, martyr and writer.

London, the 24th, 7th mo., 1681

FRANCIS AND GEORGE ROGERS
JOHN NEWENHALL AND WILLIAM HOWELL

I have received yours of the 3rd ditto about 6 days since, by Thomas Phillips, your sugar boiler, whom I understand you have sent over to be perfected in his art, and according to your desire concerning what they would have to teach him, etc. But I found their demands and like to be so difficult and tedious to effect that I thought

[61]

best to close with G[eorge] White, who, I believe, really is both skillful and honest, especially considering that you lay great stress upon his quick dispatch, that you may be at work again, which I should think is also a matter of great consequence, and I closed the [deal] rather because G[eorge] W[hite] was to do some work, I think to make bastards the 22nd inst., which T[homas] P[hillips] said he was most desirous to observe, and that would not come again to be done in 3 weeks.

So after pretty much arguing and pleading we agreed that I must pay £20 down, and that he will give T. P. of it 50s back, and I immediately paid him £10 in part. And T. P. desired £10 for his use, which I paid him also. The 21st I think he began; and I hope he will mind his business and lose no opportunity, that he may return to you as soon as is possible, which I shall endeavor to effect. I shall pay him £10 more if he desire it and take his bill on John Fenn, and if in anything else I can be serviceable to you I shall be very glad of your commands. . . .

"Bastards" was inferior sugar, from syrup refuse, reboiled. Claypoole wrote Claridge that he was "out of cash" for him, once he had paid that correspondent's bills. He added, "I believe thy good word to A[bel] Ram might sometimes procure bills to be sent to me."

He wrote Chare and Mitley on the 26th urging them to be quick in disposing of the furs Valentine Archer (Unity) had taken in his ship, fearing, as always, a collapse in the market. At the same time he complained of the high prices asked in London for good pelts. "They are bought up here at extravagant rates," he wrote. The best minks were now priced at 5s.

He wrote again on the 27th to the Rogerses. He had spoken to Thomas Phillips the day before, he said, "who says that he is now sensible that he wanted instruction in [sugar] boiling, and does not question but through George White's skill (whom he does very much approve of) that he shall be perfected in the art in three weeks time, and then intends to be gone from hence. He desired me to write to you to send to Bristol for another stove, for there will be a necessity for two stoves."

London, the 29th, 7th mo., 1681

JOHN SPREAD

. . . The 19 hhds. sugar per the *Supply* [Thomas Edwards, master] for account of T[homas] Cooke, I received long since in good condition, but they are come to a miserable market. . . . I also received by Captain [John] Foy [master of the *Dolphin*] for account of the said T. Cooke 4 hhds. sugar and 1 barrel of beaver [skins], and by the *Welcome* [probably the ship that took William Penn and his friends the next year, but not necessarily; there were several of that name in the colonial service] 750 pieces of 8, whereof I have given him an account long since.

Beaver is fallen within these 3 months about 20%, and is expected will fall much lower, for a vast quantity is expected from Hudson's Bay. The 126 skins I sold for $7\frac{1}{2}s$ per lb. weight, 179 lbs. The pieces of 8 were right; I sold them at $5s\ 3\frac{1}{2}d$ per oz., which is better than to send them for Cork at $6s\ 5d$, for the hazard and loss of time is worth near 3%, and I remitted the last £200 at $9\frac{1}{2}$.

I never traded to New England myself and am loath to begin now; there is such great loss by returns. [The ships had little goods to bring back.] But I have spoken to some of my friends to correspond with thee, but at present they are fixed and loath to alter, but be sure I shall make use of every opportunity of recommending thee to such as I know to be fair dealing men, and I hope thou wilt be so kind as to do the like for me, which, with my true love to thee is all at present.

I am earnestly desired by a friend of mine in Worcestershire to make inquiry for one William Mumford, a stonecutter in Boston, whether he be living or not, and, if living, that in thy next letter he may write a few lines, and it may be attested by some that comes over in the next ship, to end a law suit for one that holds an estate during his life. . . .

John Spread had been a merchant in Bristol but, as the letter shows, was now established in New England.

Was beaver losing its appeal to the wealthy class? Penn had agreed to send King Charles two beaver skins a year, which he did faithfully. Or was this a defense Claypoole set up for himself in advance, in case his sales did not satisfy his client?

To Anthony Heywood on the same day he wrote that he had received the letter of attorney to prosecute Thomas Jarvis for the £450; however, he heard that Jarvis would not come to England this year but had sent for his wife to go out to join him in Virginia. A note along the side of the page here says that a copy of this went per Captain Edward Daniel (the alternate master of the Biscay Merchant?*) for Jamaica.*

The next letters were purely business, to Avery, to Claridge, and in Haistwell's handwriting to John Mason that Claypoole was sending some mum in the next ship to Exon. Mason was a trader in either Exmouth or Exeter.

Two months before, Claypoole had suggested to Claridge to wait before buying land in Pennsylvania, to see what influence Lord Baltimore might have. This, or some gossip he had heard, caused Claridge to hold up a letter he had written asking for land, for on October 4 Claypoole wrote, "I did not deliver thine to William Penn because thou forbid it, and that I should say nothing to him from thee."

London, the 4th, 8th mo., 1681

MARCUS VON MIDDOCK

... Thou says there is bill of loading for a pack of hammels, No. 4, and a barrel of hogs' bristles, but there was no such bill enclosed, so possibly there was a mistake and may come by the next. Hammels [coarse cloth] are very low, I believe have not been in less esteem in England these 20 years. I have not sold 1 ell of thine nor of John Brummer's yet, though have had many chapmen [to see them]. Not a man will give me 4*d* an ell, unless they take the best pack, and above 3¾*d* they will not give for thine. So let me know what I shall do. . . . Harfords and osnaburgs are very low and like to continue yet, for French cloth comes in in great plenty. . . .

In spite of tariffs and legislation, a large section of the English public was prosperous enough to demand the fine materials and the fine wines of France.

To Chare and Mitley on the 4th, Claypoole wrote that he had tried to avoid buying "catts" as much as possible, "but sometimes must take some or else lose all the rest; and now this day I bid £176 for a parcel, there is 18 bears amongst them which must take for the sake of the rest, for Hazelwood gives any price and would buy all. They have run up foxes, minks, etc., to 4½s per piece, good and bad, and woodchucks 7 and 8s per piece running [runnions: mangy animals], otters near 20s if good." Claypoole had sent a message to Edmund Holt, who said he could not pay, "indeed, I believe now in this dead time of trade he cannot do it."

London, the 7th, 8th mo., 1681

WILLIAM CHARE AND GEORGE MITLEY

. . . I was yesterday at Theophilus Smith's, that now I had occasion for money for William Chare's account; and being I had waited so long according to his desire, I expected he would pay me the bond of £80, and urged him to it with what arguments I could, but he said he was not able to do it, and that he had not £5 over but that he must of necessity pay next morning, and desired me to write W[illiam] C[hare] that he might have it still at interest, which he thought might be the easier granted by reason T[homas] Chare had given £100 to his daughter on day of marriage, etc. . . .

I have bought another parcel of furs of T[homas] Glover and farther do not intend to proceed, for I have 2 fatts packed which shall enter tomorrow on board the *Phoenix*, William Cutter [master], whom I could hardly persuade to take them in. But I promised them a pair of gloves of a crown [value 5*s*], and 6 R[ix] D[ollars] freight.

I was loath to lose this opportunity, because winter comes on and we have but little time to spare for sale, so 5 or 10*s* may not be ill bestowed. [Claypoole added that he had two other fatts with Archer —the captain he had mentioned in his letter of September 27.] . . . These 2 fatts will come to about £330, and I do expect they will send for their money tomorrow. And I must not put them off, for now it is counted a great favor to sell a man a parcel of furs for present money, there is such a striving for them. . . . Exchange for Hamburg 35*s* 5*d*.

A fatt was a large tub or barrel.

On the 7th he wrote Marcus von Middock again—an annoyed letter this time, since Middock had drawn against him for £100, and Claypoole was already out of cash for him. Besides, he had sent those hammels, "a coarse, troublesome commodity"; Claypoole could not accept this £100 bill, "so hope thou wilt not take it unkindly, all things considered. With my love to J[ohn] Brummer and thyself. . . . Harfords, £38 per roll, brown hempen hammels, if good, 4d per ell."

The next day he wrote to the Rogerses in Dublin, "Thomas Phillips intends to be gone in about 10 days; I have advised him to go by coach to Minehead." This way could save him as much as two weeks on his trip back to Ireland.

[65]

London, the 11th, 8th mo., 1681

WILLIAM CHARE AND GEORGE MITLEY

This serves chiefly for cover to invoice and bill of loading of 2 fatts of furs by the *Phoenix*, William Cutter, master, for your account ½ and my account ½ part, amounts to £327 9s 4d. The ship would be gone tomorrow if the wind was fair.

The freight is high considering too that I gave the master a crown for a pair of gloves, but both he and the broker doth affirm they could have put 11 R[ix] D[ollars] in cloth in the room thereof. It is a rich commodity and the winter draws on. . . . The bears are very cheap, else I would not have bought them. I hope we shall not lose by these, but rather than to send them to Danzig or Copenhagen, sell them for a R. D. per piece. . . .

Several short letters were copied, one by young Haistwell: "My master James Claypoole" had sent John Heywood two barrels of mum as he had requested, at £3 5s per barrel, or £6 10s, and would Heywood please pay for the mum sent six months before?

There was one to Edmund Travis at Manchester dated the 13th. They had tried to sell his cloth, but a principal linen draper had seen it and would not give more than 6d a yard for it. "French cloth comes in now very cheap." To Von Middock on the 14th he wrote he had had his letter written in Dutch by Aurend Brummer. The goods had come but were attached by the customs so Claypoole could not get them. Could he sell those hammels for 3¾ d, which was all he could get?

To the Rogers brothers the next day he wrote that Phillips had concluded his business and was to leave on the 17th, also that he had paid George White £20 more—he does not say for what. To Chare and Mitley on the 21st he wrote that he hoped to hear of the arrival of Valentine Archer, who had sailed with the earlier consignment of furs, "and for William Cutter I hear he went from Gravesend and the wind is fair." He did not intend to buy more furs, and was content with the sale of the ginger. "I cannot have time this month yet to look over T[homas] Chare's letters about your demand of warehouse room, etc."

London, the 22nd, 8th mo., 1681

SAMUEL CLARIDGE

. . . As for my country house, it is a small place to keep my children in and does very little hinder me in my concerns, for I very seldom go till a Seventh Day [Saturday] in the evening, and come to London again 2nd Day in the morning. And I have a servant [Haistwell] and my son James at home, so that I think no business of consequence is neglected. I have positively bought 5,000 acres of land of William Penn and am to pay him £100 for it next 3rd Day, and I know not but that I may buy the quitrent off also for £20. . . . Here is a ship going to Pennsylvania, the passengers going away tomorrow, and in the spring William Penn intends to be there himself. . . . [The ship was the *John & Sarah*, Henry Smith, master.]

So on Third Day, or Wednesday, Claypoole got his land and, shortly after, the elaborately engrossed deed. As was usual, this was written twice on one piece of vellum and cut apart to make a wavy line, the best way to guard against counterfeiting of deeds. Penn kept one part, Claypoole the other.

When he was made treasurer of the Free Society of Traders, he felt he had to own 10,000 acres, so the following spring he bought another 5,000. He managed this sale with some other London merchants, however, so he did not have to pay the entire extra £100 himself.

London, the 22nd, 8th mo., 1681

FRANCIS AND GEORGE ROGERS

. . . I sent the books by Robert Scotting and do intend the next ship that goes, to send some of Samuel Fisher's books for a trial. I am like to be a great loser by helping to print them. . . .

London, the 22nd, 8th mo., 1681

JOHN CURLIS at Hertford

I desire thee to send me word per first [post] after the receipt of this, whether Sir Thomas Clutterbuck be at home or no, for I must take a journey on purpose to speak with him and I would not willingly lose my labor.

London, the 24th, 8th mo., 1681

RICHARD GAY

. . . [Claypoole had drawn 300 milreis upon Gay's account, which at 6s 6d per milreis was £97 10s.] I have sold no more of thy wine, but

[67]

I have some customers on hand now that I hope I shall sell 2 or 3 pipes to, however, [if] the wine proves good. And the French wines this year prove extraordinary bad, so that I am still in hopes of disposing of it to some content. I wish thou would send 10 pipes more of the red, if very good, and one or 2 pipes of white. I believe it cannot do amiss, and if thou please to interest me ½ therein, viz., in 11 or 12 pipes, advise me thereof, and draw the money upon me and I shall pay thy bill.

But if your Barraberry and Carcavelos wine be very good this vintage, I would be concerned the ½ of 20 pipes if thou please, and let them be full gauged, 130 gallons at least [to the pipe] and deep colored. . . .

Claypoole added that people complained that the wine was too strong and said that there was brandy in it.

After this he made another attempt to reestablish friendly relations with William Rogers. After the usual notices about bills he added, "I hope thou wilt not so give way to prejudice as to leave thy old correspondent without a cause. However, I am, as I have always been."

London, the 28th, 8th mo., 1681

Dear Brother Norton Claypoole

I writ to thee by my sister thy wife, who went hence about 10 weeks since, who I hope, with your son James, is safe arrived long before this time at Burlington, to your mutual joy and comfort. I have not in a long time had any [letters] from thee, though ships come pretty often from New York or New Jersey or Maryland, by one of which ways I believe thou mayst send almost every month in the summer.

But thy silence makes me still more doubtful of thy honesty and good intentions, and seems as if thou wouldst forget thy old friends, that helped thee in a time of strait here, which if it should so prove, as I should be sorry to see, then assuredly the character of baseness and ingratitude will be fixed upon thee, and the hand of justice will find thee out.

The advancing that £150 to Major Wallis that was lent thee, has been and is, a great prejudice to me in my affairs, for I have been and still am, out of cash all the money to this day, for my brother Claypoole [John] has only paid some interest, as I writ thereof formerly, and I doubt he will never pay more, for he will not suffer me to speak with him, nor give me any answer if I write to him. And as for Doctor Peachey, he never intended to pay 1d of the £30, nor interest. But Major Wallis has lately with a great deal of trouble got £17 of him, which is £10 part of the principal, and £7 part of [what] the interest came to for four years, and for the other £20, he has a year's time given him.

He does very much exclaim against thee, and indeed I think he is a great sufferer by thee and ought to be remembered, and as soon as thou art able, have some part of satisfaction with the rest of the creditors. Now as to the debt by bond to Major Wallis, my cousin Cromwell has given thee £50 as a legacy, which my brother Claypoole is to pay, but he will pay none of the legacies.

However, if thou will send me by the next ship that comes, which possibly may be this ship, a right letter of attorney, witnessed by some that comes in the ship, that will attest it here, I am in hopes that I may prevail with him to pay it, especially considering that I have offered them a release from that bond, he paying the ½ the interest then due, when he pays the £50. So I desire thee, brother, not to fail, but send me an authentic letter of attorney by return of this ship or by some ship from New York.

And I desire thee to write at large what encouragement there is to remove from hence with a family to dwell in those parts, and what commodities is most proper and profitable to carry with one, and in what time a man may, if he arrive there in the 7th month, with the help of 3 or 4 servants, clear ground enough to afford corn and feed cattle for a family of 15 or 20, what safety or hazard may be expected from the Indians, in what time and with what charge a house with 10 or 12 rooms, and barn and stables, etc., may be built. In what time an orchard will bear, what sorts of trade is now amongst them, and what like to be as the people increase. But especially give me advice of merchandise, what quantities and what sorts are most vendable, and what returns may be expected. And whether New Jersey or Pennsylvania be most advisable to settle in.

I desire the more particular and large account, because I have purchased of William Penn 5,000 acres in his country, and I know not how I may be disposed in my own mind in a year or 2 time, to remove thither with my family. However, in the meantime, I purpose to send over my attorney with some servants, to build and plant, etc., and to provide cattle and other necessaries, that if I ever come there, my land may be still improving, or some part of it, and not lie wholly waste. And if I should send over one of my sons as overseer, and some servants, what sort of servants may be most profitable. And anything else thou canst think of, may be for direction, and how the country is as to heat and cold, how long winter and summer, what fruits grow, what plenty of things and what inconveniences there is, which we know not here, as hazards by wild beasts, snakes, serpents, or flies for biting or poisoning, that we [may] know beforehand what may be expected of good or bad. So not doubting but thou wilt be both able and willing to give me a satisfactory account in these particulars, and much more than I can think of to mention at this time, I conclude with my love to thyself and wife and son.

Also advise me about thy own condition, how settled and where, etc.

Apparently the Rogers brothers had written Claypoole, asking him to get further information from George White about sugar boiling, or refining, for which they were willing to pay a fee. On the 29th Claypoole wrote them, sending White's answer on the back of the sheet of paper he was using. Being responsible for hiring White, he was naturally anxious to praise him. "I think he writes very honestly and reasonably. He might have earned a guinea and given you a slight answer, but he is honest and would take nothing. But if you send him 6 neat's tongues, he being a housekeeper, may be acceptable. . . . I doubt [am sure] William Rogers has left me and deals with James Hemmings [in Basinghall Street, London], but he has never hinted anything of it to me."

Neat's tongues had been offered Claypoole a few weeks before this and had been accepted for a later date and cooler weather "unless they have taken salt."

London, the 7th, 9th mo., 1681

RICHARD GAY

. . . I cannot yet fasten any of thy wine upon those customers I expected, nor have I heard since from Matthew Bridges, but I hope thy next will advise that the *Christiana* is arrived. I should not have writ at this time but to enclose a letter from Charles Jones, Junior, of Bristol, advising of his bill drawn on thee for 493½ mills, payable at 21 days to myself. . . . We have news that the Algerians have declared war with France, so that we may expect that they will have peace with us, which may encourage trade. . . .

He then wrote the Rogers brothers on the 8th the continuing bad news that sugar remained low in price, 19s to 21s per cwt., and only 22s for the most desirable kind, muscovado. He had heard that Sir Thomas Clutterbuck had been made a justice of the peace; "he was lately at home but I could not go till this week." He had found out that he was not coming to London.

To Chare and Mitley he wrote that he was afraid the moths would get in the furs if they were not sold soon and he could not collect for the barrels of mum.

In a letter to Charles Jones, Jr., wealthy Quaker merchant at Bristol, Claypoole gave the exchange rate "at 6s 5¾d per milreis," which amounted to £159 17s 5d.

London, the 8th, 9th mo., 1681

WILLIAM ROGERS

. . . That which thou calls prejudice in me ought rather to be accounted true and brotherly love, which has been as is manifest too far extinguished in thee by jealousies and evil surmises. Thou speaks of and writes of a willful, envious, idolatrous spirit, and a blind zeal that could put fire to a faggot to burn a heretic. I am no such man, I assure thee, but thou knows not what spirit thou art of thyself. I have never blasted thy Christian reputation, but vindicated thee in all things so far as I could according to truth, but in that where truth was against thee, I hope thou would not have me be for thee.

I can truly say it would be a joy to me to hear of thy recovery to that condition which thou wert once in, that love might abound as heretofore. I have never been straitened in serving thee, nor am to this day, but as free as formerly and do desire the continuancy of our correspondency unless it be prejudicial to thy concerns in any particular which thou may acquaint me of in a friendly way and take my answer. My love to thy wife and children.

A letter to Abel Ram praised William Alloway as a "very sure man" and mentioned Christian Devonshire of Minehead. Then young Haistwell wrote to a new correspondent in Lancaster and copied the letter himself.

[71]

London, the 12th, 9th mo., 1681

HENRY COWARD of Lancaster

My master James Claypoole has received thine of the 31st past in which thou gives order for 6 barrels of mum, so in answer thereunto, on the 9th current, I sent 6 barrels to go aboard the *Anne and Ellen*, Henry Thorpe, master, for Liverpool, who is . . . a careful man, so I hope they will not be abused. We took special care to pick out those which are very good, so I do not question but they will give content. The price is £3 3s per barrel, is £18 18s, free of all charges on board.

We sell [the mum] for most part here in town to those that sell again, at £3 2s 6d per barrel, and others £3 5s per barrel, and country chapmen, £3 7s, so that I do assure thee the price is very reasonable.

My master meddles but little in the mum concerns, so at any time when thou hast occasion, I will take care to send that which is very good. We expect new mum from Brunswick in a month's time. . . .

Claypoole was allowing Haistwell to act independently and take over the small mum orders, such as this, and Haistwell was being the eager young merchant. Unfortunately, Coward was to prove unsatisfactory.

The next half-dozen letters contain little of interest; Claypoole had measured some linen sent by Edmund Travis, and the piece lacked 6 yards; good brokers wanted 6% to 7% to insure young Charles Jones's cargoes to the Delaware and New York rivers. To Samuel Claridge on the 22nd he wrote, "Thine to William Penn I should have delivered, but thou positively forbid it." He had also practically balanced accounts with Chare and Mitley, with a debit of £1,800, but he had £1,720 coming in and later another £100.

To William Smith, or Smythe, of Dublin, the one who had been "undermining" him, saying he had neglected business to live in the country, he wrote a friendly letter: "I know not but that Richard Gay's concerns is all well. I heard he has been sick, but is recovered again."

Nevertheless, he was worried about Gay and confessed to the Rogers brothers, "I hope all is well with Richard Gay; I know nothing amiss of him yet, but, however, I shall be more shy of him for time to come."

London, the 26th, 9th mo., 1681

SAMUEL CLARIDGE

. . . Thomas Rudyard is agreeing here with a great ship for Pennsylvania, and I hear there is another going from Bristol, and in the beginning of the summer it is expected there will go 3 or 4 ships more from hence. I must send some servants to improve my land, if I could tell where to get some that were likely to do well, and should be glad of a little advice from thee, which with my true love is all at present from—

The bill against the Earl of Shaftesbury was brought in by the Grand Jury IGNORAMUS.

This legal word, literally "we do not know," which Claypoole put in larger letters, was written across any unproved accusation.

Claypoole had a double interest in the event. He must have known that his brother John and probably his brother Graveley were working under Shaftesbury, and he also knew that Shaftesbury was one of the Whig leaders, trying to exclude the Catholic James from succession to the throne. The Quakers would naturally be in sympathy with this more liberal-minded party. William Penn was a Whig, but he managed to remain a friend of the king and of his brother James, a devout Catholic.

To Aurend Brummer, Claypoole wrote that old mum was selling at 40s a barrel; he had 60 barrels of his own left, and as to the 50 barrels coming over with Wilkin Vogelsang, he was satisfied to have them. Brummer, he went on, should have said something about the price he wanted for them.

London, the 29th, 9th mo., 1681

JOHN CASSAWE of Bremen

. . . [Claypoole had received the ten barrels of mum and sold six, hoping to dispose of the remaining four very soon.] [The mum] came in a very seasonable time, for people did very much desire new mum, or else it would not have sold, for it is very indifferent. I have sold some for £3¼ [£3 5s], and some £⅛ [£3 2s 6d] per barrel. I accept of thy kindness in receiving them, but I do not desire mum by commission; the trouble is much and if one would do that one would do it for one's own account rather than for another. The linen trade is very bad, that hempen hammels will not fetch 4d per ell. . . .

The next letter, to Samuel Claridge, carried one of Claypoole's usual complaints—he was out of cash for the account, £400 in this case. He also wrote that the Earl of Londonderry had not paid, and he demanded the 10% commission "according to custom, which on both the bills comes to near £3, which is my just due, for I took his bills at a very low ex-

[73]

change, 8%, when I had 10 of others." Claypoole also wanted the postage charges paid.

There were short letters to Abel Ram and Robert Rogers, and then an important one about the redemption of some Quakers who had been captured and sold into slavery by pirates.

London, the 3rd, 10th mo., 1681

THOMAS COOKE

. . . I have but this day received the rest of money for the sugar, £32 19s. I expected to have heard from thee about insurance. I have gotten something done for Robert Rogers, but I presume thou commits that affair to Robert Stepney.

Yesterday I was at the Meeting of Sufferings when D[aniel?] Baker's wife brought a letter from thee, directed for Friends of the Men's Meeting of the City of London, which was given to me to read to the Meeting, where was G[eorge] Fox, A[lexander] Parker, William Gibson, and divers others, which, after they had considered and debated the contents, ordered me to return thee an answer in the name of the Meeting, viz., that it had been more proper for thee, writing from or in the name of the ½ Year's Meeting, to have enclosed thy letter to me or some other elder Friend that belongs to the Meetings of Business and Sufferings, than to R. Stepney, a young man whose society is with others, and comes little amongst us. Especially considering there was mention made of a report of Friends here that was scandalous, and it was left open for him to read to D. B.'s wife.

Then as to that report, that by reason D. Baker had an easy employ in Angier [Algiers] it has been thought fit to let him stay there and to release others in his stead; it was evilly surmised of us, for we had no such purpose, but have still been endeavoring his release, in which his wife has been and is satisfied, and did declare to the Meeting she had been no occasion of that report. . . . William Mead and John Osgood are now transacting that affair by the order of the Meeting and have liberty to engage for D. B. and his youngest son to the value of £400, besides the national county money and some money that is in his wife's hands. So that if £500 will do, he and his youngest son may probably be redeemed.

And also we are endeavoring the redemption of Robert Barret to the value of £120, so that for these and some others we have engaged all our money within a small matter, and if we will go farther we must disburse the money ourselves or have another collection.

So I desire thee inform the Friends at Dublin and Cork that they may be satisfied of our honest endeavors and good intentions and not receive such reports concerning us, and farther, this I must say, that the Meeting did not take it well but looked on it as an indiscreet thing in thee to communicate such a matter to R. S. rather than to some elder Friend.

When anything is effected as to the releasement of those mentioned, I intend to write thee again. . . .

London, the 3rd, 10th mo., 1681

Francis and George Rogers

. . . I have been this week at Sir T. Clutterbuck's in Hertfordshire, about 24 miles from hence, and prevailed with Gawen Lawrie to go with me, and found him at home. And after we had dined (for the cloth was laid when we came) and discoursed awhile about other matters, I proposed to him to state the account by reason I was come on purpose, and had gotten my friend G. L. to go with me, who was a merchant capable to advise us both. But he absolutely refused to enter on that subject, pretending that he could not do anything in it by reason his clerk, who had the papers and knew it all better than he, was not at home.

But he promised that if I would come next week to his house with William Penn, whom he pretends to have a great esteem for, that then he would examine the account with me. So if I can get W. P. to go with me, I intend to go next week. He would have had us stayed all night, but seeing he would not discourse about the account, we would not stay, but went away late, that by riding in the night we endangered ourselves, and my coat on post or trees was torn almost from my back. . . . John Story is dead and buried near Kendall.

John Story was one of William Rogers' anti-Quaker collaborators. The Clutterbuck controversy was never made entirely clear; it had to do with some combined and unsuccessful business venture, and the Rogerses, to cover their losses, had tried to seize the ship at least partly owned by Sir Thomas. They wanted to have the matter of Claypoole's commission, £20, referred to an impersonal group of businessmen, but, as he wrote next, he was not sure they would win. This letter was copied in by a new clerk, who carelessly omitted words and even phrases.

London, the 6th, 10th mo., 1681

FRANCIS AND GEORGE ROGERS

. . . I writ you in my last that I had been at Sir Thomas Clutterbuck's, and since I have so far prevailed with William Penn that he is like to go with me in a few days. You often insist upon the ketch, and the letters you writ about it, as if it had been in my power to obtain it for the balance of the account. Sure I gave you a reasonable answer to that letter of my proceedings long since, and that was that after I had tried a considerable time, with a great deal of pains and all the ways I could devise, to deliver it myself, and could not compass it, I sent it [the letter] him by a careful hand and afterwards a copy of it, I think twice, and he sent me an answer a long time after by his man, that he would not part with the vessel, but valued it [at] a considerable rate and intended to fit it out for his own occasions.

I perceive you still insist upon it to have a reference and my commission for that account. [Quite naturally, Claypoole did not want to lose that £20.] I am certain, if ever it come to a reference, it will not be for your credit, for I have as just a right to it as you have to anything you enjoy, having earned it 5 times over to serve you in that particular, and I do believe it were more plausible and reasonable for me to demand £20 more upon that account (all circumstances considered) than for you to demand the return of that.

But I believe it is wholly George Rogers' doings, and if I had an opportunity to speak with him, could (as I suppose) easily prevail with him to acquiesce. But seeing you will have it referred, it is equal it should be referred here at London where the transaction was, unless you will impose upon me to have it done at Cork. In that case I know not who to choose but yourselves to do what you please.

Clutterbuck has often, both by message and writing, offered to give in appearance if I would enter in an action. I could not formerly, nor can I yet tell you that I will not concern myself further to serve you in that affair, for I was always in hopes, and am so still, of getting to an end of it at last, to some reasonable satisfaction that I may thereby be clear. . . .

From this it would seem that Claypoole was to have, or had already had, a commission of £20 for collecting Clutterbuck's debt, and the Rogerses wanted it back, having already given up any hope of being paid.

London, the 6th, 10th mo., 1681

MARCUS VON MIDDOCK

Since thy going from hence have not heard from thee, but I hope thou art safe arrived at Bremen long before this. [Claypoole then gave him the bad news that he was out of cash for him, nearly £240.] ... Thy hammels prove bad, this pack as the former, so that no man will give me 4d per ell for them, and the bristles are short and soft, very bad so that I cannot sell them. I wonder thou shouldst send such and call them very good. [He hated to sell the hammels for 3¾d, but that was the most he could get.] ... I hope thou hast paid the balance of my account in thy hands to Aurend Brummer, being 22 R[ix] D[ollars] and 13 groat [groschen], which is all.

To the other Brummer, John, of Bremen, Claypoole wrote on the 9th. He hoped that in two or three months, when ships began leaving for Jamaica, Virginia, and such places, the price of linen would pick up.

Next day he wrote the Rogerses, trying to coax them into a good humor: "I am in hopes that William Penn will go with me next week to Sir T. Clutterbuck, but cannot yet get his promise. He is extraordinary busy about his new country and purchasers present [themselves] daily. I have bought 5,000 acres and intend to send over some servants and possibly one of my sons." *There were details of bills, and he had had a letter from Richard Gay; the* Christiana *had arrived.*

London, the 13th, 10th mo., 1681

JOHN CASSAWE

... The 10 barrels of mum by Herman Elsers [the *Clarke*] were very acceptable to me, and I wish there had been 20 of them. ... I would send some goods, as tobacco and vitriol and cotton, but that the people that trade in those goods spoil the market.

I would have a parcel of gammons, about 50, but they must be put into a small fatt, as a hog's bristle fatt, and hid under the mum or linen, that they be not seized, or in mum barrels which are like the other. And the master of the ship must be true and not betray one, for they are forbidden here. . . .

Claypoole was now an enthusiast of the colony, for which he was to work the rest of his life. He wrote on the 13th to a now reluctant Claridge: "If thou hadst not forbid the delivery of thy letter to W[illiam] P[enn], thou mightst well think I would have given it him. And as to thy judgment of the letters from New Jersey, that they are to decoy people, that is known to be otherwise and that the chiefest of them come from very honest, faithful Friends."

London, the 13th, 10th mo., 1681

WILLIAM CHARE AND GEORGE MITLEY

. . . As for Hazelwood's friends selling 1,400 minks, I know where he had 1,000 that I refused, sure they were not all good, among which was 600 bad ones. The truth is he gave such prices for such goods as I durst not venture to do, else I might have had more than he. You must not find fault with some slight goods, for that could not be helped; our market was so quick, as I wrote before, that men would not suffer their goods to be culled. I am not for sending foxes for Danzig. . . .

London, the 16th, 10th mo., 1681

DEAR BROTHER EDWARD CLAYPOOLE

. . . I perceive thou hast had a good issue of thy contest with the executors and that justice has taken place to thy great satisfaction and vindication, which I am heartily glad of, and did acquaint thy friend William Harding therewith, and Thomas Hinchman, who were also glad to hear it. [Did Edward, at least, win his case against his brother John as executor for Cromwell Claypoole's estate?] . . . I perceive thou expected to hear from me by Aubenny [of the *Experiment*] and some others and was therein disappointed. I wish I had then writ to thee, but I hope Strutt [of the *Concord*] will not be long after them, and then thou wilt be satisfied both as to advice and accounts. And indeed I should have writ thee again before this time, but I thought I had writ till I examined my copybook of letters, or else I should not have been silent thus 3 months.

As to my concern with William Lewger, I am satisfied in thy care

therein hitherto and desire thee it may still be prosecuted to a conclusion, for delays are dangerous; he may break or die and then all is
lost. . . . I am glad to hear that my sister is delivered of a daughter and
is well in health. The Lord is the author of all our mercies and bless-
ings, and He is worthy our whole heart and affections and all rever-
ence, obedience, and praises forevermore. Here has been a great glut
of unpurged sugar . . . [and he was hoping Edward would send some
cotton or scraped or scalded ginger but not aloes, which were a drug
on the market, hardly worth 12*d* a pound].

I have bought some land in Pennsylvania, 5,000 acres, and shall
want some advice how to improve it. I have some thoughts of sending one of my sons over with some servants and a little stock to build
a house and get cattle and corn, etc. Pray let me have a few lines
from thee about this particular. . . .

*To this, Claypoole added the market price for cotton-wool, white
11d, and yellow 10d per pound. Ginger, white, scraped, was 35s; scalded
20s per bag.*

*To Ralph Weeks he wrote he had received the muscovado sugar and
the aloes, and asked him to send white or yellow cotton, these being
good commodities. He was out of cash for him too, £220, but he hoped
to sell his sugar soon.*

London, the 16th, 10th mo., 1681

JOSEPH GROVE

. . . [Claypoole's last letter was by John Strutt with the invoice
and the bill of lading for the account of Samuel Clay and himself and
some others of the owners of the *Amity*. The sugar they would have
to sell cheaply, but he was sending out to the West Indies some linen,
hammels, and osnaburgs.] John Jones owes me about £4 ever since
the 6th month [16]80, and now writes no more to me. I desire thee
speak to him about it. I hope thy next will advise of the sale of the
wine which is left at Barbados, and what I may expect of that sent
to Jamaica.

I would not have thee stand upon price much, but sell it off, for old
wine will be brought in there very cheap, and the longer ours is kept
the worse it will be. . . . I have some purpose to send thee for my own
account 20 or 24 barrels mum in 2 ships in a little time. . . .

Since the above written, I have sold our 4 hhds. sugar in ½'s at

2 1*s* [per cwt.], but must pay brokerage and allow £3 14*s* tare and stay 1 month for the money.

Sent per the *Carolina*, Capt. Harding, in the Downs.

The tare was an allowance for the weight of the receptacle, to find the net weight of the merchandise.

Still on the defensive with Chare and Mitley, he wrote them on the 16th about some furs he was sending, "I believe indeed I might sell this parcel readily for £5 profit here, but I hope they will come to a good market [in Germany] and produce near 20% advance." He was sending them off the following day.

London, the 19th, 10th mo., 1681

RICHARD GAY

. . . I am glad to hear the *Christiana* was safe arrived and have acquainted the assurers the adventure was over. I take notice that I may expect remisses for thy account from Cornelius Van Jerusalem. . . . I have at last disposed of thy wine resting, about 16 pipes for £100, whereof I may send thee an account quickly. The wine is not yet delivered but will be in a few days; the money is to be paid in a month. . . . I accept of thy love in sending me a box of oranges.

London, the 20th, 10th mo., 1681

FRANCIS AND GEORGE ROGERS

My last to you was the 10th current. Since have yours of the 8th ditto; the 1st side is from George Rogers, which contains many reflections and accusations about your affair with Sir T. Clutterbuck, which I never did deserve nor was guilty. It would take up a great deal of time to answer every particular, which, however, I would do and much more to satisfy you. But at one time or another I have writ what I should now write to vindicate myself, which I do believe would satisfy any reasonable man void of prejudice.

I writ that I had been at Sir T. C. his house, and he would [not] treat with him [me] for want of his servant, and since, I have been endeavoring to get William Penn to go with me there, and there is still some probability of it. But last week the Lady Clutterbuck, who lodges about the Strand, told my man probably her husband might come to town about the end of the week. So yesterday, soon after I received your letter, I got William Penn to go with me (for whom Sir T. C. pretends an extraordinary respect and esteem), and William P. stayed near the house while I went to see whether Clutterbuck was at home, but so it is that he came not to town but sent his steward, who was not then at home. His wife told me she did believe her husband would not come till after next week, and she knew not when Percifull, his clerk, was to return to him, but promised she would send in day or two to my house, that so I might discourse with him about the account, and know certainly when he would go to his master, that so I might go with him. For otherwise it will be in vain for me to go if he be not there.

I tell you plainly, if I had not a great respect to you and your business, I would not thus perplex myself about that which is never like to have a satisfactory end. The time that I have spent about it, and the pains I have taken about it, besides the care and perplexity of my mind in this business, is more than I ever wrote to you, or than you can be easily persuaded, especially George Rogers, who has such ill thoughts of me, as if the like was hardly to be found among Turks or Jews. Truly I believe, if I should do nothing else but solicit this business for ½ year together, it would not expiate with him, unless I could obtain what he desires, which possibly may never be in my power to do.

I must needs say if all my correspondents were as hard to please as G. Rogers and so full of evil surmises, which produces such smiting of the tongue, which may be called words like sharp swords, I had rather be a plowman than a factor. . . . [Claypoole continued that Thomas Phillips was detained at Minehead by contrary winds.] If you should employ Robert Stepney [master of one of the ships called *Endeavour*], to treat with Clutterbuck, indeed I believe it would signify nothing, though he is capable enough for other business, for Clutterbuck is a high proud man that is not to be dealt with as other men, and if Gawen Lawrie and I and William Penn can do nothing with him, surely R. S. can do nothing. . . .

London, the 27th, 10th mo., 1681

JOHN BRUMMER

. . . [Thou] writes strangely as if thou wert angry and as if I had not followed thy order to sell thy linen for 4d, but had mixed it with other men's, which thou writes is not honest, wherein thou hast gone too far, for I never mixed thy linen, but kept it apart from the 1st day to this, and not one piece mixed. And that I have not followed order is also a mistake, for it has not been in my power to sell it for 4d per ell ever since I had thy order. . . .

And that thou shouldst not accept my bill would be very unkind. But I hope thou wilt be better advised, and besides it will be more damage to thee to have it be protested than paid, and I will not bear the loss, besides the disgrace, which is of more consequence. And in the meantime, if I have not done as an honest factor, I will answer it before any man and give the satisfaction.

I kindly receive thy advice concerning my relations in Germany. I desire thee to remember me and my wife to them, and that we are all well.

London, the 27th, 10th mo., 1681

WILLIAM CHARE AND GEORGE MITLEY

. . . [Claypoole starts with accounts of a sale of mink and sable, which balanced their debts and credits.] [I] have not had time yet to look over Thomas Chare's letters, but may do it within a month. . . . There is a cheese in a small cask, which I desire you to send without opening to Hans Christopher Mauks. . . .

London, the 27th, 10th mo., 1681

MICHAEL BILBY of Hull

. . . [I] understand the *Swallow* frigate is to be freighted for Lisbon for Richard Gay's account, and that there may be £500 needed to that end. . . . [Richard Gay, Claypoole explained, had ordered him to pay £200, but the "effects," the goods to cover that much money, had not come to hand. However, he expected a letter which might bring further orders.] In the meantime, it troubles me the vessel should be delayed, for it may be a great damage to him. . . . [I] am loath to go beyond order, yet if the ship might be dispatched, but [by] thy drawing £100 on me at present, let it be at 20 days and I will accept thy bill and pay it. I say, one hundred pounds. Figs, new, 15 to 16s. China oranges at about 20s per chest.

A brief letter to James Freeman stated that Claypoole was supplying the lowest price for "white and golden spirits of scurrigrass" and also for Daffey's elixir. The first was a volatile spirit made from scurvy grass, supposed to be antiscorbutic, the other a nostrum named Elixir Salutis, popular as a cure-all, recently invented by an Anthony Daffey. The copier forgot to fill in the prices.

London, the 27th, 10th mo., 1681

SAMUEL CLARIDGE

. . . I can never yet get sight of Thomas Roberts since he came for England, though his father has often promised me he should come to my house, or I should be sent for to him. I desire to know what thou wilt have me do about thy account with him. I perceive thou hast received £3 for interest and postage of the Earl [of Londonderry?]. I hope thou clears me of the extraordinary postage of those bills as well as interest. I am now about £180 indisbursed for thy account. . . .

To Thomas Cooke he wrote that he was sorry to find him discouraged about his sugar account, but that was every man's case as well as his; New England sugars were going for 18s and 19s a cwt. Some sugar would waste more if it were green or packed loose, or if it rained. Then he went back to the plans for releasing captured Friends and promised to advise Cooke when they were free.

London, the 3rd, 11th mo., 1681/82

FRANCIS AND GEORGE ROGERS

My last to you was the 20th past, since have yours of the 8th and 13th ditto, with a letter of Sir T. Clutterbuck's to you, which have perused, and one from you to be delivered him, which have taken a copy of; and there is another sealed letter, but not directed, which suppose is for William Penn, which may deliver him when he comes to town, which will not be in less than 14 days. Last week Sir T. C. his clerk came to my house and pretended he would have come sooner, but he was sick. He said it would be in vain for me to go into the country for his master without him, for he had the papers and was sure his master would do nothing without him.

So I desired to know when I might go, that I should not lose my labor which he promised positively should be on the sixth day of this month. So then we are to go together. Shall do my endeavor to get G[awen] Lawrie [to go] with me, but for W. P. there is no hopes at present. I should not have writ you now, but I doubted by my long silence you would have concluded I neglected your business. But, however, cannot drive it on faster than I do. . . .

At this time something seems to have happened to the partnership of Chare and Mitley. Perhaps Chare decided that Mitley was too easygoing in collecting money that he, Chare, was sure Claypoole had owed the firm for some time.

London, the 3rd, 11th mo., 1681/82

WILLIAM CHARE

. . . [I] have yours of the 23rd ditto and shall according to your order correspond with William Chare alone for the future. I am of thy mind that it may not be proper to buy any more furs at present. I have been lately to see a parcel, wherein was 646 otters at 14*s*, 380 martens at 2½*s*, 36 red foxes and 6 cats at 4*s*, 16 woodchucks at 3½*s*, and about 40 bad minks, but have not closed, so now shall wholly desist.

I take it very kindly thou hast accepted my bill protested by Mark Middock. I must desire the same for a bill of £100 on John Brummer, for Middock writes that he would not accept that on him. They do like a couple of knaves, for they have drawn me in to be £350 out of cash for them. But they shall pay it to 1*d*, for I have good security in hand. So I desire thee when those bills are due to recharge on me including the commission, protest, postage, etc.

Shall go to T[heophilus] Smith again shortly and then shall threaten him, and I shall mind [Edmund] Holt and Arding, etc. . . . I have not yet perused T[homas] Chare's letters about warehouse room, but I reckon to do it next week. [John Swinton was to get employment at Amsterdam and so pay his bill, Claypoole added.]

London, the 7th, 11th mo., 1681/82

FRANCIS AND GEORGE ROGERS

. . . Here is also verbatim copy of a letter from Sir T. C. which received but this day. His man never came at me, but promises by the middle of next week to call me to go with him to his master, and then I am in hopes shall have W[illiam] Penn with me, for he is come to town and has almost promised me. You little think how many errands and messages I have about it, almost every day more or less. Yours to W. P. I delivered and he said then he intended to go with me. . . .

To Claridge, Claypoole wrote that he had seen Gerard Roberts and had been promised, again, that he should see the son in a few days. The son, keeping himself well hidden, was making conditions, and Claypoole wanted a letter of specific advice.

On the 9th of January he wrote Richard Gay again that some of the money from the sale of the wine had been paid, and that the box of oranges had come "and were very few of them rotten."

London, the 13th, 11th mo., 1681/82

JOHN BRUMMER

. . . [I] have thine of the 31st ditto with copy of thy several letters to me and mine to thee, which thou needs not have been at the trouble of, for I have them all by me. I hope my last letter will satisfy thee better than the former, for thou built on a mistake, that I had mixed thy linen with Marcus von Middock's, or that I would not sell thine without his. I assure thee I have offered to sell thine alone, and would never have refused the selling of ½ a pack, and was many times offered 4*d* per ell. But since I had thy order to accept it, could never be offered it again, and under 4*d* thou never gave leave to sell, so that it was wholly out of my power to raise money to discharge thy bill, or after I had paid it, to [re]imburse myself. So it was no such occasion of offense for me to draw £100 on thee, when I had been 45 days indisbursed, and did really want the money by reason of other disappointments.

In this thou hast not done either like a friend or a merchant . . . and as for Mark Middock who has suffered my bill to be protested, he has done like a knave, and so shall tell him in due time. But he values me the less, because his effects will not answer what I have accepted from him. He has ill rewarded my kindness in accepting his last bills for £100.

I have a chapman or two that will come tomorrow or the 16th to see the linen, but I doubt they will not give 4*d* unless I should allow 3 or 4 months' time. . . .

[85]

Claypoole then mentioned a Martin Elkin or Elkins, who seemed a possible customer for the linen but who already owed him £25 on some former transaction. However, if this were paid up, he would consider him, but the deal was "more trouble than the commission is worth, 3 times over." However, if Brummer insisted, he would—after receiving the money—deliver the goods to him, though "of all the men in England I could wish rather I had never seen him." Then he added a postscript: "I have sold a little of it at 4d an ell, not many packs."

To William Chare on the 13th he complained, "I wish I had never undertook the business for Christian Pitch, etc., for I have such a base fellow to deal with that I doubt the trouble will be intolerable."

London, the 13th, 11th mo., 1681/82

JOHN CHRISTIAN PITCH

I have not in a long time written to thee, being in hopes still of giving thee some good account of Van Baselar. But he has put me off from time to time with such excuses and pretenses that it would be tedious to give thee a particular account thereof. And now this morning, since Theodore Jacobson has spoken to him, he is like a madman, and did swear and curse at such a rate as I have seldom heard a merchant, without any provocation of mine, and said, swearing by God thou wert a knave and a rogue, and he would prove thee so, and though thou hadst sent to T[heodore] Jacobson, yet he valued thee not, thou mightst send to the devil and his dam too, he cared not.

He would not refer it nor account with me, but keep me in law 20 years. So I told him I should advise with counsel and enter an action and arrest him, which he said I might do, and he would give in bail. So I went to Theodore Jacobson and told him the whole passage, and he desired me to come to his house with all the papers, that he might see how we might fix thy demands on him, and he would assist me, that if possibly we might end it without law. So in a few days I shall go to him, and we shall consider together what course best to take.

Following this lively episode, the letters settled down into the usual routine reports of bills received, dispatched, and accepted and the state of the various correspondents' accounts.

London, the 14th, 11th mo., 1681/82

JOHN HODGSON

. . . [John Nanfan had not paid Claypoole one penny of a £100 bill which Claypoole had previously asked Hodgson to collect.] I have been dunning of him ever since, and several times threatened to arrest him, so I got £50. And then the 8th month last [October] £30, so have received in all £80; and for the other £20 both myself, my man, and the goldsmith's man have taken a great deal of pains, and threatened him often, and at last sent a sergeant to arrest him. So then he came no more to the Exchange and now they say he is gone into Lancashire. . . .

To Abel Ram he wrote a letter about bills and added a note. "My brother Wingfield desires advice about his affairs, which thou may please to write in thy next letter to me." He added the exchange for Dublin, which was 10% to 12%.

London, the 17th, 11th mo., 1681/82

FRANCIS AND GEORGE ROGERS

. . . As to Clutterbuck, it seems I had not advised you of the sending your letter about the ship, but truly I thought I had done it. However, it is most certain, after I had most long endeavored to speak with him and could not, I sent your letter to a friend of [at] Hertford, John Curlis, a shoemaker that worked for the family and was acquainted with Sir T. C., to deliver it himself, which was done about the middle of the 6th month, and in my letter to T. C. I was very earnest to have his answer, but could get none till a considerable time after.

He would not part with the ship but fit her out for himself. And as for his being at Bristol, I never could tell whether he was there or no; however, I gave you timely notice thereof, and it was more proper for you to [have] given order for William Rogers, than for me. [To arrest Clutterbuck when he was away from home?] Before your last letter came to hand, W[illiam] P[enn] promised to go with me, which I was loath to reject, so we went out of town together and yesterday we were at his house. And there we both agreed to refer the whole difference to W. Penn, and tomorrow come fortnight we are all three to meet together in London. I believe he will not fail us, for he has an extraordinary respect for W. P.

I thought on this agreement not fit to show him the letter, so I keep it by me and a copy of it, and shall deliver it hereafter if there be an occasion, but I hope there will be none, for we [are to] refer all your demand[s] on account, my commission, and your disbursements on the ship.

I have spoke to W. P. about 5,000 acres of land for you, and shall get the writings perfected in your name. . . . I suppose W. P. will write to you himself, but have not seen him this day.

London, the 24th, 11th mo., 1681/82

FRANCIS AND GEORGE ROGERS

. . . I spoke to William Penn about 5,000 acres of land for you, and he said he had written to you about it and would wait for your answer. Sir T. C. has sent me word this day that he shall not come to town till the 3rd day next month, so we may appoint the 4th or 5th day to meet him, which I shall advise with William Penn about. . . . Persecution is very hot at Bristol and so continues. About 50 of the chief Friends in prison, whereof I suppose you have from others a more particular account than I can give you. We are yet quiet here but greatly threatened.

London, the 24th, 11th mo., 1681/82

SAMUEL CLARIDGE

. . . [There is] great persecution in Bristol and many other places in the nation, but as yet we are quiet, only threatened. We want several Irish posts, and the ships are still detained in the Downs by contrary wind. There is 7 East Indiamen arrived counted worth £700,000.

London, the 24th, 11th mo., 1681/82

JOHN MASON

I have received thine of the 9th ditto, which is chiefly about the loss of the last mum sent. I have not had an opportunity to speak with the master, nor do I think that it will signify anything, for he knows not me nor I him, nor have I any pretense on him. Thou shouldst abated it out of the freight. However, I am not obliged either by law or custom or equity to make it good; I having done my duty in sending them tight and well-conditioned aboard and sending thee timely advice, I run no farther hazard. And so it is in wine and mum and all commodities unless the buyer bargains that the seller shall be at hazard, and in such cases there is allowance accordingly. However, I shall not be strict with thee but bear a part, so in thy next let me know how many gallons were wanting. . . .

The next letter was apparently written by Claypoole's son James.

London, the 27th, 11th mo., 1681/82

WILLIAM CHARE

Per order of my father, I write this to advise thee that Christopher Smith is arrived safe at Yarmouth so has not insured anything. Arding says that he will pay in a month, abating the 20s, also [Edmund] Holt says he may pay sometime in 3 weeks or a month. But as for [Theophilus] Smith, he is angry and says thou need not be so hasty, for T[homas] Chare gave his daughter £100. Last post my father advised T[homas] Dennison he had order from thee to accept his bills for £1,000 as formerly. . . . When any ship bound for Barbados is ready to go from this port, shall advise. . . .

London, the 31st, 11th mo., 1681/82

WILLIAM CHARE

My last to thee was the 13th current. Since have thine of the 10th, ditto, to which I ordered my son to write a few lines. . . . I shall expect my ½ of the 20 [Rix] dollars for the counterpane, for T[homas] Chare told me he would bring it to account, and perhaps he might give it to Sir Richard Dutton. If thou wilt write to him to Barbados, I will send thy letter; there is seldom a month but a ship goes, and if thou hast never a correspondent there to order him to pay the money to, thou mayst send thy order to one of my correspondents, Joseph Grove, merchant, at the Bridgetown.

I hope Mark Middock will pay my bill; I am £140 out of cash for

[89]

him, besides that £100, but I have effects for all but about £20. I have not lately writ to him, nor will ever have to do with him if I can once get clear. . . . [Then referring to his ginger] I have not [had] 1*d* for interest of money from the 3rd month last, nor for hazard of sea and debts, nor commission nor charges, nor yet fully my principal. The charges of that commodity, I see, swallows up all the profit, so 'tis a miserable trade, and will not find water to wash one's hands. . . .

As to thy demand of £69 8*s* 5*d* [word undecipherable] for commission of goods sent out and warehouse room, I have spent almost a whole day to search letters but cannot find anything express as to those particulars. However, I am fully satisfied that T[homas] Chare never intended to charge me with either of those articles, for in many accounts under his own hand he expresses goods sent away, but nothing for commission and for warehouse room.

I am certain he would have scorned to charge me with it. . . . [Claypoole then wrote details of accounts covering seven years, of beaver skins sent overland to Moscow and other furs by sea to Archangel, and how much he had lost on all these deals.]

By some discourse I had with thy brother, he never intended to charge me with 1*d* for it; if thou dost insist upon an arbitration as to those 2 particulars, I desire it may be done here, because I am acquainted with nobody at Hamburg I can refer my case to. Smith [probably Christopher] and Hume are arrived, Archer cast away, and Cutter missing. [The last three were shipmasters of the *Mary*, the *Unity*, and the *Phoenix*.] The wind has been easterly 3 days.

London, the 4th, 12th mo., 1681/82

FRANCIS AND GEORGE ROGERS

. . . T[homas] C[lutterbuck] sent his servant to acquaint me that he was sick in the country and could not come to town till about the end of next week, and then he would bring his papers and meet us to join in the arbitration, which I acquainted William Penn withal. But he being engaged to go out of town about 40 miles hence before the middle of next week, I desired him to write to Sir T. C., which he did very effectually, and I sent my servant and horse with it yesterday. My man came there about noon but could not till next morning have his answer. He would not read the letter for fear it should discompose him. So this day he bid my man give William Penn and I for answer that he was sorry he had disappointed us, but it was merely through sickness, and that seeing he could not come, he would refer it wholly to W. P. and what he determined should be performed—which I this day communicated to W. P. who has it under consideration, whether it may be proper to end it without hearing both parties, to which I shall have his answer in 2 or 3 days. T. C. was very ill and bid my man several times desire us to pray for him. . . .

London, the 4th, 12th mo., 1681/82

Dear Friend Charles Marshall

. . . I heard thou wast coming to town, and since, I have expected thee almost every week. My wife and I were well affected with thy letter and refreshed in a sense of our mutual love, as we have often been, which still remains as formerly very sincere to thee and thy dear wife, and our hope and belief is that nothing shall ever interpose to make a separation. I am sensible thy exercise and travail on truth's behalf is very great, and so likewise is thy reward, and the Lord's work has prospered with thee to the comforting the hearts of his children. We had this day at our house the good company of dear G[eorge] F[ox], G[eorge] W[hitehead], William Penn, and his wife. I did not mention writing to thee but I know their love is to thee. . . .

Charles Marshall was one of the eminent writers and preachers of that day, and a martyr as well. He subscribed £25 to the Free Society of Traders, and he bought 1,000 acres of land from Penn, later sold to Richard Whitpaine.

To [James] Freeman, Claypoole wrote: "I hear that the persecutors go on very violently yet against Friends, "but the Lord will bring away their wrath in due time, and this as well as others will turn to the advantage." He also wrote that Freeman could have his three jars of aloes at 12d a pound.

Letters to Claridge and Ram were copied on the 7th, complaining that because of contrary winds there had been no Irish mail for three weeks. Claypoole asked Ram to deliver a receipt that he enclosed from his brother Wingfield Claypoole to a Captain Fitzgerald. The same day a letter was addressed to William Chare, and after notes about bills Claypoole wrote: "Holt came to me this day and entreated me not to disgrace him about the £35, for he would pay it me honestly in a month, or 6 weeks at furthest, for he said his trade would be much quicker than now it is."

London, the 10th, 12th mo., 1681/82

JOSEPH GROVE

My last to thee was the 16th, 10th month, per [John] Harding [*Carolina*], who went from the Downs but 12 days since, to which I refer thee. I intended to have sent thee a parcel of linen for our account in ½s, which indeed now is extraordinary cheap as ever I knew it. But sugars are so low here that there is no hopes of any profit, but a prospect of loss, so I shall forbear awhile till I see how our wine is like to sell. I am afraid we shall have but a poor account of it, there has been such abundance of claret and other sorts sent away at low rates, and if we have sugars from Jamaica, unless they be very good will yield but 22s per cwt., which formerly would have yielded 27 or 28s per cwt.

Cotton-wool or ginger are better commodities; especially scraped ginger, if good, will yield above 25s per cwt. . . .

Claypoole added that he would send the account if the ship stayed a few days longer, but the net proceeds of the sugar sale would be £32. He was sending by Joseph Wasey (master of the Grayhound*) twelve barrels of "right Brunswick mum." He wanted it sold from the ship, preferring not to risk having it spoil by standing about waiting for a higher price. He had accepted Ralph Weeks's bill and would soon be out of cash for Grove about £40, with "effects" for only £6. He would do all this out of "respect" for Grove, but he wanted some goods sent him to sell.*

Claypoole had been asked to arbitrate in a dispute between Samuel Claridge and Gerard Roberts, a merchant in Gracechurch Street. Claridge was convinced that Roberts owed him £20; Claypoole did not think he owed him anything, and his explanation was long and complicated.

London, the 11th, 12th mo., 1681/82

SAMUEL CLARIDGE

. . . Thy hard words against Gerard Roberts for not paying thee £20 when he owes thee nothing, I do not understand. I believe he will complain of thee to Friends in Dublin. . . . Let me have thy answer to

Thomas Roberts's objections, or else how can I be thy arbitrator? I must hear both parties that I may do justice; so I desire thee be not reserved, but let me know thy mind plainly, and what thou are sensible are mistakes, let be owned on thy part, and what is wrong on their part, let it appear, for I would do the thing which is right. . . . We are glad to hear thy wife is safe delivered and in good health; our love is to you both.

Gerard Roberts was a friend of George Fox and a witness at William Penn's wedding in 1672. Thomas may have been his son.

London, the 11th, 12th mo., 1681/82

FRANCIS AND GEORGE ROGERS

. . . Clutterbuck's man was with me 2 days since and told me his master was very sick, could not turn nor remove himself in his bed, and did desire that William Penn would forbear ending that business till we could meet here in London together, which he said might probably be in a month. So I asked him about the ship, what his master said still to that letter so long since sent him, and said I had another letter of the same import and would send it. He desired me not, for he [Clutterbuck] would neither read nor hear letters, so it might be lost. So I know no remedy but patience. But I desire to know in your next, that in case he should deliver you the ship for what he owes you, if you intend, however, to dispute my commission.

The method of Friends taking up land of William Penn is by deeds of conveyance, for which the purchaser pays about 12s.

If it be for 5,000 acres, which is called a whole share or Proprietary, for that we pay £100 and 50s per annum quitrent, to begin in '83 or '84 (I cannot tell which). They that will pay no rent must pay £120 presently, and so for a lesser quantity proportionable, and he that can settle some few families, I think about 6, may have his land all together, and every purchaser of 5,000 acres is to have 100 acres by lot in the first city.

The concessions or fundamentals for government are to be perfected this day and then to be engrossed and signed and sealed by the governor and purchasers, which, if it may be permitted, I shall send you a copy of, and then may write you more at large, if you intend to be concerned, as also about our Pennsylvania Company. . . .

This is Claypoole's first mention of the Free Society of Traders in Pennsylvania, which was to cause him so much work and grief in the future. A small notice appeared in the Impartial Protestant Mercury *in April saying that people could subscribe and learn details about the Society at Bridges Coffee House.*

At this point, young Haistwell copied a letter he had written the previous December 31 in an attempt to collect a small debt for one barrel of mum, which must have cost the office, in time and energy, far more than the debt was worth.

London, the 31st, 10th mo., 1681

JOHN PIERCE of Windsor

By the order of my master I write this to satisfy thee that Joseph Ryves [Reeves?], who is dead, bought three barrels of mum for thee, and paid but for two of them. The first was delivered the 13th of May, 1679, to pay at 2 months, but the money was paid the 9th of June, and the 10th day [of June] another barrel delivered and the money received the 8th of July, and the 9th day [of July] the 3rd barrel was delivered to Joseph Ryves for thee and to this day my master was never paid for it, which I shall make appear thus. When six weeks or two months (as near as I can remember) was expired, I went to J. Ryves in St. Paul's Churchyard for the money, and he was gone from thence. So I went to his lodging and demanded the money, and he told me he had not received it but promised me to write to thee and bid me call again. So accordingly I called again about a fort-night after, and then he said thou hadst been in town, and he thought thou hadst come to our house and paid it. But I told him it was not yet paid and my master was not willing to be put off any longer.

So after that I called when he was upon his death bed and spoke with him, and he said he wondered thou didst not pay it, and about four days after that I heard that he was dead. And then I writ a letter to thee but never received an answer. . . .

Haistwell plodded along, explaining in detail. Unfortunately young James Claypoole had sent Pierce a receipt with the wrong date on it; it was really for payment of barrel Number 2, but being dated after the

[94]

delivery of barrel Number 3 it could be read as a receipt for that. It looked rather hopeless, but Claypoole Senior took a hand, dictating another letter, which is undated.

JOHN PIERCE

[Claypoole hoped that the above would satisfy Pierce that his son James had dated the receipt wrongly.] So this in short is the matter, if thou received from me 3 barrels of mum and paid but for two of them, thou knowest in thy conscience there is one still owing for, so let there be no shuffling, but do the thing that is right. . . . and that which makes me suspect it the more is that in two years of time thou would give me no answer till I signified my resolution to go and get thee arrested. Thy answer I desire in a short time, either directed to me in Scots Yard by London Stone, or else to John Poynting. . . . John Poynting hath given a great character of thy honesty, and I should be glad to find it true. . . .

Then followed a final letter from Haistwell himself.

London, the 16th, 12th mo., 1681/82

JOHN PIERCE

My master enquired lately of John Poynting for an answer to the foregoing, but he said he had not received any but was doubtful that the original was miscarried. Therefore I send the copy. So be pleased (without further entreating) to return an answer. Also expect to be prosecuted according to law. For my master, James Claypoole.

To these letters he signed his own name, Edward Haistwell, but in each case scratched it out. To some letters he added a line of his own short-hand.

On the 18th, Haistwell sent a letter to John Hammond concerning a bill that had come in between nine and ten o'clock at night, about which he could do nothing that day, as "it was late before the post came in."

Letters for the next several days were entirely about bills of exchange, though in one to Michael Bilby, Claypoole remarked that he was sorry to hear that "the master of the Swallow is put back again and delayed by contrary winds."

WILLIAM CHARE

... I never received thy letter of the 30th December, so desire to know the contents of it. ... Christian Pitch has of late writ to Theodore Jacobson about Van Baselar, so I have a partner in that troublesome business. But I doubt we shall never end it without going to law. I have accepted thy bill for £109 to Harmon and Henry Rentzells being to discharge my bill on M[arcus von] Middock, and here underneath is account of the prices of silk, and next post I intend to write to him the account. I desire thee to cut [this] off and give to Christopher Mauks, which may suffice at present. ...

24 ozs. per lb.

	s		s d
Ardas of Aleppo	9s	to	9s 6d
Ditto of Smyrna	9s	to	10s
Liege ordinary Aleppo	15s 6d	to	16s
Ditto Smyrna ordinary	15s 6d	to	16s
Ditto Burma	17s 9d	to	18s
Ditto Sherbasee	18s 6d		
Tripoli Belladine	17s 6d	to	17s 9d
Ditto Bayreuth (Beirut)	17s 3d	to	17s 6d
Acra	16s 6d		
Bias	16s		

Ardas was fine Persian silk, Smyrna was Turkish, Sherbasee was Persian silk, Belladine was a white silk, Acra was imported from Acre, and Bias, or rather Beas, was from northwest India, the Punjab district.

London, the 21st, 12th mo., 1681/82

SAMUEL CLARIDGE

... [After mention of bills of exchange] I have sent a small box marked J. C. per the *Deborah*, Christopher Howard, master, for Dublin, with 10 books of Samuel Fisher's works; they are very well bound and I hope amongst Friends they will sell. I advanced towards the printing £30, merely for the service of truth, and am like to be a great loser. We sell them here for 12s per book, so there should be 14s, but I leave to thee to abate something rather than not sell. I have also sent 10 of the same to Cork. . . .

Claypoole had written the previous September 10 that he had "about 30" of these great folio volumes. Besides the ten mentioned here, another ten were being bound when he left London the following year. He gave one, signing his name in it, to Thomas Ellwood. On the 25th he wrote the Rogerses that he was sending ten of Samuel Fisher's books and added, "I expect William Penn in town next 2nd day [Monday] and then we will consult how to proceed with Sir T. C."

London, the 28th, 12th mo., 1681/82

JOHN SPREAD

. . . I am sorry thy 9 hhds. sugar came to so bad a market. I kept it in hopes of amendment for was bid but 18½ and 19s per cwt., and would willingly have taken 20s per cwt. for a long time together. Now lately I have sold it about 14 days since to Joseph Strutt at 20¼s per cwt. as per the enclosed account, the proceed of which being £62 11s 1d. I have carried to the credit of thy account current. . . . [Claypoole had not the time to send the equivalent of this amount in goods; the ship for New England was leaving too soon, but by the next he would send pepper and allajac, probably ellagic acid from gall nuts.] As for cloves, mace, and nutmegs, they are excessive dear, especially nuts, above 10s per lb. by reason of ingrossing in Holland [in modern terms, the Dutch were cornering the market], and we do expect they will fall.

I have received thine 19, 7th month, 6, 8th month, and 16, 10th month, and have sold Thomas Cooke's 8 hhds. and 3 tierce [of sugar]. . . .

This sent per Captain Peter Clark [the *Society*].

London, the 2nd, 1st mo., 1681/82

WILLIAM ALLOWAY

. . . As to thy desire to know what success Friends have had at court about their sufferings, I can as yet give thee no answer, for as yet they are only in hopes and know not what may be the effect thereof . . . money is very scarce here with us at present.

[97]

WILLIAM CHARE

... I shall expect thy letter to Sir Richard Dutton at Barbados and shall send it by the first conveniency. ...

As to the returned minks producing but £4 13s, it was because they were very much eaten with moths. They lay a long time at Richard Gawthorn's for sale, as if they had been his, and he asked 12d per piece for them. But they would not sell but grew worse and worse, so we sorted them and took out 100 of the best, and the other 300 he said if I would not have them home, he would give them to the dustman. So some of them was thrown away (how many I know not) and the rest were sent to William Baker, and he sold them for me. ...

I observe what thou writes about the commission and warehouse room, thou seems to slight all my objections as if they were of no force. But I am certain that if I could have a fair hearing by men unbiased, they would be regarded. Thou says that warehouse was never made use of for any particular private concern; thou saidst thou wouldst look back but 7 years, and now thou adds to that promise and says 7 years of thy brother's life. But that will not hold water. ... [Claypoole went on for some time repeating what he had written before. William Chare had said he wanted an arbitration in his own city of Hamburg.] As to referring it there, that is not equal, for they are thy friends and intimates, and I know no man there. But here it is more equal, for here thou hast variety of intimate friends as well as I, so let it be referred here and choose a man or two, and I will do the like. But if thou wilt not do that then I tell thee plainly I will not be imposed on. ... The fur trade was not so encouraging as to pay £8 sterling per annum for a warehouse; I have used my warehouse often for furs and beavers and never charged him [Thomas Chare] with 1d yet. It is worth £8 per annum also. In short, I say still it is unkindly done. ... I desire thee to consider the matter a little farther and propose that which is moderate. ...

The next day Claypoole wrote a brief letter to Samuel Claridge, mentioning that he was out of cash for him but also bringing in the name of "John Wallis the goldsmith that keeps my cash." This would have been the Major John Wallis in the 1677 directory, one of the "goldsmiths that

*keep running cashes," whose place was at the Angel in Lombard Street
and to whom Norton Claypoole owed money.*

*There were other business letters to Ireland. In one to James Freeman
he wrote, "I hear the persecuters are very violent still, but doubtless the
Lord will in due time restrain their wrath and preserve them that trust
in Him." On the 9th he was writing to Bordeaux.*

London, the 9th, 1st mo., 1681/82

WILLIAM POPPLE AND ROBERT STEWART

... I have used my utmost endeavors to get the £50 of Nanfan, and
at length when he had put me off several months, I employed a sergeant to arrest him, but he could not be found and I hear he has taken
sanctuary at Whitefriars. So I advised John Hodgson thereof that he
might get the £20 of the drawer.... [Here followed the usual excuses
of the men who could not pay.] I have had no courage to the wine
trade this year, they being generally bad as I heard long since, and
things so dubious and uncertain here. One while they come in without interruption, another while all seized with a great deal of violence
and strictness. Besides, they are often forced to swear them off for
port wine, etc.... [There was a special duty on French wines which
would not apply to wines from Portugal. But French goods, in spite
of laws to discourage importing them, were beginning to come in
again.]

I am desired by William Penn, who is my singular good friend,
whom I suppose William Popple has also some knowledge of, to
write to get about 1,500 or 2,000 vine plants to carry with him to
Pennsylvania, a colony in the West Indies near Maryland which the
king has given him, lying in 41, 42, 43 degrees of northern latitude,
whither he intends, God willing, with his family and servants and
many people this summer. He desires of those that bears the best
grapes, rather than the most. I suppose you know better than I the
way of sending them safe in open hhds. with earth, and whatever the
charge is, I shall repay you and be obliged to serve you in a greater
matter. You will also thereby very much oblige him. There is several
vessels now at Bordeaux which John Moore is concerned in, and he
tells me they will any of them take them in if you use his name. The
masters' names are John Leffield [*Guannabow*], Thomas Gadsden
[*Elizabeth & Mary*], William Harwood, Thomas Hawes....

FRANCIS AND GEORGE ROGERS

... Sir T. C. is likely to recover, but has been near death, and writes William Penn [he] has had 100 ozs. of blood taken from him. I sent the other day to enquire concerning him, and his wife sent me word she was going to him into the country and that I should hear from him next week. .... I know not yet what probability there is of my going for Pennsylvania, for I never intended it, but I have bought land, and if I see my way clear it is possible I may go. Yet not suddenly, and if ever I should intend such a thing, you may be sure I will give you and all my correspondents timely advice thereof....

As to the settling of a company in Pennsylvania, we have had many meetings and debated about it, and brought matters now so to bear as we think will give general content. The proposals or articles are transcribing, and next week we shall come to a conclusion either to desist or send copies abroad, and then I shall advise you further....

There were several short letters for the Irish mail, and then one written as though there had been no trouble between Claypoole and his Hamburg correspondent.

London, the 17th, 1st mo., 1681/82

WILLIAM CHARE

... Arding puts us off still, but I am in hopes of getting 50s [£50?] of him. [Humphrey] Blowers seems to be much concerned that he cannot get his money at Hamburg to pay thee there and would put me off longer on farther answer. So I was short with him and told him I would not be delayed on such an account, but if he did not in a little time pay me the money, he might expect another kind of message. So then he promised positively in 14 days to bring the money, which was, I think, 5 or 6 days since. I sent this day to Theophilus Smith to threaten him ... but his shop is shut up and he not to be spoken with so that it is to be supposed he is broke.

On the 21st Claypoole wrote to Samuel Claridge, "I wish thou wouldst get Thomas Holme to arbitrate it for thee [in reference to his letter of February 11] for I see it is not likely that I should please thee. He may be a very fit man, being honest and of a good understanding." This shows that Claypoole was unaware that Holme at that moment was either on his way to London or preparing to come. Exactly one month later Holme was made a commissioner by Penn and was on his way to Pennsylvania.

That week's Irish mail took a few more letters, one to Daniel Savery about Miles Forster, last heard of in the debtors' prison in spite of Claypoole's pleas for leniency. "I have not seen Miles Forster a long time, nor do I know what I shall do farther in that affair, but do really think it will be more for your satisfaction and profit to be favorable than severe, though he has done amiss and provoked you, and not to be excused."

London, the 21st, 1st mo., 1681/82

FRANCIS AND GEORGE ROGERS

... I hope R[ichard] G[ay] will stand good, or else I shall lose above £70 by him, and now he has ordered me to accept William Smith's bills for his account for £200, but I, having no effects, have writ to William Smith that he may draw his bill on R. G. payable to me, and I will negotiate it. His 30 pipes and 6 quarter casks [of wine] rendered but a very poor account, 10 of them decayed and many very ill tasted, that the net produce was but £22 2s 8d, and I do not remember that he ever gave me order to carry it to your account, but to dispose of it otherwise. If you insist on it, I will search his letters, and I think it will appear that I have neither been unkind or parted with it to my [your?] own wrong.

I have not heard since from Clutterbuck, but in the morning my man shall go to his lodging in the Strand.

As to planting my land in Pennsylvania, I have had divers considerations in my mind, which way to proceed, but cannot come to any result. Sometimes I am thinking to send one of my sons as an overseer, with 2 or 3 servants, to build a little house and plant an orchard and garden, and get some cattle, and ground cleared for corn, and so to go on raising of corn and cattle. And other times I am thinking to send some honest poor Friend with a servant or two to act for me as my attorney, that if I should have an inclination hereafter to go thither with my family, I may have a house and some provisions ready. I conclude on neither as yet because of some objections which I cannot get over, and [besides] the settling [of] the Company [the

Free Society of Traders] wherein I hear may some encouragement be offered for my going there myself. And one grand objection is that I may not possibly like the house nor situation, and so not care to dwell in it.

When we have concluded our business and all things else relating to the Company, we shall send copies thereof to divers parts, and among the first, to you at Cork, and then shall write you more at large about this business. . . . I believe what goes or comes from Pennsylvania must be entered in England because of the Act of Navigation. . . .

By the Navigation Act all ships coming from or going to the English colonies from Europe must call at an English port. It would be interesting to know whether the "objections" he could not get over came from his wife and daughters, reluctant to start life again in a wilderness.

London, the 28th, 1st mo., 1682

FRANCIS AND GEORGE ROGERS

My last to you was the 14th, ditto, since have none from you. This from Maskolin Alcock [master of the *Increase*] came to my hands but this afternoon. Sir T. C. has writ lately to William Penn that he will meet him in London next week, and then the difference between you shall be ended. . . . [Claypoole then reports on the bills of exchange, adding the unwelcome news that he was about £1 10 out of cash for them.]

The articles for the Pennsylvania Company are printing and I hope will be done by next post, and then either Philip Ford or myself will send you one. I cannot tell what to write you about the deeds for land, but yours will be like mine and others, which are approved on by men skilled in the law. And as to improving of land, there I can say little at present, but do find myself more and more inclined to go, so that I believe it will be my lot to remove with my family before a year be past, whereof I shall write you farther. But let me desire you not to think of removing your business from me upon this account, for I shall give you three months' notice of the time I fix on going. I have not signified this much to any of my correspondents, so desire you to keep this to yourselves. . . . I have subscribed £100 in the Company's stock; hope the same of you and others. . . .

WILLIAM CHARE

... Arding puts off very shufflingly for week to week. I hear no farther of [Humphrey] Blowers yet; I think thou had best write him a threatening letter. The 31st falls due Thomas Dennison's bill for £120 for thy account, and I am now £43 out of cash for thee. ... Thou seems to make light of my objections to warehouse room and commission. .... [Claypoole repeated what he had said before, especially to the arbitration not being in London.]

However, if thou art not willing to have it referred here, but rather desirous, as I am, that we should end it privately between ourselves, that so there may be no breach but our love and friendship continue, propose moderately and ingeniously in thy next what thou wilt have and I shall most readily consent to it. ...

Thy letter to Sir Richard Dutton I shall send to Barbados, but it will be long before I can have an answer, it's possible four or five months. Vale. (Tripoli Belladine is at 17½s per lb. Have enclosed a price current; it may go free. When hast perused it, please give it to Christopher Mauks.)

Claypoole sent the letter to Sir Richard Dutton, for on the 31st he wrote Chare again, asking for a copy of it. "We commonly send 2 copies to Barbados, besides the letter," he explained. Richard Dutton was governor of Barbados at this time.

Claypoole was beginning to change his former attitude about paying these extra sums of money, though he was clearly in the right. He added that if William Chare would mention a moderate sum they could come to an agreement.

London, the 31st, 1st mo., 1682

MARCUS VON MIDDOCK

... Thou says thou art not willing to accept my bill, though it be for thy own account, and but part of what I have long disbursed here for thee, which is very unworthy, not like a friend or a merchant, and if I had served thee according to thy deserts, I had refused to accept thy bills and might have kept my money to serve my own occasions and not have it lie dead thus at thy will and pleasure. When I drew that £100 I was near £240 indisbursed for thee and had been so some months, and I had not liberty to sell thy linen at market price to imburse myself. And I then told thee that I would not have drawn but for want of money, and then when my bill became due, thou mightst if thou hadst occasion, recharged again upon me, which was as fair as a man could offer his own brother. So thou hast neither done fairly nor honestly in refusing my bill, and when it comes under the consideration of others will not be for thy credit.

As for thy hammels, they are all resting, not a piece sold, and whereas thou sayest I may take 3⅞d per ell, I do assure thee I can find no man, unless for time [to give] more than 3¾d. But at 6 months' time I could sell at 4d. The hogs' bristles are a mere cheat, and thou dost not well to commend them when thou knowest they do not deserve it. Those that are honest and knows the commodity affirms they are such trash as the like is hardly to be seen, and 5d per lb. is the most I can get for them. I desire thee to appoint thy correspondent here to view them and see whether it be true or not. And let me know in thy next whether thou hast paid the balance of my account in thy hand to Aurend Brummer.

More trouble about hammels appeared in the next letter on the 31st to John Brummer. Claypoole said he must sell Brummer's hammels for 4d an ell; he could not get 4⅓d except at four to six months' credit. But he consoled him by saying he could only get 3¾d for Middock's goods. "They do use very little now of that sort of linen now in this land, or send to the West Indies. French linen is so cheap, there is few cares to buy such coarse linen as hammels."

London, the 1st, 2nd mo., 1682

Samuel Claridge

. . . Our book of articles for the Pennsylvania Company or Society is printed and I did intend to send thee one this day, but Thomas Holme told me he purposed to send 2 to Dublin, one to thee, and one to another. . . . For land, which William Penn sells in Pennsylvania, he gives every one their deeds when they pay their money, which are made hard [cash] by Thomas Rudyard. . . . I hope we shall get subscriptions, so as to encourage the settling of a company for trade there. Here are many have signified their good liking to it and will be concerned, and we have advice from Friends of divers counties in

England that will join with us. Our book will be ready for subscribers to begin next week. I do intend for my own part to be concerned £100 at least. . . .

London, the 4th, 2nd mo., 1682

FRANCIS AND GEORGE ROGERS

. . . [I] have little to add but at this time to convey the Articles of the Pennsylvania Company which I suppose upon perusal you will easily understand. If you are satisfied so as to subscribe, you must order someone to do it in time and send your vote against the 29th next month, when the subscriptions is to be confirmed, by depositing 5%, and the three general officers, the treasurer, and committee [are to be elected] as per the 5th Article.

There are some here privately talked of that are intended to be nominated at the General Court, for president, deputy, secretary, etc., but at present I think it not convenient to mention them. But by next post we expect William Penn in town, and then I expect he will either write to you himself, or join with Philip Ford and I to write to you and other Friends of Cork, in advice to you about this business. In the interim, please to communicate it as far as your freedom to Friends or others as John Hammond, Thomas Cooke, Robert Rogers, etc. . . .

London, the 7th, 2nd mo., 1682

JOHN CASSAWE

. . . The enclosed I send to [by] Captain Bruce [the *Dove*]. As to cotton and other goods which we used to send to Bremen, I have no mind at present to send any. I have entered the 20 barrels mum and received 10; the others lie on board. Have received all the gammons of bacon, which was not well cut; there was too much fat. There should have been in every 12 lbs., 2 lbs. of fat more cut off. They will give not above 5d for them. The mum is but indifferent, had far better from Brummer in winter. The invoice I have not yet examined but hope it may prove right.

Thou may draw on me by way of Amsterdam and Hamburg. I accept of thy pudding and 2 pieces of dried beef, but Herman Bute says that Captain Bruce must have them and he has delivered them to him. . . . Mum is sold here for 55s to £3 free of all charges.

Claypoole, however, never sold this sweet beer as cheaply as this but got as high as £3 7s a barrel. He may have been annoyed because the ship's captain got his present.
After some letters to Ireland he wrote again to Bremen.

London, the 11th, 2nd mo., 1682

AUREND BRUMMER

[Claypoole had sold Brummer's clapboards and received £391 19s 11d for them but had to pay the shipmaster Wilkin Vogelsang a few charges out of it.] . . . Have received all the mum out of Daniel Dietien [*St. Peter*] pretty well conditioned. He is an honester fellow than Vogelsang. . . . [Vogelsang, shipmaster and merchant as well, sent his barrels of beer partly empty, so Claypoole had to use five barrels to fill up the other forty-five, in an order of fifty.] Advise me by the next whether it is possible to turn my wheat and rye into money in a month's time, and for what price, and how much then I must lose by it, so then I shall speedily resolve whether to keep it or dispose of it [referring to the grain Claypoole had ordered the previous summer, still in the warehouse].

London, the 11th, 2nd mo., 1682

HENRY SMITH

. . . I received thine of the 18th past, wherein thou desires me to buy and send by the 1st ship that comes from London to Dublin a parcel of cloves, mace, nutmegs, and cinnamon, which have all bought according to direction. . . . I cannot yet get the 8 double barrels of anchovies, there being very few in town and those not good, and dear. [At this point Claypoole got into a muddle as to whether Smith wrote "capers" or "copperas"; if Smith's letter confused Claypoole, certainly Claypoole's answer must have confused Smith. In any case, he did send the spice.] Nutmegs are 7s 6d, cloves 7s 11d, mace 13s 3d, cinnamon 6½s. . . . I will suspend buying until further advice.

The same day a letter went to John Hodgson saying that John Nanfan, who still owed £20, was broke and in a place of protection, so he was sending the bill of exchange back, hoping it could be collected from the drawer.

London, the 18th, 2nd mo., 1682

SAMUEL CLARIDGE

. . . I am much inclined to go with my family to settle in Pennsylvania, but I think it will hardly be till the year 1683. In the meantime I am willing to serve my correspondents with the same diligence as formerly. I hope thou wilt still be my friend with Abel Ram. We are going on with the subscriptions of our Company or Society of Pennsylvania, whereof I suppose Philip Ford will advise thee the needful. My eldest son [John] is going with Thomas Holme to assist him in surveying the country; we expect they will be gone from Gravesend this week. . . .

London, the 19th, 2nd mo., 1682

JOSEPH GROVE

. . . [Claypoole enclosed a copy of his last letter, dated December 16; he was worried at not hearing from Grove and was doubtful of his health. Ralph Weeks owed him about £22, and he hoped Grove would remind him. He added the news about his son John.] I have bought 5,000 acres of land and may probably be concerned in the Company or Society, of which I send thee a book enclosed, and one of William Loddington's. So if the Lord clears up our way, I hope I may remove next year with my whole family thither. But in the meantime I am willing to serve my correspondents here and shall be often advising them how I proceed, and when I go away shall leave a letter of attorney with some honest, able person to take care of my concerns, till I can clear all here. I hope I shall hear from thee by John Strutt; if not, be sure do not omit the next opportunity, for I shall expect every ship to hear from thee. . . . I shall send thee more goods, for though I am like to remove, yet I intend to continue my correspondency with thee as long as I stay here, and also when I come to Pennsylvania, for we have a prospect of a considerable trade between Barbados and Pennsylvania.

We calculate there will go thither from hence above 1,000 Friends this year. After midsummer then 2 or 3 ships will go from London, then William Penn and his family goes, Thomas Rudyard, Christopher Taylor and his family, and many others. Then two ships from Bristol and 5 from Wales, so that if the Lord bless us and prosper our way, the country will be planted in a little time.

I may write thee more at large but cannot, the ship being in some haste, now preparing for Gravesend with my son. . . .

Here is a letter from my correspondent William Chare of Hamburg to Sir Richard Dutton, the governor, for £5 sterling, made payable to thyself, which I desire thee to seal and direct and deliver and receive the money, and send it me in some commodity, distinct from my own concerns.

Sent per William Emberley [the *Prosperous*].

William Loddington was a prominent Friend in Buckinghamshire, who wrote a pamphlet entitled Plantation Work: The Work of This Generation *to encourage emigration. Many individual Quakers, indeed entire Meetings, felt that emigration was running away from persecution. The ships from Wales went from Liverpool, and one, the* Lyon, *sailed from Chester.*

The sequence of dates was broken here, and some earlier letters were copied into the book.

London, the 14th, 2nd mo., 1682

HANS CHRISTOPHER MAUKS

. . . [I] have thine of the 24th past to answer in which thou ordered me to buy a bale of Tripoli silk for thee, which I have accordingly done yesterday. It is upright Tripoli and very fine of thread as ever I saw. If it comes well to hand, I do not doubt but it will give thee good content. It amounts to, according to the enclosed invoice, £190 12s 8d, and I had it the cheaper for paying present money. . . . tomorrow shall put it on board the *Mary*, Edward Hume [master]. He intends to be gone next week. . . .

Claypoole wrote William Chare the same day, telling him he was sending the silk to Mauks, consigned to Chare, according to Mauks's instructions. He also wrote to Barbados.

London, the 14th, 2nd mo., 1682

RALPH WEEKS

My last to thee was the 16th, 10th month, per the *Carolina*, Captain Harding. . . . I intended to send thee some ox bladders, but was advised by some that well understands the packing of aloes that nothing is so good to send it in as calabashes small and great, and the drugsters or any trade that uses it, esteems it better in those shells than in anything else, and they can take little or great shells as they have occasion. For bladders, they are apt to break, and the aloes being soft and liquid, they come to run one among another, so hereafter send in calabashes if they are to be had. . . .

London, the 15th, 2nd mo., 1682

FRANCIS AND GEORGE ROGERS

. . . As to my sending servants this year to Pennsylvania, I can come to no result in my mind till 2 or 3 months is over, that we see what subscriptions there will be for the Company, and who will be chosen for officers, about which I suppose William Penn, Philip Ford, and myself may write to you next week. . . . My son John is to embark next week for Pennsylvania with Thomas Holme, to assist him in surveying the country. Now if we had his sea bedding, etc., would save us some money. However, please to send them and they may be useful hereafter.

London, the 20th, 2nd mo., 1682

DEAR BROTHER EDWARD CLAYPOOLE

My last to thee was the 16th, 10th month. Since then have thine of the 23rd ditto, with the 14th, 12th month, and 4th, 1st month, wherein thou mentions nothing of Lewger. But I hope thou does not forget that business, for it is a matter of great consequence to me. I take notice Charles Sawyer will pay thee, which is well.

I forgot the case with the 2 pair of spectacles but intend to send them if I can now. We received the shoat last week, and it is to be killed this day. It is a brave hog but far bigger than I expected, and we do kindly receive thy love. . . . [Here were some details of bills.] [Joseph] Ball is arrived [master of the *Hope*], and yesterday came thine by [Thomas] Aubenny [the *Experiment*]. Shall enter thy 12 hhds. sugar and dispose of them, I hope, at a good price, for our market is very quick for such sorts, especially 1sts and 2nds, they having been wanted for some time past.

Since the above written, I have been at Gravesend with my son John, who is gone in the *Amity*, Richard Dymond, master, for Pennsylvania to be assisting to the general surveyor, whose name is Thomas Holme, a very honest, ingenious, worthy man. Have fitted John out with all things necessary, and his employment is very creditable and if he be diligent and sober may come in a few years' time to be profitable. However, it will be a present maintenance and keep him from ill company.

[I] have bought 5,000 acres of land of William Penn, and we are endeavoring to settle a society for trade, according to this enclosed book of articles. There has been subscriptions already for near £10,000, but we laid that aside, not having agreed on all particulars, and now the next week we shall begin to subscribe according to this book. Divers persons have desired that if the stock be considerable, so as that we shall proceed, that I might be one of the principal officers, as deputy, for there are 2 chosen for president and treasurer. Which am inclined to accept of if they choose me.

However, I have a great drawing in my mind to remove with my family thither, so that I am given up if the Lord clears our way, to be gone next spring, it may be about a year hence, I know not of any sooner time. In the meantime I am very willing and desirous to serve my correspondents here and shall do it with the same care and diligence as formerly, and thee in particular, brother. I hope thou wilt not lessen or withdraw thy business, for I shall be writing thee almost every month how my mind stands as to this matter, and if anything should come near the time of our going away, I shall certainly leave a letter of attorney with some very honest, sufficient man, to answer all bills, and to make full returns both to thee and all others, so that none shall have any cause to complain of me, for I shall do justly and honestly by all people. I have accepted thy bill for £30 so have included it in the account.

I send thee enclosed 2 pair of spectacles in a case, cost 5s. Advise in thy next what I might have 2 Negroes for, that might be fit for cutting down trees, building, plowing, or any sort of labor that is required in the first planting of a country. I hope to carry 10 or 12 servants from hence, and many people that love us well are inclined to go when we go. William Penn himself and family goes this summer, and probably about 1,000 people, and he is so much my friend that I can have anything in reason I desire of him, so that I have as much encouragement as any man whatever. But I look not at all [at] that, but at the hand of the Lord, who I believe will bless us this way.

I had a letter from brother Norton this week, dated the 16th, 10th month, from New Deal in Delaware Bay, where he is settled in a plantation. He writes his wife and child was come, and he was going to fetch them home. Brother Wingfield is like to go with us to Pennsylvania, and has promised to subscribe £50 in the Company's stock, and I hear my brother John is much inclined to it.

Pray, brother, in thy next, give me what advice thou canst about carrying things necessary for our first settling and planting, and consider if there may not probably be a trade between Barbados and Pennsylvania. We hope to have corn and wine and cattle, if the Lord blesses us, in a few years. So with mine and my wife's dear love to thyself and my sister and children, I rest, thy loving brother.

I have sold the hhds. sugar at 23*s* per cwt., came to £10 15*s* 6*d*. Excuse me for thy account till next opportunity, for time is short at present. I wonder I hear nothing from Joseph Grove; I have considerable effects in his hands, so if thou canst, advise me how it is with him, I am afraid he is dead.

A short letter in Haistwell's hand to William Chare on the 25th asked him to write to the debtor [Humphrey] Blowers, "for he is a mere shuffler. I should not have writ this night, but to caution thee concerning Charles Turner, for I hear a bad report of him." [A Charles Turner had bought £100 of Free Society stock.]

Three days later another letter went to Chare. "I know not what to do with Blowers unless I arrest him." Otherwise the letter is very much a repetition of the one he sent on March 3. "If thou dost place it [the ancient charges] to my account, I shall not allow of it, however, but consider of some way to right myself." It was unworthy of Chare to go back to 1673, which was during his brother Thomas' life, adding up charges. And as to the warehouse, Claypoole could prove it was used for other goods than his furs.

A short note to John Cassawe in Bremen said that they had shipped by the Love, *Paul Bendix, master, seven blocks of tin, which came to £57; the ship was to sail the next day from Gravesend.*

London, the 29th, 2nd mo., 1682

FRANCIS AND GEORGE ROGERS

... I am to go to Kingston to meet William Penn, who is at Windsor.... Sir Thomas Clutterbuck is not yet come to town, but his wife sent me word yesterday that he will come in a little time, and go to the king at Windsor. I will follow that business with all diligence, but you have not told me yet what I may trust to about the £20 commission.... [Then followed some talk of bills of exchange.] Our ship for Pennsylvania went out of the Downs the 23rd.

London, the 29th, 2nd mo., 1682

ABEL RAM

... I have some purpose, through the Lord's permission, to remove hence with all my family to Pennsylvania, but not till 1683. And in the [mean]time I am very desirous to serve thee as formerly, and I hope thou wilt not withdraw.... There is at Kingston, 12 miles from hence, to be sold a freehold estate with about 23 acres of land, which lets for, with a barn, £28 per annum, a large house, coach-house, stable, brew-house, etc., a brave orchard and garden walled about, excellent well situate[d] for good air, and gravel ground, and not far from the Thames, may be worth very well £40 per annum. They ask £900 for it, but possibly £800 may buy it. The dwelling is fit for a London alderman or knight or gentleman of £1,000 per annum. If thou art inclined to buy it, I may enquire further.

Surely the property so delightfully described was the house that Claypoole rented or owned, modestly mentioned earlier as "a small place to keep his children," to which he frequently went for weekends. Abel Ram was an alderman in Ireland—which explains Claypoole's writing that the house was worthy of a man in that important position. He would naturally not say it was the house he was living in, which he would have to sell the next year. He was trying hard to win Ram as a permanent correspondent; therefore any services he offered must not have a personal motive behind them.

London, the 29th, 2nd mo., 1682

SAMUEL CLARIDGE

... [I] have accepted thy bill for £150 to Abel Ram's order; of late he sends all his bills to others; I have not had one from him in a long time. I am not like to go to Pennsylvania till the year 1683, so I hope that is no discouragement. He shall have warning enough between this and then, that his business in my hands shall not suffer. I have many bills drawn upon me payable to him, but he endorses them to others. . . . I hope as thou hast an opportunity with him thou wilt stand my friend. . . .

The same mail took a letter to Robert Rogers at Cork, listing bills to £300, mentioning that he might go to Pennsylvania. To Robert Avery on May 4 Claypoole wrote, "Concerning the Angier [Algiers] captive we have been in daily expectation of a peace with them. So yesterday came the news of its being concluded and this day is confirmed, but we have not the particular articles yet."

The previous December Claypoole had written a long letter to Thomas Cooke about ransoming the Quaker captives. Buckinghamshire "Upperside" Meeting had also collected money for this and sent it to him through Penn's good friend Thomas Ellwood. Now, apparently, the rest of the captives would be freed without ransom. They were, however, treated well by the Algerians and allowed to hold their religious meetings in peace.

London, the 6th, 3rd mo., 1682

FRANCIS AND GEORGE ROGERS

. . . As to what you write about the proceed of Richard Gay's wines, which is the chief contents of both your letters, I am sorry you have taken so much pains to so little purpose.

But I account it the fruit of George Rogers's strong conceit of his own infallibility, as if he were the only wise man, and all were blind that did not see with his eyes. . . .

A long explanation followed; the unfortunate Gay's wines were bad, a bill had been protested, and Gay had contradicted himself as to who was to have the money for the recently sold wine. Having paid the brazier and plumber for that copper, Claypoole was £180 out of cash for the Rogerses' account.

London, the 6th, 3rd mo., 1682

HENRY SMITH

. . . [Having read Smith's order for capers as copperas, Claypoole sent for a sample and got, naturally, ferrous sulphate.] Now I perceive it must be capers. If the ship be not gone and that I can get the anchovies, I may send them. The box [the spices] is gone by Thomas Summers [the *Blessing*] and sealed with my seal, marked H S and directed on parchment to thyself, and come to, with commission and charges, £10 10s 9d, for which thou mayst pay Samuel Claridge, to be placed to my account, £11 10s 9d, or else send me a bill [of exchange] for that & the anchovies and capers.

I did kindly accept of thy love in the neat's tongues, but they were very bad, many of them scarce worth boiling, so I accounted somebody had cheated thee. Samuel Claridge sent me some once in the pickle, and I got them dried here and they were the best as ever I had from Ireland. If thou sends me any more I must endeavor to requite thee, but let be new and large, for the small ones are the worst, the last proved old, little, hard, lean, and rusty. . . .

London, the 6th, 3rd mo., 1682

WILLIAM ROGERS

. . . I am sorry I had not the opportunity of speaking with thee again before thou went away. I immediately accepted thy bill for £50 for F. and G. Rogers. . . . If thou hast any such cider left as thou gave me two bottles of, I desire I may have an order to thy factor here for 6 or 8 dozen, but I hope thou wilt take no more of me than of my brother, though I do not sell it, I give it away. . . .

This was clearly another overture to resume their old friendship, for if Claypoole wanted cider to give away to his friends or clients he would be more likely to get it from his brother Graveley, whose business was largely cider making. The letter was badly copied; Claypoole was probably suggesting that Rogers buy his cider from Graveley.

He wrote Thomas Dennison that he had paid out over a thousand pounds for him, and to William Chare he noted that their 238 Canadian foxes had been sold.

He wrote John Hodgson about the £20 left over from an old debt, originally £100. "[I] set a sergeant to arrest him [John Nanfan], and he appeared no more, and seeing I cannot find him to speak with him, I send thee the bill." Claypoole was hoping he could get the £20 from the original drawer, "which, if he be honest, he will not scruple to pay."

On the 16th he wrote Robert Avery that he still had no particulars of the peace with "Angier." To Abel Ram he wrote, "I perceive you buy

land for ½ the price there in Ireland, that it is here sold for near London,"
probably thinking of the house he wanted him to buy. Ram must have
objected to paying £800 or £900 for 23 acres in a London suburban
village.

London, the 16th, 3rd mo., 1682

SAMUEL CLARIDGE

... The Earl of Londonderry has been at my house, and also his brother. He would have me take his bill, but considering how troublesome their bills have been formerly, I refused it. I am engaged to thee for thy kindness in speaking to Abel Ram to continue and increase his business with me. . . . I shall speak to William Penn for one of the books of Laws, and Frame of Government of Pennsylvania when [he] comes to town, which will be in 8 or 10 days. I suppose it is printed, yet I have not seen them yet, though my hand is to both. . . .

The Frame had been signed by Penn on April 25 and the Laws on May 5; together they were an extraordinary pair of documents. Penn's whole thinking was that the will of one man should never hinder the good of a whole community; though given dictatorial powers, he deliberately gave them up for himself and his successors. Government was for the freedom and happiness of the people.

London, the 20th, 3rd mo., 1682

FRANCIS AND GEORGE ROGERS

... I have complied with your order to Joseph Ruddock for £58 for a copper [in connection with sugar boiling] and £5 for lead, which, with your bill to James Freeman for £40 which I have accepted and is near due, will put me indisbursed for your account above £220. . . .

In my last I sent you copy of W[illiam] P[enn]'s letter to Clutterbuck. Since, I cannot hear of his coming to town, but I shall still be mindful of it. Advise if my books be come to hand, which is all at present.

Claypoole wrote William Chare again on the 23rd. Charles Turner had promised to pay the bill of £300. He "intends to continue a cor-

respondency with thee, but I cannot advise thee to trust him far, unless thou hear a better character of him than I can have."

Another letter went to the Rogers brothers on the 23rd, again asking them to send his son John's bedding and to let him know if they had received Samuel Fisher's books. "Richard Gay has sent me 8 pipes of excellent good wine, which are cellared, and writes that he will speedily remit you all that is your due, and that you should not pretend to any of the proceed of the wine more than what I have paid you. I hope your apprehensions concerning him will soon be over, and that he will acquit himself as an honest man."

London, the 23rd, 3rd mo., 1682

WILLIAM ROGERS

. . . I have received of John Barnet [Rogers' London factor] 7 dozen and 7 bottles of cider, and one a little broken, about half full, and another had leaked about half out, so I account 7⅔ dozen, which at 8*s* per dozen will be too dear, especially considering the smallness of the bottles. I believe 12 will hold but 10 quarts, so let me pay but 7*s* [per dozen], will be £2 13*s* 8*d*.

It was typical of Claypoole, perhaps typical of commercial practices of the age, to haggle over petty details; in this case he was risking, for a few shillings, a business relationship he had been at great pains to keep friendly.

To Robert Rogers on the 23rd he lamented, "a good bill and good exchange is hard to meet with . . . enclosed is a bill for £20 drawn on thee by thy mother, which I send thee for thy proper [personal] account; at 8%, is £18 10s 4d."

To John Mason of Exeter he wrote that he was sending him some new mum by the John's Endeavour, *John Tendall, master, so their previous quarrel about leaking barrels was over.*

London, the 27th, 3rd mo., 1682

FRANCIS AND GEORGE ROGERS

. . . I thought good to write you for cover to this enclosed from Samuel Carpenter, who has sent me for your account by Charles [Christopher] Newham [master of the *Employment*] 8 butts and 8 hhds. of muscovado sugar. The master has been at 'Change, but the ship not yet come up; I suppose in 2 or 3 days will be entered at the Customs House. I will do my endeavor to sell it on board, but if I cannot must house it at the key, which I believe will be most for your profit (though it be more trouble to me). For M[askolin] A[lcock] gives a high character of his sugar and much of it cost 14*s* per cwt. and S[amuel] Carpenter uses not to send bad sugar, and when we sell unseen we expect it bad, and the buyer does suppose the worst. So that when we have any assurance that our sugar is very good we count it not equal to sell it unseen.

However, seeing your order formerly has been so positive for selling on board, I am resolved to sell it so, if can be offered a reasonable price, which I think may be about 20*s* per cwt. And I shall show the buyer my invoice of the price and advice of the goodness, etc.

William Penn comes to town next week, and then I hope F. R. will be here also. Sir St. John Broderick has not consigned his wine to me, but to his son.

The same Irish mail took a letter to Samuel Claridge, regarding a bad bill. "If it be without the bonds of London, each protest is 5s and noting [endorsed for nonpayment] 3s and less I never paid. . . . I shall observe what thou desires about the books of Pennsylvania and the quitrent deed, etc., but I have not seen that book of the laws yet, nor do I know that [it] is printed. W. P. will be in town next week, and then I may speak with him. . . ."

London, the 30th, 3rd mo., 1682

JOHN SPREAD

. . . Enclosed I send copy of the 9 hhds. of sugar per Thomas Barrett [the *Horne* or *Herne*] for thy account, the net proceed of which is £62 11*s* 1*d*. And here is bill of loading and invoice of one hhd., one bale, and one box of merchandise per the *Thomas & Susan*, David Edwards, master, consigned to thee for thy proper account, amounts to £63 3*s* 1*d* so that I have overbalanced the sugar account by £0 12*s*. These goods have been a pretty time bought, for we expected Edwards would have been gone above a month since.

But nutmegs was fallen before I bought them, about 2*s* 6*d* per lb. The pepper is of the best sort, and for such thou must sell it 1*d* better than most that is sent. The money falls much short of what I expected, so I have not sent the East India silks nor bone lace, but hope what I have sent will please thee. But indeed the encouragement [for trade] is but little either from Barbados or from New England, for sugars are very dear there and cheap here, from 20s to 22s per cwt.

We are fixing of a company for trade in Pennsylvania by a patent from the governor, William Penn, according to this enclosed printed book. We have subscribed between £5,000 and £6,000, and till the 29th next month the subscriptions go on here. Then we shall provide a cargo upon the company's account and do hope to have a ship arrive there before winter. And then for 6 months after, subscriptions will be taken there to enlarge the stock. So that if thou, or any friend or acquaintance of thine, have a mind to be concerned, you may send your order about subscribing.

I hope through the Lord's assistance to be there next year with all my family. I intend to embark about the next first month, called March. They have chosen Nicholas More president, John Simcock deputy, and myself treasurer, which was done yesterday. Also an agent and 6 factors to manage concerns here, and 12 for a committee in Pennsylvania; per next ship may write thee more full, but at present I am in haste, so must conclude.

Spread was not a Quaker, or Claypoole would not have translated the first month as March. Quakers were anything but welcome in the Boston of that time. The Committee of Twelve to live in Pennsylvania included such prominent merchants as Robert Turner, Thomas Brassey, Thomas Holme, John Bezar, Francis Plumstead, Griffith Jones, Anthony Elton, James Harrison, John Blunston, Isaac Martin, Walter King, and William Haige. Joseph Martin of London was to be chief agent at home, with Philip Ford as deputy, and assistants William Sherlow, the goldsmith Sir John Sweetapple, Edward Pelrod, and the wine merchant Thomas Barker. Plumstead did not come.

London, the 3rd, 4th mo., 1682

THOMAS COOKE

. . . I send thee enclosed the writ of error and seeing it was thy desire to have 10s given to my servant, and did not mention which, I have given each of them 5s, for they were both employed about this and the former business. But thou need not have been at the charge, for I am willing to do any such thing without gratuity.

I am landing and housing thy 10 butts of sugar, which I must do for here is no chapman presents. I have spoken to some, but they will not buy. . . . The *Patience*, Emmanuel Hudson, is expected in a month. [In other words, more sugar would be coming to an already glutted market.]

London, the 3rd, 4th mo., 1682

FRANCIS AND GEORGE ROGERS

. . . [I] have paid Joseph Ruddock's bill for £58 [for the copper boiler]. Have received this day bills of lading and invoice for 10 hhds. muscovado sugar and 12 hhds. by John Jewell [the *Expedition*] which ships are come, but whether in the Downs or River of Thames I cannot yet hear. Those by Christopher Newham [the *Employment*] and Edmund Scot [the *Hare*] I am taking up and housing, which there is a necessity for at present, for no chapman offers to buy. Have spoken to some and they will not buy; besides, the sugar is so good that it must certainly be more for your advantage to sell it in the warehouse than in the ship, I believe 5% difference beyond all the charges. You may be sure I will use my utmost endeavor to obtain the height of the market and [find] good men, and save what charges I can.

They [the sugar] will be housed at the keys, so little charge in carrying. William Penn was at Windsor yesterday and is expected in town this night.

He wrote to Claridge the same day, telling him he had spoken again to Philip Ford about the Pennsylvania deeds. "He tells me he will send it thee, but shall remember it again, and the pieces [of] kenting for thy wife." Kenting, sometimes called cloth of Kent, was a very fine linen, mostly used for neckwear and kerchiefs.

London, the 3rd, 4th mo., 1682

WILLIAM CHARE

. . . I perceive he [Charles Turner, about whom he had already warned Chare] has consigned thee some sugar and intends to continue a correspondency with thee, but I believe he will take offense if he may not have credit hereafter, wherein I can give no encouragement, for he is a young man of little experience, and has too many sorts of trades to thrive. . . . [Claypoole added he would try to get some furs when they came into the market.]

The sale of the 90 bags of black ginger I refer wholly to thee. I desire thee send my account as soon as thou canst, and then if there be no other remedy I must refer my case to the Court of Assistants. [They were senior members of the various City companies, such as the Goldsmiths, Fishmongers, Merchant Taylors, etc., who met to manage the affairs of the companies. This was a powerful threat, if Chare understood the importance of livery companies.]

Holt has paid £10 more and I suppose will pay the rest in a little time, but Blowers puts off for a month and then promises to bring me the money; if not, I intend to prosecute him. I delivered Charles Turner the particulars of the linen, and I delivered thine to John Moore. If they should want credit for £500 at any time, I mean he and Thomas Barker, thou mayst safely do it I think. They are accounted sure men, and I would not question them for £1,000. . . . I doubt Arding will pay nothing; I wish thou wouldst get Nat Wood to dun him, which is all.

The Moores were among the most prominent merchants in London; a John Moore was a knight. Thomas Barker had just been made assistant to the London agent of the Free Society of Traders in Pennsylvania.

London, the 13th, 4th mo., 1682

FRANCIS AND GEORGE ROGERS

My last to you was the 3rd ditto, since have yours of the 30th past, which is chiefly about the proceed of Richard Gay's wines, wherein you very much wrong me. . . . [Claypoole had sent them an account of goods totaling £570, and Francis Rogers, at least, had had some objections.]

As to your cautioning me in friendship as to R[ichard] G[ay], I took it very kindly, and I did not ill-reward your kindness, or do anything amiss, according to my judgment, in telling R. Gay you were disgusted he had protested my bill for your account. It was nothing but what you yourselves or anyone else in the like case [would have done]. I have never endeavored to exasperate him against you, nor you against him, nor had I any such end as you surmise. But your wicked jealousies will return on your own heads, for I am clear in the sight of God and shall appear so before all just men, if ever it comes to trial. And I must tell you I believe R. Gay does not deserve those reflections you cast on him.

You often insist on it that I intended to convert that money to my own use, which was not so, for I have accepted some hundreds of pounds for his account lately. . . . F[rancis] R[ogers] gives other gross reflections on fair dealing, and G[eorge] R[ogers] says he complies with every particular of his brother's, and that his brother sees my disingenuity with his own eyes, and as if I had neither good manners nor breeding.

It seems you are both agreed to run me down at an extravagant rate. I expected no better from G. R., for as the tree is, so is the fruit, and as the fountain is, so is the streams. But I am grieved to see that F. R. should so far drink in his brother's spirit as to murder me in his heart, both as a Christian and a merchant, and I do know the Lord will require it at his hands.

Then as to the words in great characters, I have no tricks nor devices but what are just and honest, nor have I been ungrateful, nor ever had 1d of yours but what have honestly deserved, and in the whole course of my correspondence with you I have been very careful of your concerns, and been always desirous to please you, and condescended to you beyond what is common. And you have sometimes, as at this time, insulted over me as if my whole dependence was on you. G. R. says he admires at my folly, [that] I should endeavor to sham you thus of, and to believe you such notorious dunces and sots. The folly is his own, and it proceeds from the pride of his heart, and I have no share in it. . . . Sir T. C. has sent me word this day that he will be in town to meet W. Penn and me next week.

Claypoole was sending another copy of that account, this time signed by two witnesses, to show it was a true copy of his books. As to their sugar, he would dispose of it with as much care as if it were his own. He then apologized that he had no time to write more and added that "Thomas Barker is a Friend that lives in Seething Lane near Tower Hill and is a great dealer who bought the wine."

He found time to write the same day to Robert Rogers, telling him that he had no "certain correspondent" in Rotterdam or Amsterdam and advising him to write to Daniel Lodge and partner at Amsterdam and to Benjamin Furly at Rotterdam.

The Lodge family were among the Quakers in Amsterdam. Benjamin Furly, friend of Penn and Fox, was a leading Quaker on the Continent, a rich merchant and an intellectual; he was also Penn's agent, and he started the great emigration of Germans into Pennsylvania.

The next letter went to the son of the Irish knight and merchant, Sir St. John Broderick.

London, the 13th, 4th mo., 1682

THOMAS BRODERICK

I received thine by Captain [William] Strong [the *Broderick*] and have entered and taken up the wine. There is 14 pipesful and ¼ cask; it proves very indifferent. We entered them filled and lost the 12% and filled them up on board, which is the most profitable way. . . . [Claypoole's complaint was that the pipes, which should have held about 126 gallons each, were not filled. However, he got an allowance of 1⅓ pipes from the Customs.]

They are lodged in a cool cellar and when they are a little fallen [settled], shall be racked [the clear wine drawn off from the sediment], and then proffered to sale. Have paid in charges about £55 already and the master £20, and must pay for rapes [the French *vin râpé*, a cheap drink made from the second pressing of the grapes] and beer and bread, etc., so that I shall quickly be out £100. Have taken care of the birds and cheese, etc. I hope to see thee here in a few days, so shall not enlarge at present. [The cheap wine, beer, and bread were possibly some extra payment for the crew of the ship.]

London, the 19th, 4th mo., 1682

RICHARD GAY

. . . There is a great difference arisen between Francis and George Rogers and myself about the proceed of thy last wine, which they insist upon ought, according to thy order, be placed to their account, so that I am like to lose their correspondency and, in all probability, have a lawsuit with them beside. [With an eye to business and his commission, as well as friendship, Claypoole asked Gay to end this dispute. He had received eight pipes of wine by the *Samuel*, Thomas Lock, master. The wine arrived in good condition and was already old for £17 a pipe. "Horse beans 20 to 23s per quarter," he added.]

London, the 20th, 4th mo., 1682

DEAR FRIEND ROBERT BARCLAY

According to thy desire of me when thou wert here in London in the year '79, I took upon me to deliver John Swinton from the trouble that attended him by reason of a bill of exchange accepted by him, due to W[illiam] Chare, and after I had used my utmost endeavors to William Chare to get abatement to part of the charges and could not prevail, no less would satisfy him than the whole sum, or to fall on J. S. again. So that besides the £4 13s 6d principal, I was fain to pay him £4 6s for charges, so there is due to me on that account £8 19s 6d which according to thy promise to me in writing, dated the 8th month, '79, I do expect of thee. And seeing I have forborn thus long, near 3 years, I hope thou wilt return me the money without delay.

If thou orders it to G[eorge] Keith may be as well, for I have a child with him, and must pay him money. Have looked for thee these 3 years at the General Meeting and should have been very glad to have seen thee, and now am doubtful shall not see thee in a long time, for I am to go in spring with all my family to settle, to dwell, in Pennsylvania. But though we may be far separated outwardly I know we shall be near one another in that life which reaches over all, wherein my love is and always has been since I knew thee, very sincere to thee, which may be easier felt than expressed by words. And I know and am satisfied in the same from thee, which I desire may never decay but increase, that we may still be as epistles writ in one another's hearts, in the reading of which there is mutual joy and refreshment.

I should be glad to have a few lines from thee, and then may write to thee again. So at present, with mine and my wife's dear love to thee and thy wife, I conclude. My dear love to my cousin Thomas Mercer when thou sees him.

Robert Barclay, author of the Apology for the True Christian Divinity . . . Preached by the People, Called, in Scorn, Quakers, *lived near Aberdeen. A friend of Penn and Fox, he was one of the twelve original Proprietors of East New Jersey and was valuable in the colonization of both New Jersey and Pennsylvania. His book is one of the great Quaker classics.*

George Keith had only recently taken over the school at Edmonton,

[123]

about eight miles north of the City. The child that Claypoole had there was Nathaniel, then ten years old; George and Joseph were still too young, and James, as we know, was in his father's office.

It would be another ten years before Keith openly broke with the Quaker beliefs. Joseph and Nathaniel followed his teachings.

John Swinton is listed in the 1677 directory as a merchant doing business in Water Lane, London. Later he went to Amsterdam.

This same day Claypoole wrote Henry Smith, to whom he had sent the capers, and asked how they were. He complained that it was hard to get good bills of exchange and asked Smith if he sent any more neat's tongues to have them new and in pickle. "One dozen large so ordered is better than 3 dozen of the little dry, lean, rusty things."

London, the 20th, 4th mo., 1682

ABEL RAM

. . . Thy bill for £70 to Symon Harrison I paid at sight, and thy bill to the Lady Shane for £100 I paid this day, and tomorrow I must pay thy bill for £349 13s 6d to Lord Chief Justice Keating. [John Keating was chief justice of the Court of Common Pleas in Ireland.] I hope thou wilt send me some more bills now, for it is long since I received any from thee. I purpose to stay in England till the next 1st month called March. My brother Wingfield is very desirous to have a few lines from thee.

London, the 23rd, 4th mo., 1682

WILLIAM CHARE

. . . Here is now a New England ship come into the Downs, so that in probability there may be some quantity of furs. Shall do my endeavor to get some good goods, if I can have them reasonable, without trash and such sorts as will not vend. . . . I have a great quantity of sugars on hand and a very bad market; such as we used to sell for 24s, worth now but 21s per cwt., am treating with William Gore for about 40 ton, would send some to Hamburg if there was encouragement; they are Barbados muscovado and heavy hhds. and butts, 15 to 17 cwt. and 9 to 12 cwt. Advise per next what demand they are in, and the tare now given. . . .

Haistwell copied a letter to Cooke, whose sugar was still unsold. He wrote that they had the "chiefest dealers" in to see it and they offered but 19 shillings. "Now I am in treaty with a Hamburg merchant, a great exporter, and am in hopes of getting 20s, but that will be the most."

London, the 24th, 4th mo., 1682

FRANCIS AND GEORGE ROGERS

. . . I have writ at this time but to advise you how far I have proceeded in the sale of your sugars. They are all landed and housed at the waterside, and yesterday I showed them and this day again to some of the chiefest buyers in our city; and the most I am yet bid for the whole parcel is 19s per cwt., although they are an indifferent good parcel. I have from another a parcel not so good by 2s or 3s per cwt., but they shall not prejudice yours, for I sell them alone or with such as are of an equal goodness, but I have not one pound to sell for my own account. I am in hopes of getting 20s per cwt., but that is the most; and I must give a month's time for the first half payment and 2 months for the last, and I am about £180 out of cash for you, besides the charges of sugar.

Sir T[homas] Clutterbuck is not yet come to town, and this day William Penn is going into the country for a few days, which is all at present from your friend.

London, the 27th, 4th mo., 1682

SAMUEL CLARIDGE

. . . Philip Ford says he will send thee the quitrent deed when he can get it perfected. My wife has bought for thee a piece of linen for thy wife for handkerchiefs; it cost just 12s. I sent my man with it [to the ship for Ireland]. We are going on with our subscriptions for the Pennsylvania Society. . . .

London, the 27th, 4th mo., 1682

WILLIAM CHARE

. . . I desire thee when thou hast an opportunity, to tell Hans Christopher Mauks that I have made full enquiry concerning Tripoli and Bayreuth [Beirut] silk and am informed that there is not such choice in town as at other times. Some fangotts there is of fine silk, but scarcely a bale. [A fangott was a bundle, especially of raw silk, of from 1 to 3 cwt.] But there is a Turkey ship expected, which in all probability may be here in 14 days or 3 weeks and then we shall have a supply of both sorts. So if I may have his order I shall take the right season to effect it. The price is 17s per lb. both for Bayreuth and Tripoli Belladine, but I am informed by those that have good experience in that sort of silk . . . that Bayreuth is more proper and profitable, and for France they send Bayreuth generally for gold and silver twist. . . .

London, the 27th, 4th mo., 1682

JOHN BRUMMER

. . . I have accepted thy bill for £120 to Nicholas Brummer's order, but I wonder thou wouldst draw £120, for it is more than the linen will produce. However, I have honored thy bill. The hammels I cannot sell; I would now take 3¾d and doubt cannot get it. However, I stand for [3]⅞d, but the next good man that bids me 3¾d shall have them. I am sorry the market proves so bad, but it is not my fault. Thou limited me when I could have sold at 4d to 4¼d, and the commodity is now in a worse demand than ever it was. . . .

London, the 27th, 4th mo., 1682

DEAR BROTHER EDWARD CLAYPOOLE

. . . I have received up the several parcels of sugar, viz., 12 hhds. per Aubenny [the *Experiment*], 13 hhds. per the *Concord*, John Strutt, and 10 hhds. per the *Carolina*, John Harding, master. [John] Hull [the *Orange Tree*] is not yet come. The first parcel I sold to divers grocers, some at 43s, some at 33s, and some at 27s per cwt., the second parcel to others at the same price. Those by Harding were not so white as the former, and indeed I could hardly get 43s and 31s per cwt. for them. But so I sold them and have received most of the money for the first parcel, and in a month's time I do not doubt but may have all the rest, they being correct men. And by John Strutt,

[126]

who is beginning to load for Barbados, I intend (both) to send thee account of wares and account current.

I am still in the same mind of removing with my family to Pennsylvania in the spring, about the first month, and shall order my business accordingly, and as soon as I can fix upon an attorney with whom to leave my concerns here, I shall advise thee thereof. I have a trusty servant [Edward Haistwell] that is very diligent and capable to do business and has about 3 years to serve, but we are not yet fully agreed about his staying here or going with me, and my son James, who is now near 18 years old, has an inclination to stay here, and I and his mother are willing he should. But we shall consider farther and in a few months come to a conclusion. [James went with them; Haistwell stayed.]

The Pennsylvania Society hath chosen me treasurer and propose to allow me £100 sterling per annum and to dwell and diet in their house, to keep their effects of all sorts, and to oversee servants and buy and sell, etc. We have about £8,000 subscribed and do expect it will be made up £10,000, the ½ of which we take in at present and the other ½ as we shall have occasion, the next year or afterwards. Doctor Harding has been at my house, but I have not had an opportunity to have much discourse with him yet. [John Harding was master of the *Carolina*; Dr. Harding was James, who was interested in the Free Society.] If thou draws upon me for £200 more, I shall readily accept thy bills. I paid the doctor £17 upon demand and accepted thy bills to him.

I think I must have 2 Negro men, strong fellows, and a boy and girl, so I desire thee that when thou meets with such as may be proper for the country and my occasions, to keep them for me. The boy and the girl may be from 12 to 17 years old, or between 10 and 15. I am very glad thou hast got a bill for £80 of William Lewger; it is more profitable than sugar, and I hope thou wilt have gotten the rest before this comes to hand.

John Bawden is my neighbor and a very correct man, but is a question whether or not his bill may be accepted. I desire thee admit of no delay but get what possibly thou canst of him with speed, or I believe I shall lose it, for he is a rogue and will be gone. . . . If thou art minded to subscribe into the Company's stock, thou may send order by Samuel Carpenter or to Doctor Nicholas More, who is our president and intends to be gone from hence in a month or thereabouts, and for half a year after the arrival of the first company's ship, the book of subscriptions will be open. I shall be in a capacity to serve my friends in Pennsylvania as well as if I was not treasurer to the Company. I shall expect thy advice, and I hope thou wilt not be sparing.... [He ended as always by sending his love and his wife's to Edward and his family.]

The reference to John Bawden is interesting. A merchant who lived in Bush Lane, around the corner from Claypoole's house, he was one of the two men to whom Claypoole turned over his business when he left, and at that time Claypoole could not praise him highly enough. He was probably annoyed with Bawden at this time. Claypoole lost his temper easily, and when he did, spoke tactlessly and harshly, but he never stayed angry long. Penn, who really loved him, recognized his weakness.

A new hand now appeared in the letter book, copying a letter to "William Alloway, Loving Friend," and dating it "London, Primo, 5th month, 1682. By the order of my master James Claypoole," etc. But this departure from Quaker simplicity was soon checked, and the next letter started in the conventional way.

Claypoole continued to woo Abel Ram. He wrote that he hoped Ram would not withdraw his business, as he did not intend to leave until next March. He mentioned his loss of half a bill for £107, so business that would bring him even £20 commission would be "a piece of justice."

London, the 4th, 5th mo., 1682

Thomas Cooke

... This afternoon I received a letter from John Spread wherein is a bill of lading for a hhd. of fish by the *Dolphin*, John Foy, master, who I suppose is in the Downs. He advises that there is in the said hhd. 320 and a quarter ounces pieces of 8 and £12 12s 6d English money and 4 pieces of gold, and that he would send 348 and a ½ ounces more; that he would send in a other ship. When they come to hand, I shall dispose of them to the most advantage I can, which is all at present.

The value of a piece of 8 varied according to whether and to what extent it had been clipped or debased. Hence the goldsmiths weighed them. Presumably these were thoroughly washed to be rid of fish oil before the goldsmiths had them; it is unfortunate that Claypoole does not mention anything about this.

London, the 4th, 5th mo., 1682

ROBERT ROGERS

. . . I hope thou dost not take it unkindly, anything that I writ in my last, for I did only show thee how the account stood between us, which I must do upon occasion or else I may be justly blamed. What I said about thy drawing so great a bill upon me when I was endeavoring to remit thy money was not to upbraid thee, but to excuse myself that I had not neglected to follow thy order. I would not give thee offense, if I had not a week to stay in England (but I purpose to stay till the next first month called March) for I always valued thy correspondency equal with any that ever I had to do with, all having been very fair and easy and pleasant, so that if I had met with the like dealings from others, I should have been more unwilling to leave my business than now I am.

There are some men so proud, insulting and conceited, perverse and unreasonable in their demands, that a man had better be a day laborer than a factor. . . . [Then followed some details about bills of exchange.] My Rotterdam correspondent Benjamin Furly is detained here by a Chancery writ, that I know not whom there to recommend to thee. My correspondent at Amsterdam is dead; Daniel Lodge is his son, but I never had anything to do with him, but would if I had occasion. I may in a little time give thee an answer about Antego [Antigua] tobacco, which is all at present.

London, the —— of 5th mo., 1682

FRANCIS AND GEORGE ROGERS

. . . The reason of my writing to you so largely the 13th, I was exceedingly troubled and grieved to see you both agreed in the judgment concerning me and to impose it upon me as if I was a liar, a cheat, and the like in several particulars, wherein I know that in the sight of God I am absolutely clear and innocent, and have given you no just cause to entertain such thoughts of me. I say still I did not expect it from F. R. and therefore was much grieved. But from G. R. who has been taking occasion against me for some years, and threatening me in an insulting way in the pride of his heart, to remove his business, I could expect no better, for I know in what ground the root of enmity goes. He is a man so nice and so high that he must not be controlled nor contradicted.

I say it is an unreasonable, unjust thing (and I will never consent to it) for you to impose upon me to refer a business in Cork that was transacted here. . . . I do hope I shall have order from Richard Gay a place to proceed [to place the proceed] of his wine account to your credit, and then I shall most readily do it. And I hope to get an end with Sir T. C. to your content, for William Penn is now in town and T. C. has promised to come and refer it to him.

As to my mentioning the several sums paid you per order of R. Gay, I do profess I did verily believe you had insisted upon the proceed of both parcels of wine and was heartily glad when I understood to the contrary. For I feared to be embroiled in a suit of law, and could expect nothing but the utmost rigor at your hands. But possibly you may not believe me, but I am counted by you not so good as a moral heathen. As to the account sent you, do not give credit to it, though if it be witnessed by my son and my servant, I cannot tell it to say to you, for they will not swear nor can I, but I do affirm it is a true copy. . . .

I observe that you are now resolved to put an end to our correspondence, and if you had been of this mind 2 or 3 years since, my business had been more easier and my life more comfortable, for I have been more perplexed with your concerns within these 2 years than your commission has been worth for 7 years past. I do assure you if I was to spend my days in England, I had rather be a book-keeper than a factor to such as you now are. I could wish with all my heart I had an opportunity to refer it to the judgment of honest good men, whether you have wronged me or I you. However, the Lord is judge between us, and to Him I leave it, before whom I am justified that I have neither intended nor done you any wrong.

There was irony in Claypoole's reminder that his two boys, as good Quakers, could not swear but must affirm instead; literally thousands of Friends lay in jail because they could not swear. The Rogerses as Quakers, and Francis as a minister, knew it was forbidden. But as usual when Claypoole had written a scolding letter, he followed it with one trying to bring the situation back to normal. He now sent a second letter, formal and chiefly about bills, though he mentioned that Clutterbuck had not yet come to town. Hopefully, he still expected him. He also wrote that sugar had fallen by sixpence to a shilling per hundredweight, which

should have cheered the Rogerses, as theirs had been sold at a better price.
The next was to the son of an Irish knight, Sir St. John Broderick.

London, the 11th, 5th mo., 1682

THOMAS BRODERICK

... The wine, filled up, was but 14 pipes and ¼ with the lees, and it is computed that there will be 15 gallons of lees in each pipe [126 gallons]. So being racked and filled up, it's probable there may be 12 pipes. One of them is unsound, worth little, the rest are like sherry, and some have a little Canary taste. But they are all foul and I doubt will not yield above £18 per pipe when they are racked. I must either sell them or rack them this week, and they must be all hooped. [New hoops were put on to tighten up the wooden containers.]

They are safe kept under locks in a cool cellar, and I shall save what charges I can and sell them for as much as I can as if they were my own. If I had thy order to use my skill to improve them, which might much advance them in sale, I would buy a butt of the best malaga and mix with them, especially some of them that are tender. However, I will not stay for thy answer if I meet a chapman to my mind. I paid the master £40 and I am £40 out for the wine. William Strong has got his ship [the *Broderick*] wholly filled, so that if he comes safe I doubt not but he will give thee a good account of the money. He sailed this day and may possibly be in the Downs tomorrow. The usquebaugh [whiskey] is in the Customs House, and they say it is Sir St. John Broderick's, as the master told them as I suppose, and will not deliver it to me, so I shall want his order. ...

London, 11th, 5th mo., 1682

WILLIAM CHARE

... Furs are so dear that I think not good to buy any at present. I have bid late within this few days for 1,000 raccoons in parcels, 2⅓s per piece and 600 odd minks, 3¾s per piece. There was some cats and red foxes which the party was willing to throw out. He stood for 2½s the raccoon and 4s the minks, and since I have not spoke with him. I suppose he is now out of town, but I expect to see him tomorrow.

Blowers is so far off that I seldom see him, but Holt I often speak to and I think he will pay. . . . Arding I doubt will never pay.

I would have sent the box by [William] Wakeling and now since by another, but they will not take it without a bill of store unless I will venture the losing of it, and I know not what is in it, but I may send tomorrow about it. I hope thou wilt get me an order from Hans Christopher Mauks to buy another bale of silk for him. I have sold my sugars at 20s per cwt. I desire thee send me my account, and then I will pitch upon one to appear for me at the Courts of Assistants.

It's probable I may go to Pennsylvania next spring. I wish our ginger was sold.

London, the 14th, 5th mo., 1682

DEAR BROTHER NORTON CLAYPOOLE

As I remember I writ to thee by my son John, who went in the *Amity*, Richard Dymond, master, for Pennsylvania. The 23, 2nd month, they sailed from the Downs, so I hope they may be safe at port long before this time. [The *Amity* arrived August 3 at Upland.] I find no copy of that letter, but enclosed is copy of one I writ thee the 28, 8th month, at large, to which I desire an answer in every particular. [The letter sent with John was not copied into the letter book.] Since that time I have taken up resolutions, through the Lord's assistance, to go hence next spring with my whole family for Pennsylvania, so have not yet sent any order for a house or planting, but intend to do it when I come there. I have a 100 acres where our capital city is to be upon the river, near Schulkyll and Peter Cock's; there I intend to plant and build my first house.

We have erected a society for trade in Pennsylvania, according to this enclosed book of articles which I send thee. We have already subscribed £10 mil [£10,000] stock, of which we receive at present but ½ part, which is about £500 [£5,000], and after the arrival of the first ship belonging to the Company, in Pennsylvania, which may probably be in the 8th month next, the subscriptions will continue for 6 months following. So if there be any friend or acquaintance of thine that is inclined to join with us, I desire thee to encourage it, for the greater orders [of] stock, the more easily will it bear the charge, for we could very well employ £20,000 stock. One,

Dr. More, a very worthy, ingenious person, is chosen president, John Simcock of Pennsylvania deputy president. I am chosen treasurer. They allow the president £150, the deputy and treasurer each a £100 per annum, agreed for 7 years to come.

We are to send over a 100 servants to build houses, to plant and improve land, and for cattle, and to set up a glass house for bottles, drinking glass, and window glass, to supply the Islands and continent of America, and we hope to have wine and oil for merchandise and some linen; however, hemp for cordage. And for iron, lead, and other minerals, we have no doubt of. So that through the blessing of God we may hope for a great increase, and it may come to be a famous company.

We have sent a messenger to the emperor and kings to settle a constant friendship and trade between us, and have sent them divers presents in the name of the Society, and do reserve about £2,000 for the beaver and fur trade and skins. We have bought 20,000 acres of land and shall have 400 acres of it [in] the capital city where our house must be built, with divers warehouses and offices.

As for the governor, William Penn, he has been and will be, very kind to us. Besides his subscription, which is considerable, he has given us the quitrent of all our land and most ample patent or charter, to be confirmed by the first General Assembly in Pennsylvania, with as many privileges as we could desire, whereby we are a corporation, a lordship and manor, having a magistracy and government within ourselves, the 3 principal officers aforesaid being justices of the peace.

Now, brother, in answer to thy 2 letters, the one dated 16th, 10th month [December], which came here 19th, 2nd mo. [April], the other dated the 29th, 10th mo., came 12, 4th mo., by post, I am glad to hear my sister and her son were come safe home, but I perceive it has been a great charge and trouble to thee that they were put on shore so far from thee. But that miscarriage must not be imputed to any of us or her relations, for we would have had her gone by [Thomas] Arnold, who was bound directly for Delaware, in which I was very earnest with her, knowing it to be a more convenient vessel and better company—William Biddle and his wife and many of our Friends going in the said ship. But she was willful and minded more the counsel of the other master [Elisha Bennett], who had some ends of his own, and we heard that she should say she was resolved she would not go with Quakers. But keep this to thyself.

I hear not one word from William Frampton of New York (whom thou sayest the 16th, 10th month, near 7 months past) thou hast ordered to consign to me about £20 worth of skins. I hope what thou writ was real and that I shall yet hear from him, though it is long first [past].

My brother Claypoole [John] will not to this day let me see him or hear from him, that I doubt shall never get 1*d* more of that bond, so thou must think of providing something towards the discharge of it. Here is a letter from Dr. Harding; he pretends thou hast done badly by him, and our maid Sarah Thomas wonders thou sends her nothing for her, etc. Dr. Peachey pays no more nor will unless by forcible means.

I expect a letter of attorney from thee, that I may recover the £50 legacy of Percival, if possible. [Percival may have been the lawyer for young Cromwell Claypoole's estate. See letter of the 24th, 7th month, 1681, to Edward.] But I hear it's like to come to nothing, for they say the estate will not pay the debts, so that legacies will not be paid. However, I would have power [of attorney] that it may not be lost for want of looking after.

I thank thee for thy advice about goods that may be proper to send, and I desire thee give me what farther advice and direction thou canst, which may be very beneficial to me. So be not sparing of thy pains, but let thy advice be large and full. Our relations are all in health so far as I know....

John Simcock at that moment was somewhere at sea, in the Friendship *of Liverpool. The making of glass got under way the following year, with the arrival of Joshua Tittery of Newcastle-on-Tyne, who came in August. But the port books show that a lot of window glass was taken over; there is no reason to suppose the first settlers filled in their windows with oiled paper, as many of their romantically minded descendants imagined.*

Dr. More and William Penn had written the "Emperor of Canada," hoping to establish trade with the northern Indian tribes.

It is unfortunate Claypoole omitted copying his letter to Norton of August 9, 1681, or at least putting the name of the captain of the ship Norton's wife and son sailed on. The blank he left after the word "captain" shows it was a ship he did not know. They could not have gone by way of *Maryland* or *Virginia; either of these routes would have taken them to New Castle before Burlington—where Norton had to meet them. They did not go by way of Barbados, transshipping to the Delaware; Claypoole knew all those ships. They went to New York and then overland to Burlington, where, with some inconvenience, Norton picked them up.*

William Frampton moved from Long Island to Philadelphia and built one of the first of the brick houses.

London, the 14th, 5th mo., 1682

WILLIAM SMITH

I cannot perfect the insurance upon the *Charity* for £300 for Richard Gay till I hear again from thee. I have agreed and it is in effect done, but I must give them account, what the burden she is of, where built, and when she sailed from Dublin, which I desire thee do not omit the next post, for I am under a promise and cannot be clear else.

London, the 21st, 5th mo., 1682

WILLIAM CHARE

. . . I gave thee the reason why I had not shipped the box. Now I am informed what is in it, shall get a bill of store and ship it in Hindmer's, by whom I intend also a good parcel of furs for our personal account, possibly to the value of £500 to £600. I have bought already near £350 worth and am in treaty for about £150 more. Them bought I have not received but shall have them sent in tomorrow or next day. There is about 750 minks, 32 otters, 260 gray foxes, between 1,100 and 1,200 raccoons, a few woodchucks and martens. I hope thou wilt pay the £200 out of the proceed of the remaining furs and ginger, but if there should want £50, do not draw upon me, but stay till money comes in. . . .

I desire I may have my account current and other accounts before these furs arrive, that we may begin again upon a clear account. I hope the remainder are all put off, and I desire the ginger may be sold at price current.

THOMAS COOKE

... I have spoke with some of the purchasers of East Jersey and do understand that they are taking in 12 more, which will make 24 Proprietors, and the price of one 24th, or half a 12th, is £350. But it's possible I may obtain it for £300 if I had thy positive order. But to treat with them and then advise thee and stay for an answer signifies nothing; in such cases a man must be resolute. They have many chapmen but they will not accept of everyone, thou mayest be assured. If thou gives me order, I will get it as cheap as I can, and do for thee as for myself, which is all at present.

Claypoole was to learn that he could not haggle over the price of New Jersey as he could over a barrel of beer or a hundredweight of sugar. In another letter copied that day, he was pursuing a policy of appeasement.

London, the 25th, 5th mo., 1682

FRANCIS AND GEORGE ROGERS

... I had given your account credit since my last for £22 2s 8d and now this day have received a letter from Richard Gay wherein he does allow thereof, so that dispute is ended. I insured for him upon the *Swallow* from Hull to Lisbon, which ship went away about the end of the 10th month [December] last so in all probability is lost. Tomorrow I am to dine with the insurers in order to agree with them, and I shall, if I can possibly, secure this money for your account, which I have advised Richard Gay of. And if no other way will do it, I intend to lay an attachment privately in your names. In such case I must have your letter of attorney to prosecute and recover the money.

I have received invoice and bill of lading from Maskolin Alcock [the *Increase*], for your account, 5 butts and 6 hhds. [sugar] in John Hull [the *Orange Tree*], and for 6 butts in George Edger, and from Samuel Carpenter for 4 butts and 6 hhds. in John Hull. I shall enter them as soon as is needful and dispose of them on shore for the most I can get, which is all at present....

Having written the previous July 4 to Robert Rogers in Ireland that his Amsterdam correspondent had died but there was a son he would be willing to use as factor, he now wrote the son.

DANIEL LODGE & COMPANY

I have not hitherto writ to you for want of occasion. Now this is to desire you to give me advice per next post in what demand Antegoa [Antigua] tobacco is with you at Rotterdam, for my correspondent at Cork expects a ship laden with tobacco from thence very suddenly, and if there be encouragement at your market, we will order her thither and so continue a correspondency with you. He is a very sufficient man and was mayor of Cork last year. Pray let your advice be particular as to last price and also what the discount and all other charges will come to, that we may calculate what we may receive sterling money here for a 100 lbs. of tobacco sold there. In this you will much oblige me, and [I] shall in anything be ready to serve you here.

London, the 25th, 5th mo., 1682

WILLIAM CHARE

... I presented thy bill for £140 to Charles Turner for acceptance, but he is very angry and will not accept it, so I have sent it to the notary and shall have a protest for it, which shall be enclosed. I told him thou were informed he is under age, and he says he is 22 year old. He urged me to recommend him as a man of credit and showed me some tokens of great business, but I am still of the same mind as I was. . . . I intend to ship the 2 parcels of furs bought tomorrow in Hindmer's [the *Loving Friend*] and also thy box.

I am minded to buy no more till I see how thou likes these. But pray do not charge 100 mark a year warehouse room, for the account will not bear it, I mean for these last 2 or 3 years. I desire thee to put C. Mauks in mind of writing to me about the bale of silk, which is all at present.

Claypoole wrote Robert Rogers this same day, saying that he had "writ now very earnestly to Holland for advice about Antego tobacco" and as soon as he had an answer would write to Rogers.

London, the 28th, 5th mo., 1682

AUREND BRUMMER

... I see there is like to be loss upon my wheat and rye, but I hope not much. I intend to dispose of it in a little time, so advise me in thy next what it may probably yield and whether it may be better to send it to the Canaries or some other place than to sell it at Bremen. . . . I have received into my warehouse the pack and bale of osnaburgs and find the contents right, viz., 88 pieces containing 4,606 ells in bale, which I shall sell for thee as well as I can. But osnaburgs are very low. The printed current [list] says £44 per roll, and indeed I doubt I shall not get £45.

I desire to know by thy next whether or not thou hast received of Marcus von Middock for balance of my account in his hands, which was 22 R[ix] D[ollars] and 13 gr[oschen] for tobacco sold by him in anno. 1679. I thought it had been paid long since, and thou gives me no answer to it.

I am like to have a bad account from the mum this year, for I have near 100 barrels resting. . . .

London, the 28th, 5th mo., 1682

MARCUS VON MIDDOCK

. . . I have been endeavoring almost every day to sell thy hammels, but they are so bad that I cannot get any to buy them. I have sold John Brummer's 2 packs last week for 3 ¾ d per ell, and if thine had been as good, they had gone also. But they are such trash as I think worse were never seen; they will not call them hammels but Brunswicks [an even cheaper and coarser cloth]. I am resolved if anybody now will give me but 3 ⅝ d to take it. . . . It has been a great trouble and disappointment to me to be thus long out of my money and to have my bill protested, wherein thou didst not do fairly nor honestly.

Thou dost not answer me whether or not thou hast paid the £22 R[ix] D[ollars], 13 gros[chen], balance of account in thy hands due to me for tobacco sold in anno. 1679. . . .

London, the 28th, 5th mo., 1682

JOHN BRUMMER

. . . I have sold thy pack of linen to 3 several men, to pay in a month or sooner, but I cannot find all by 5 or 6 pieces. I believe Vogelsang had kept some of them, for he had broken open the packs and mixed them together, and soiled them with mum and blacking. [In spite of this dreary account, the sale amounted to £131 1s.]

JOHN CASSAWE

... I have great damage upon the bacon, 9 resting, and of those that I have sold, was 10 stinking ones, so bad that they were not worth 6d per piece. I believe they were of thy own drying (and killing), so that it is right and just that I should have an allowance for them; the stinking ones were great ones and the little ones were the best. I suppose the 10, one with another, might weigh 13 lb. per piece, which is 130 lbs....

And as concerning the hogs' bristles, if thou wilt not sell them under 7d per lb., it is in vain to open them; they keep better closed. If they be good, they may yield 6d per lb., but if bad, not above 5d....

London, the 1st, 6th mo., 1682

FRANCIS AND GEORGE ROGERS

... I committed an error in my last advice about your sugars; you have none from Masculine [Maskolin] Alcock in Hull [the *Orange Tree*] but 11 from Samuel Carpenter. You have 2 butts and 10 hhds. in Robert Scotting [the *Katherine*] sent by Page.

Richard Gay is come from Lisbon and I perceive is under a cloud, so I shall endeavor all I can to secure for you the money due by the insurers, which is by agreement £308 to be paid in 2 months. But the £8 will be charges. ... I have advised with Thomas Rudyard and done the needful hitherto. I am very ill at present, so excuse my brevity. R. Gay said he would write to you.

The insurance money was what he had placed on the ship Swallow, which never arrived. Its loss seems to have given the final blow to Gay's already shaky business.

All letters at this time are in Haistwell's handwriting and so must have been dictated. Possibly Claypoole had suffered another attack of his gallstone trouble.

In another letter the same day to Chare he announced that he had sent the furs off in Hindmer's ship (the Loving Friend*) in three fatts, or large containers, and excused his short letter as he was not very well.*

London, 5th, 6th mo., 1682

FRANCIS AND GEORGE ROGERS

. . . I have landed part of your sugar, but most of them are yet on board. I have been endeavoring to sell them but cannot get 20*s* per cwt., but am offered 19*s* and if I can get 6*d* more, they shall go; ordinary sugars will now yield but 17*s* and 17½*s*. I have been endeavoring these 8 days with all diligence to get the money into my hands, which is due by the insurers to Richard Gay, and have offered them for the rest of the time, which is but 7 weeks, to abate 2 per cent, but none would pay, so I entered actions against them. . . .

I am still of the same mind to embark in spring for Pennsylvania. We want servants for the Society, of all capacities. There will go three ships this month; in one goes William Penn, in another the president and servants for the Company. The 3rd is Thomas Hudson, a great ship gone yesterday with passengers. Which is all at present.

Hudson's great ship was the Elizabeth Ann & Catherine, *250 tons, which left August 4 and arrived in Pennsylvania September 29. William Penn went in the* Welcome, Robert Greenway, *master, 284 tons, leaving the Downs the end of August and arriving October 27. The* Jeffrey, Thomas Arnold, *master, with the president of the Free Society and many of the artisans they had under contract, left September 21 but crossed in the almost record time of 29 days.*

London, the 5th, 6th mo., 1682

RICHARD GAY, at John Gay's at Southstock [South Stoke] near Bath
. . . [I] am glad to hear of thy health and safety with thy friends and do advise thee to be very careful who thou admits to see thee, or how thou goes abroad. For here is such reports concerning thee as was expected, and attachment laid upon the insurers, and I believe they will lay [in] wait for thee amongst thy relations, where, they will easily conclude, is the most likely place to find thee. So indeed I think it were best to go somewhere else for 2 or 3 weeks, and do not direct any letter thyself, nor have any letters directed to thy brother, but [to] some other name.

The 26th past I got some of the insurers to a dinner and with great difficulty persuaded them to pay £78 per £100 in 2 months, and I gave them my obligation that in case the ship arrived at Lisbon by the 26th, 12th month, called February next, I shall pay them all their money back again. And since [then] one of them is dead, that writ £50, but is supposed has left a good estate. I have been very earnest to get the money into my hands and offered them 2% abatement, but not one of them would pay, so I entered an action in thy name . . . which the attorney says will do the business. . . .

I may hereafter send thee a map of Pennsylvania and William Penn's book about it, and the laws agreed on and what other papers may be necessary for thy perusal. And indeed, I should be heartily glad of thy company in the spring, if it might be so ordered. I must go on with my actions against the insurers in thy name, so I must have a letter of attorney. I have sent thee one enclosed, which I desire thee to seal and deliver before witnesses, and return to me next week. . . .

London, the 5th, 6th mo., 1682

ROBERT ROGERS

. . . I have enquired farther concerning Antego [Antigua] tobacco, and am informed that this is the best market, and so like to be, unless there should be some great quantities arrive, which are not expected. It may probably yield here 4d per lb., as I am told by several, and I have a chapman, an alderman, that would buy a cargo. . . .

London, the 5th, 6th mo., 1682

SAMUEL CLARIDGE

. . . [I] have thine of the 29th ditto, which cost 2s 6d postage and might have been half saved. In one was the 2 bonds; in the other was a few lines to William Penn concerning a purchase of a 24th part of East Jersey, which I shall deliver him when he comes to town, which will be next week, as I hear. Then I shall take care to have it rightly done according to direction. . . . [The rest of the letter was about bills of exchange, with a short postscript: "We want servants for Pennsylvania."]

A letter to William Alloway copied the same day said it was not fair for George Danter to write a wrong date upon a bill to gain time. It was dated July 11 in Limerick, and Danter had written it August 4. No one seems to have done anything about this bit of trickery.

London, the 5th, 6th mo., 1682

DEAR BROTHER WINGFIELD CLAYPOOLE

I have received thine of the 28th past and 1st and 2nd present, and have writ earnestly to Abel Ram to get in thy money, in particular the £100 of Theodore Jones, and to give me his answer about it. I have accepted his bill for £18 18s payable to thee, which is ready for thy disposal. I am sorry to hear thou art not well; I have been very ill these several days, can hardly do business, and now at this time could not write, but that there is a necessity for it. Pray remember my true love to sister [Dorothy] Holled and cousin Dorothy. I hope to have time to visit her before I leave England. . . . If thou canst do any service amongst the persecuted to help the suffering Friends, I shall take it very kindly, and may be a comfort to thyself. I am going to Kingston, and then to Epsom, to try the waters for my health. . . .

Letters for a time were brief. However, one to John Hammond on the same date must have included some printed matter about the new colony, for Claypoole wrote: "If any are desirous to serve the Pennsylvania Company, please to give them one of these printed papers. I intend thither next spring. William Penn is going away in a few days, and 3 great ships for Pennsylvania."

London, the 8th, 6th mo., 1682

WILLIAM CHARE

. . . I hope these furs will give good content and find a good market by Michaelmas. Blowers has got a ship and has promised me now to bring me the money in a few days. Holt puts off still, but I think he will pay in a month. The reason I did not send the box was for fear of seizure, and I knew not what was in it, so got a [bill of] store for it till lately. . . . I sent to Charles Turner this night, but he is gone into Yorkshire. I showed him nothing of thy letter but what I thought necessary to palliate him, and he makes ill use of it through his folly. But thou needs not repent losing his correspondency, for I look upon him still as at first. I like him never the better for bragging. . . .

London, the 12th, 6th mo., 1682

SAMUEL CLARIDGE AND ANTHONY SHARP

. . . [I] have spoken with William Penn about the purchase of the 24th part of East Jersey, and he said he had a letter from you and would write you an answer. Also I spoke with Thomas Rudyard and some others of the Proprietors, and they all say that you must advance £100 more or else you cannot purchase, which is £350 for cost, and £50 toward a stock for the general good, which every 24th part must advance. So when I have your answer, I may proceed accordingly. . . . William Penn is going from hence in a few days, and many other Friends for Pennsylvania. With my love to you both.

To Richard Gay, still in hiding, he reported on the 17th that he was crediting the Rogers brothers with £250, hoping to get it back from those reluctant insurers, adding that an officer from the lord mayor had appeared and attached all of Gay's concerns in his hands up to £1,000.

Claypoole wrote William Rogers about the sad state of Richard Gay's affairs and Gay's own indebtedness to him. William was to sign a letter of attorney to him so that he could salvage something in London. He reminded Rogers: "I desire thee let me know what thou wilt abate upon the cider, by reason many of the bottles holds but one pint and ¼."

London, the 18th, 6th mo., 1682

WILLIAM CHARE

. . . I took up the two packs of linen last week and have sold the Harfords, 3,000 ells, to Tobias Garbrand at £35 per roll. . . . We had an unhappy mischance with the pack of checks, for so they are called here [Claypoole had had a bit of trouble getting the linen through customs as ticking but had managed], . . . but the worst was after it was in the cart, with a bale of Holland [linen] of another man's. The horse went a little back and fell into the river and was almost drowned, and the carman also. The pack soon sank to the bottom, and before it could be gotten up was thoroughly soaked. So I sent it to the whitsters [bleachers] to be dried, and now it is gone to the calenders to be calendered [sized] and made up again. I doubt [I am sure] the charges will be above 50s; besides, the linen may not be so salable, but I am informed that the wharfinger must pay all the damages by reason he had not a curb upon the side of his wharf to secure the carts. I shall take advice and do what is requisite therein....

London, the 19th, 6th mo., 1682

ROBERT ROGERS

... I am still advised by several able men, and knowing in the commodity, that this is the best market for Antego tobacco, better than Amsterdam, or any other of our neighbors, and I have several chapmen ready against it come.... I will consider how to advise thee to an honest and safe correspondent [to take Claypoole's place when he left], but I am still of the mind to stay in England till the spring, which is all at present.

London, the 19th, 6th mo., 1682

THOMAS COOKE

... I can now give thee certain advice about the purchase of East Jersey (of the 24th part). It cannot be purchased under £350, and £50 to advance towards the stock, which makes their stock £1,200. ... I have taken up the 2 hhds. of fish and found the pieces of 8 and gold all right, according to John Spread's advice, and have sold the pieces of 8, 1,028 pieces, weighing 881 ozs., at 5s 3¼d per oz. is £232 3s 9d English money, and the gold came to £18 7s 5d; is in all £250 11s 2d.

The fish makes my house stink so that some of my friends will not come to see me, so thou mayest be sure I will sell it as soon as I can. We boiled a couple of them and they are very good....

Presumably they boiled the fish that came in the barrel with the Spanish coins and the lump of gold!

The letter to Chare ten days later began with a new kind of dateline, a style soon suppressed.

London, the Primo, 7th month, 1682

WILLIAM CHARE

... I am glad that Hindmer is arrived and that the furs proved to content. I shall look out some more according to thy advice. There is no getting any money of Blowers till he has made a voyage, he is so poor, and to arrest him now he is going to the Canaries might ruin him, so I had rather take some blame upon myself than use so much severity. . . . [Humphrey Blowers had just been made master of the *William & John*. The London port books show it was at that moment loading in the Thames, so Claypoole's kindly counsel prevailed.]

I am endeavoring to sell the checks and ask 32*s* per piece for them, but am offered no more than 30*s*, but am in hopes to get 31*s* per piece. Osnaburgs and Harfords does rather advance than decline.

London, the 5th, 7th mo., 1682

ROBERT ROGERS

... I entered the pink [a small ship] yesterday at the Customs House, and this day the tobacco, viz., 18,000 lbs., paid present money, £137 15*s*, and having had divers customers and tried our market, I thought best to strike the iron while it was hot. So I have sold it all to Alderman Booth at 4½*d* per lb., and tomorrow we shall begin to land and deliver them to him. Here is more expected, so I was the more resolute in selling, after I had tried the most I could get. I was this afternoon on board and do hope by what the master says it will prove free from damage and then it may render a good account.

I have been trying to sell the dust gold. There is 20 ozs. less 4*d* weight; but [it] will not yield near £4 per oz.; the most I can yet expect is £3 17*s* per oz. But I have not yet sold it but shall try some others. I stand for £3 19*s*. I shall save you what I can in the charge of the tobacco, but there is no saving the customer but without great charge both to ship and goods. . . . I understand thou hast a vessel with sugar may come here if there be encouragement. Our market is very low at present; unless it be good, will not yield above 17*s* per cwt. and so to 19*s* and 20*s* per cwt., . . . and now it comes from Barbados at high freight, as £7 10*s* per ton. It's possible it may rise.

Thy man John Lathum is well and intends to write to thee next post, which is all at present.

Exchange for Dublin, 7 to 8%.

I hope thou will not insist upon my 'bating ½ my commission because thy man is here, for I assure thee it is no ease to me, but it may be a benefit to him to be informed in a business he understands not. However, I may abate something.

London, the 5th, 7th mo., 1682

THOMAS COOKE

... The Proprietors of East Jersey will not sell 24th part under £350, and £50 towards the stock for the good of the whole. So if thou will not give that £400 for principal and stock, it is in vain to write about it. I cannot at present give thee any further account of their proceedings, nor do I know how the people are settled that dwell there, but I intend to get information against next post and send it thee.

Thy letter to George Cole is delivered, and the other shall be sent to Jamaica, which is all at present.

The various Coles were among the biggest of the London merchants. One, George, lived in Bartholomew Lane, another in Scots Yard by Claypoole's own house.

London, the 5th, 7th mo., 1682

FRANCIS AND GEORGE ROGERS

... [I] have yours of the 11th, 15th, and 22nd ditto. As to Richard Gay, I think he is very cordial to you and had rather you had the money than anyone else. I was amongst the insurers today, and they say that they have not been summoned yet upon the attachment, so I am in hopes that they will not prosecute, but that I may receive the money without obstruction. ...

Sir T. C. has so often deceived me, that now William Penn is gone, I can no more hope for anything from him but must give it up as lost, and do desire you to signify in your next that you have nothing to claim upon me on that account. I mean of the commission we had some dispute about, for I would not have any differences hang thus long between us; and I hope what I have done and may do, in saving the debt of R. G., will fully compensate, if there was any neglect as to Sir T. C. ...

I have been trying the market for your sugars, and now I have sold them to John Fleet at 18s per cwt.; it was the most I could get. Some of them was pannells. I bought a parcel to ship for Hamburg of ordinary [sugar] at 14s per cwt. I have consulted with William Rogers about R. G.'s money and got such writings as we thought necessary.

Philip Ford says that your deed for the land is ready and your deed for the quitrent, and that he has writ to you to send him the money. We hope the *Welcome* with W. P. is gotten away clear.

I have accepted your bill for £100 payable to George Moore. I cannot learn what R. G. failed for, but some say for £6,000 or £7,000. I know not whether he be yet in England or gone for Ireland, but suppose he is very private. . . .

London, the 5th, 7th mo., 1682

DEAR BROTHER WINGFIELD CLAYPOOLE

. . . I have . . . received of Edward Cooper my sister [Dorothy] Holled's £5 and sent it to Katherine Clinton, according to this enclosed receipt, which pray give her with my true love and tell her I would have writ to her but had not time this night. But I intend to visit her before I leave England. I observe thy order as to Brother Graveley but he has not sent yet. . . .

I desire thee to get me some good servants for Pennsylvania, either husbandmen, coopers, bricklayers, or almost any other trade.

London, the 5th, 7th mo., 1682

RICHARD GAY

My last to thee was the 22nd past; since have thine of the 13th and 26th ditto, with the judgments and release which shall be made use of if there be occasion, but never to thy prejudice. This enclosed is from Robert Hubbold; he says he has a letter from thee in England.

There is nothing done about the attachments on the assurers yet, but all things remain as they did. It might be well if thou couldst discharge this proud Witham's account and get Robert Hubbold into a good opinion of thee; he pretends thou mayest safely discourse with him, and what he would do for thee; but I cannot advise thee to trust any so far. It is late, so excuse my haste.

London, the 12th, 7th mo., 1682

ROBERT ROGERS

... I have now delivered the tobacco. I have not yet perfected the bill of parcels, by reason we have not agreed yet upon the tare. But the net weight at the scale, allowing 2 ⅓ lb. per bundle tare, is 9,917 lbs., comes to about £187, charges to be deducted. . . . [Claypoole had posted a notice at the Exchange that the ship was ready to take on freight and had spread the word but found few people ready to send anything. Therefore in a few days he would buy and load her with hops, balks, spars, and hoops—a freight less profitable than he had hoped for.] I shall send the chairs and couch and stands, etc., for thy wife.

London, the 12th, 7th mo., 1682

SAMUEL CLARIDGE

... The writings for East Jersey are perfected. I read them all over myself and saw them signed and delivered, and subscribed as a witness, and they were to be recorded in Chancery and is expected will be ready tomorrow. But I doubt he will not deliver me all the writings for £200 [deposit?], for there must be £50 advance towards the stock. . . . Philip Ford told me that the quitrent deed was perfected and he had either sent it thee or writ to thee to send for it. I would have thee comply with the £50 subscribed by P. F. per thy order, and I believe thou wilt have no cause to repent it. My purpose of going in the spring is still the same; about the 1st or 2nd month, if the Lord permit.

A new hand now appeared, large and angular, and headed the next letters in a worldly and un-Quakerlike fashion, writing the month as September.

London, September the 19th, 1682

ROBERT ROGERS

... I have some difference with the buyer of the tobacco about the tare but hope I may send thee some account of it next week at farthest. I cannot give any encouragement for sending sugar to this market, it being worth from 16 to 20s per cwt. We have been endeavoring hitherto for getting freight for the *Elizabeth* [Thomas Gouldney, master] but very little presenteth, so intend tomorrow to go buy the balks and spars, and deals and rafters, and load her, that she may be gone the last day of this week.

The hoops I have bespoke already, the 12 bags of hops I shall look after tomorrow. The best [hops] are above £5 per cwt., and I shall buy for thy wife a dozen of cane chairs and a couch, with a table and stands of olive wood and a barrel of my best mum.

London, the 19th, September, 1682

FRANCIS AND GEORGE ROGERS

. . . I cannot possibly send you a perfect account of the sugars yet by reason I have a difference with the buyer about the warehouse room and wastage, while he refused to receive it after it was sold for 2 or 3 weeks, which I hope will be ended tomorrow. And there is above £200 of that money unpaid. It is the same man that bought this last parcel, and I cannot to this day get him to take it, but he promises me afore this week is out to receive it.

I hope the £250 allowed you on Richard Gay's account is so well secured that you cannot be deprived of it. The insurance money is almost [a word left out here], and then I shall try what strength there is in their attachments. I am told by the attorney that nothing but a statute of bankrupt[cy] can prevent me, and against that there is no offense [defense].

Have enquired about insurance but cannot [get] a full answer; some talk of 2% to insure the men's persons from the Turks; for the ship and goods 3% out. But you do not write whether [you want the insurance to be] out and home, or only out.

London, the 19th, September, 1682

SAMUEL CLARIDGE

. . . [I] have this day paid John Heywood £233 6s 8d for thine and Anthony Sharp's ⅔ of a 24th part of East Jersey, the whole being £300 principal and £50 stock. I have not paid for the writings but shall pay for them and send you account thereof, and I would know how you would have the deeds sent, and [it] is recorded in Chancery in the name of Thomas Warne. I have had a great deal of trouble about it and could not get an end of it till this night at 8 o'clock. . . .

The new clerk was muddled. The price of the 24th part was £400—see letter of the 5th, 7th month, 1682, to Thomas Cooke. One third of this would be £133 6s 8d, two thirds for Claridge and Sharp, £266 13s 4d. This actually is what they bought.

London, the 19th, 7th mo., 1682

JOHN CASSAWE

. . . [I] have thine of the 15th July and 30th August to answer; have sent thee 8 blocks tin in Daniel Dietien, marked J.C. No. 1 to 8, containing, as underwritten, £80 5s. He was gone away before I expected, but here is a receipt will serve as well the money. May draw on thee next post. I desire thee to send me by the 1st ship for London before winter, for my account, 20 barrels best mum, 15 whole and 10 ½'s, and I will order the money in due time. Be sure send no more than 20. D. Dietien is gone this day to Gravesend. Excuse me that I write English, being late. Thou must not forget the gammons bacon.

London, the 19th, 7ber, 1682

WILLIAM CHARE

. . . Turner runs very high and pretends thou hast above £500 effects of his and would have the checks, paying the charge and standing to the damage. . . . I am to go see a great parcel of furs to-morrow. It is very late and am weary, so cannot enlarge at present.

He must have been weary, and no wonder, since he had not finished the business of Claridge's East Jersey deed before 8 o'clock that evening and after that had written three letters. The Chare letter is full of gaps where words are left out.

However, in two days he was feeling well, for he wrote to his friend John Goodson, who sailed in the Jeffrey, *Thomas Arnold, master.*

London, the 21st, 7th mo., 1682

JOHN GOODSON, Dear Friend

I hope by this time you are safe in the Downs, which I should be glad to hear by a few lines from thee, and how you all do on board, and what order they keep. We pleaded much with the master for abatement for thee, either in commodity or that ½ passenger [fare] but could not prevail. He said thy accommodation in the gun room was worth as much as the president's [Nicholas More] in the cabin. He promised that Edward Cole should keep his place with thee all the voyage, so I desire thee to insist upon it that he may not be turn[ed] out, for he is a civil man and will not wrong any but may be wronged by others. I gave the boatswain half a crown to be kind to him and spake to the mates and to the president the like, so I hope he will be well used.

Here is the indenture for Edward Cole, who is to serve me 4 years, which I desire thee to lay up safe for me till I come to Pennsylvania, and here is the bill of parcels for the goods in the chest and bundle, being ironmonger's ware, tools for working, and some materials towards the building of a house, which let him take a copy of, and the other things were committed to his care, being in his name—chest and a case, a bundle and an iron pot. Here is also one of the bills of lading for the freight and passage. He arriving in health in the country, I expect he should enter upon my land where the first city is intended to be built [Claypoole expected the site of Philadelphia to be confirmed by the time the ship arrived], and there with the advice of William Penn, Dr. More, Thomas Holme, Ralph Withers, and thyself, I would have him to begin to build a house that may receive us, if it please the Lord we arrive there in the 2nd or 3rd month next. If it be but a slight house like a barn, with one floor of two chambers and will hold us and our goods and keep us from the sun and weather, it may suffice.

I would also have some trees planted at the right season, for an orchard, between the trees [already] growing, which may be either lopped or sawed off near the top or root, as is most advisable. But for grubbing up, I think that may be left till I come with more help. I need not name the fruit trees, but I would have all such sorts as our neighbors there do plant. But principally I would have him look out for earth to make bricks and prepare as much as he can in the most convenient place to work upon in spring.

I write to my brother Edward Claypoole of Barbados to send me one or 2 good stout Negroes in the spring, and I hope to bring a carpenter, a husbandman, and some other servants with me. I would have a cellar under the house if it may be.

As to his maintenance till I come, I know not how to advise but must leave that to him and to the advice of my good friends there. I hope he will be wise and save and do what he can for my advantage, and then I shall be the more engaged to do for him, and the more peace and satisfaction he will have in his own mind.

Truly my desire is that we may all have an eye to the Lord in all our undertakings, Who is the great provider for all and the preserver of all, that we may so live in His fear that we may honor His name and truth and in our whole conversation answer His witness in all people. So shall righteousness establish our nation, and our habitations be in peace and safety, even [as] in Jerusalem, that is a quiet habitation and has salvation for walls and bulwarks. I know the Lord will keep us, both from our inward and outward enemies, if we trust in Him and walk in His counsel. We have found it so, that in all our troubles and trials and exercises He hath been with us and has not forsaken us, and His name has been, and is, our strong tower, where we fly for safety as the righteous did in all ages.

So my friend, let us look to the Lord and trust in Him and wait for His presence, that we may feel the renewing of life daily, and so live in the dominion of His power, over that which would not have him to reign, that He may be glorified by us, for which end we were created. And this being kept, we have access into His presence and are sensible of His care over us and preserving power, Who commands the winds, and the seas, and they obey Him, and is a deliverer in the mighty waters. It may be well if all that profess truth on board [all who were Friends] and others that are willing might meet together two or three times in a week, to wait upon the Lord, that you may be comforted together, as we have been many times, and can say we never sought His face in vain. So that you will be kept in the savory life and be a good example to others and keep down bad spirits that they shall not have power.

My love to Isaac Wheeldon, Nathaniel Watson, thy wife and maid Mary, and what other Friends there is. With my true love to thyself, I rest, thy friend and brother in the truth.

Post—Remember my love to the president and his wife and Captain Arnold. I sent by the president 2s 6d to Edward Cole and Isaac Wheeldon his 20s. I intend to write Edward Cole if I have time. Mary Penington, William Penn's wife's mother, is dead and this day to be buried.

FRIEND EDWARD COLE   London, the 21st, 7th mo., 1682

I hope by this you are safe in the Downs, which I should be glad
to hear. I have given some directions in my letter to John Goodson
about building a house and planting an orchard, and trying of earth
for bricks, which must be all done in season. And if John Goodson['s] carpenter helps thee, thou mayst other times help him,
wherein agree with John Goodson, doing that which is equal. Take
advice of Dr. More, Thomas Holme, Ralph Withers, and John Goodson, and if William Penn be not over busy, apply thyself to him
sometimes.

I would willingly have a cellar under the house, for I shall bring
wines and other liquors that the heat may otherwise spoil. I intend
to order my brother at Barbados to send in the spring 2 stout
Negroes, and it may be, a boy and a girl also, and in the 1st or 2nd
month I intend, through the Lord's assistance, with my whole family
to embark for Pennsylvania, and if I can, get a carpenter or two and
husbandman. It's possible I may bring 6 or 8 men with me and all
necessaries for husbandry, etc.

Be sure do thou write to me by the first opportunity and put John
Goodson in mind to write to me, and if thou sees my son John, tell
him we are all well and expect to hear from him. Write what things
is most wanted for my concerns there and what kind of land my lot
is, and how it lies as to the river, etc., and what water and trees, and
all things needful to be known, when thou hast got a hovel to keep
thee in safe, and provision without much charge for food. Thou
wert best buy a cow and a sow or two for breed[ing], but in all
things get good advice.

For what thou wants for food, etc., thou mayst sell the linen or
what else can be best spared. Thou wilt see by the invoice what they
cost, and I hope they will yield near double. The linen may yield
near 6d per yard, but sell it as well as thou canst with good advice.
The length is [in] half ells, as 62, is 31 ells, that is, 38 yards [and] ¾,
and let me know whether or not the ironmonger's wares prove well.

Remember my dear love to William Penn; I hope to write him
by this ship or else by the next, and to Thomas Holme and Ralph
Withers, with my love to thyself, I rest. Show this to John Goodson
and read mine to him. Thine to thy wife I may carry tomorrow or
next day.

[153]

Ralph Withers took over, until Claypoole himself arrived, the manage-ment, or rather mismanagement, of the Free Society of Traders.

Cole followed Claypoole's directions literally about the house, which was a great disappointment to the family when it arrived. Claypoole brought over Cole's son as an indentured servant.

One would expect that, as treasurer of the Free Society, Claypoole would have written many letters asking for subscriptions. The letter book contains only one, to a well-known Gloucestershire family.

London, the 21st, 7th mo., 1682

DEAR FRIEND THOMAS LOVEDAY

I . . . should have given thee an answer before this, but that I have been at Gravesend and otherwise hindered. As to the £75 which was paid me upon the Society's account, for thine and William and John Loveday's subscriptions to the Society, each £25, I do acknowledge I received it, and that you had receipts but for half the money, and for the other half, I accounted with Philip Ford, and he intended to allow it thee and them. But now I shall account with thee for it.

So if thou art willing and they also, to have your subscriptions doubled and made each £50, I shall send thee 3 more receipts each for £12 10s. [They would then each have receipts for £25, or the re-quired down payment of half their subscription.] But if that does not please thee and them, then without any further advice send a receipt signed by thee and them for £37 10s, and I will pay it to whom thou wilt.

Our president with above 50 servants belonging to the Society is going away in a great ship for Pennsylvania; we suppose it is this night in the Downs. It is about 500 ton, called the *Jeffrey*, Thomas Arnold, master. William Penn and those Friends in the *Welcome* we hope may be near half way thither. There have been divers false reports to discourage people, as if a ship from Bristol with Friends was cast away and that Carolina was seized by the Spaniards. But all is well and like to prosper, so with my true love to thee, I rest.

Claypoole treated the purchase of land in the New World or stock in the Free Society like any other commercial transaction. Apparently in this case, if the Loveday brothers pulled out of the whole affair, Clay-poole would credit them with their original £37 10s payment, using it to pay their bills. The Lovedays, however, kept their original subscription; they are down in the list of Society subscribers for £25 each.

A business letter to William Rogers came next, with a mild pleasantry at the end: "Let me know what I must pay John Barnard [Barnet?] per doz. for the cider, or else I will conclude thou art so kind as to give it me."

Hans Christopher Mauks is now spelled Maeks and so remains. James was trying to buy him a bale of the best silk, getting the price down from 16s 8d per lb. to 16s 6d, to send it in the Merchant's Delight, William Wakeling, master, to be ready to sail in five days.

To Chare on the 22nd he wrote that he had bought some furs and sorted them himself, so they would all be good. But as for the checks—the goods that had fallen into the river—he could get only 30s a parcel for it.

London, the 23rd, 7th mo., 1682

DEAR BROTHER EDWARD CLAYPOOLE

[A note written above the letter says: "Sent per the *Bachelor*, Roger Bagg, in the Downs, who sailed the 25th."] That on the other side [of the paper] is copy of my last, which was the 27th, 4th month. Since have thine dated 20th and the 26th May with the copies, 15th June and 4th July and 18th July. The 23 hhds. of sugar I have received up in good condition, viz., 10 by Hull, 8 by Singleton, and 5 by Witheridge, and have sold them all and received most part of the money, viz., 5 seconds at 42s 6d, and 8 seconds at 42s, one third at 32s, and 9-3rd [nine thirds] at 31s, of all which I intend to send thee a particular account by John Strutt and an account current. He is gone to Gravesend and may sail to the Downs in 8 or 10 days. This I send by the *Bachelor*, Roger Bagg, now lying in the Downs for a wind, and I have paid thy bills drawn upon me which are due, according to thy advice.

I am very glad of the £80 bill from Lewger; I wish thou mayst get such another and so clear with him. I suppose James Harding has sent thee those things he was to buy, for I paid him the money upon demand. I received the hog by [Thomas] Singleton in good plight, and both my wife and I do receive it very kindly. I have shipped the copper in John Strutt [*Concord*] with the skimmers and ladles; it is about 350 gallons. . . .

I have insured £380 for thee from Barbados to London in 3 ships

[155]

mentioned at 2 guineas %, £300 subscribed by Alderman [Richard] Alie, and £80 by Nehemiah Bourne, both very substantial men.

My purpose of going with my family to Pennsylvania is still the same as advised in my last. I purpose to be ready to go on shipboard about the end of the 1st month or beginning of the Second month. In the meantime I shall be looking out for servants which may be proper to take with me, as two carpenters, a bricklayer, a husbandman, and 2 laborers. I have sent by Captain Arnold (who is in the Downs bound for Pennsylvania) an honest man to build me a slight house, and plant an orchard and clear some ground with the help of a carpenter that is going with another friend. My man is a brickmaker but has skill in planting and husbandry, and a piece of a carpenter; he is an honest, industrious, solid man, of about 47 years old and one called a Quaker.

For his assistance and for my use and service I desire thee to provide me 2 good stout Negro men, such as are like to be pliable and good natured and ingenious. I question not but thou knows better than I do which may be fittest for me, and I hope thou wilt be so kind as to let me have those which are good likely men, for some I hear are so ill natured and surly that a man had better keep a bear, and some again, so ingenious, diligent, and good natured, that they are a great comfort and benefit to a man and his family. And my family is great and I have 3 young children [Nathaniel, aged ten, George, eight, and Joseph, five] so that it may be very prejudicial to me to have bad Negroes.

I would also have a boy and a girl to serve in my house; I would not have either of them under 10 years or above 20. But principally observe their nature and capacity. If I have them in the 3rd or 4th month in Pennsylvania may be well, but the men I would have sent by the first opportunity in spring, directed to John Goodson at Upland in Pennsylvania, chirurgeon to the Society of Traders, or in his absence to Ralph Withers, to whom I have given a letter of attorney, to be deputy treasurer to the Society till my arrival.

I hope thou wilt get in the money of Lewger and send it me in good sugar, if that be not too troublesome for thee, but I leave that to thee, either to send bill or goods. And for buying the Negroes, I intend by John Strutt to send thee a letter of attorney, to receive my effects of Joseph Grove and several others. Further, as to thy corresponding with me, I desire it may continue as it is, and I shall take all necessary care therein, even to the last day. And when I go away, shall leave my letter of attorney with some diligent, honest person, that may be as capable to serve thee as myself, and if I have a part of the commission, I will be security for him.

I have something of that kind under consideration with my servant, who has now about 2 years and ¾ to serve. He has been very true and diligent in my business and has learnt so much that I could leave all to him for a year together, if I was not to remove. Besides, there is a young man proposes to be his partner, him I know very well to be diligent, honest, capable, and sufficient, that they will neither want money nor credit. So I desire thee, brother, do not promise or engage thy business to anyone, but let it continue as it is, and for the future I hope my proposals shall be as well to be accepted of as anyone's. My man is about 24 years of age and the other, 28 years; they are both solid and sober and not given to any extravagancy and are called Quakers. It's possible they may dwell in my house where I live now, if we can agree. I intend to write thee again by John Strutt, so with my true love to thyself and my sister, I conclude at present.

In the ship bound for Pennsylvania in the Downs is the president of the Society with about 60 or 70 servants, besides many other passengers. It is a great ship, near 500 tons and never was at sea [the *Jeffrey*]. We reckon there may be near 1,000 people gone this year. There is some probability of my brother Wingfield's going with us to Pennsylvania; he is resolved upon it if he can get his concerns from Ireland. As to our coming to Barbados to stay 3 or 4 weeks, he likes that well, but I know not yet how it may be. I have endeavored to get thee a servant or two, but as yet I cannot, but I doubt not to get some before I go away.

Sent copy per Strutt the 12th October.

Claypoole underestimated the migration. Penn reckoned an average of 80 persons to a ship, and the first year he wrote there had been twenty-three ships "with passengers"—nearly double Claypoole's figure. Moreover, people moved in from other colonies and came north from the West Indies.

On September 26 he wrote to Claridge in Dublin, "Thomas Rudyard is gone from hence yesterday towards East Jersey with old Samuel Groome." Rudyard had been lawyer for Penn, and sales of Pennsylvania land were often made in his office in Lombard Street. He and Groome were among the original *Proprietors of East New Jersey, and Rudyard had been made deputy governor.*

They did not go with other Friends in the Jeffrey *but in a ship bound for New York, the* Globe *(Samuel Groome, Jr., master), which arrived November 13. They were both delighted with the country but, like Claypoole, complained of the lack of builders and farm laborers.*

London, the 26th, 7th mo., 1682

THOMAS COOKE

. . . I have received from John Spread a bag sealed up for thy account, containing 951½ pieces of 8, ounces 823½, which I have left at a goldsmith's, who has offered me 5s 3¼d per oz., but I hope to get more. They are heavy pieces and not of the right sort, else I could get 5s 3¾d per oz.

Being thou offered but £300 for 24th part of East Jersey, I could not bargain with any of them; they would have £400 in all, viz., £350 for the purchase and £50 towards a stock. Now I hear all the shares are sold and there is not one part to sell. I have enquired of them that I might advise thee concerning the country and their settling, that I might advise thee thereof, but they refer me to a book printed by them which I suppose thou hast.

John Spread writes of sending more pieces of 8, and when they come may advise thee thereof and dispose of them as well as I can. [He also wrote that he had sold the fish in which the coins came for 10s a cwt.]

To William Chare he wrote that Chare's half of the five fatts of furs shipped with Captain Wakeling amounted to £431 and he was sending the bale of silk in the same ship, the Merchant's Delight.

London, the 26th, 7th mo., 1682

JOHN CASSAWE

. . . [He had sent him the eight blocks of tin with Daniel Dietien —this time spelled Detyne—which came to £80 5s 2d.] I have not yet sold any of the hog's bristles, but I hope I shall sell it in a little time. I would willingly have 20 barrels of mum in the first ship, viz., 15 whole and 10 halves, and [for] the money thou mayst draw upon William Chare. And do not forget the gammons of bacon, that I must have in lieu of those that were nought. [As usual, Claypoole had calmed down; in his letter of August 1 he had called them stinking.]

To Mauks he reported having sent an excellent black otter and the bale of silk in Wakeling's ship; the whole amount was £266 0 8d.

London, the 29th, 7th mo., 1682

AUREND BRUMMER

. . . Thy osnaburgs I have sold and received the money, 4,606 ells at £45 per roll, £138 3s, and have paid thy bill for £100 to William Chare. [Claypoole then asked whether Von Middock had paid that old bill of 22 rix-dollars and 13 groschen] . . . and I desire my account current, and of all things, including the charge of the corn to that very day. As to the 11 barrels [of mum] remaining betwixt us, I cannot sell one of them; I still let people taste them, but none will buy any of them, they are so thin and stale. I have sold some lately for the East Indies, and so if thou wilt let them go upon account at 30s per barrel, I will take them to myself and send thee account, but I know not whether I shall be able to sell one here or there.

Now as to my wheat and rye remaining, it is my desire and order that it may be sold forthwith for what it will yield, that I may see what I shall lose by it, for I am past hopes of getting anything now by it. As to the charges, I hope thou wilt in friendship spare me what thou canst, that I may come off with the less loss. . . . [Tactfully he ended by giving an order for some fresh mum. He had not heard from Brummer and concluded he was either ill or on a journey.]

London, the 29th, 7th mo., 1682

WILLIAM CHARE

. . . This serves chiefly to send bill of lading and invoice of 5 fatts of furs in Wakeling, who, I suppose, goes to Gravesend tomorrow, the wind being fair. They are for our account in halves as formerly and amount to £861 2s 8d, whereof thy half is £430 11s 4d.

Here is very few left at this market, and a great ship came from Hudson's Bay that has not £20 worth, in so far as I can hear, so that none can spoil our market. . . .

A letter of September 30 to Robert Rogers in Ireland included bills of lading for 200 small spars, 80 balks, 200 bundles of hoops, one dozen cane chairs, one table, two stands, and a barrel of mum. These were "shipped aboard the Elizabeth, *Robert Davies, master, who set sail for Gravesend this day." This ship, or another ship also called the* Elizabeth, *was captained at other times by the Quaker shipmaster Thomas Gouldney. "Hop continues at £5 and £5 10s per cwt., those that are good, so that my master did not buy any," Haistwell wrote.*

A letter to the Rogers brothers assured them they would soon have their completed accounts. It also said, "I hear no further of Sir T. C., nor do I expect now. However, I will go to him again if you desire it."

Another letter went to Robert Rogers, saying little but to confirm the sailing of the Elizabeth, *"the wind being fair easterly."*

London, the 6th, 8th mo., 1682

JOHN BRUMMER

. . . I send thee account of the 2 packs of hammels, which I would have sent 2 months since, but I was in hopes of finding the pieces that were wanting, amongst other packs in my warehouse. But I cannot find one piece, so am still of the mind that Vogelsang has them short [he had accused Vogelsang of this before], and then we were in such a hurry of business that it was passed by and forgotten. I have put 21s to account for the wanting pieces, which I think may suffice, considering it is so much lost to me. . . .

Claypoole wrote Richard Gay, still in hiding, that he had sold his wine, so he would make up that account and send it to him, and in connection with trying to straighten Gay's affairs and pacify the Rogerses, he wrote them about the legal difficulties with the insurers. He also said he was having trouble with the man that had bought their sugar, but the dispute was only about an item of 40 shillings.

London, the 11th, 8th mo., 1682

DEAR BROTHER EDWARD CLAYPOOLE

[A note at the beginning said the letter was sent by Benjamin Norminton (Norington) to Joseph Strutt at Gravesend.]

The foregoing is copy of my last per the *Bachelor*, Roger Bagg, master. [With some optimistic news of bills of exchange, he wrote that Edward had a balance of £195 16s 3d with him.] . . . The money for the sugar is all received to about £40, which is safe, I think. The copper I hope will please thee. . . .

Here is a pair of silk garters enclosed, which my daughter Mary made and sends to thy daughter Mary for a token; she was not very well else she would have writ to her. Here is also a little silver box with ten shillings of new small money, which my wife desires my sister [Edward's wife] to accept of. [William] Emberley [*Prosperous*] and [John] Hill [*James & Mary*] is come, but [William] Beeding [*Friendship*] not heard of yet. I am landing the sugar; one hhd. of seconds they have seized and sent to the King's Warehouse, which may cost 1 guinea [to get out]. They are worse now than ever. . . . I wonder I hear nothing of Samuel Carpenter of that bill which was made payable to me; it's possible it might come by Beeding. However, I intend to enquire after them both.

I never sell thy sugar by the name or sort but by the goodness. Our relations are all in health so far as I know, which, with mine and my wife's true love to thee and my sister, is all at present.

I desired thee to send me to Pennsylvania 2 Negroes, but I am since informed that men without women will not do well, which stands to reason. So I desire to have one man and one woman.

Remember my love to Samuel Carpenter if he be not gone; I intend if I have time enough to write to him by this ship, as also to Joseph Grove. I would also have the boy and the girl I wrote for.

The time of Carpenter's arrival in Philadelphia is not known, but his certificate was dated August 23, 1683. He made himself so comfortable in a cave in the Delaware River bank that the Board of Property had difficulty getting him out. He became one of the colony's richest citizens and with a small group of other wealthy merchants tried, unsuccessfully, to establish a "bank for money" in Philadelphia.

London, the 13th, 8th mo., 1682

WILLIAM CHARE

. . . I have spoke to Charles Turner about the checks, but he will not receive them on fair terms. I would have 31s per piece for them but cannot obtain it. 30s I am offered, but without thy advice I will not take it. He is a very shuffling, bad lad, and thou mayst be glad thou art clear of him. I hope our furs by Wakeling are arrived, the ship having had a fair wind these several days. I should be glad to hear that the furs give content and come [to] a good market. It is true the winter is near, but they may have time enough, before the frost begins, to dress abundance of furs.

I would willingly have refused the cats, but then I could not have made so good terms for the rest. I must have advanced [the price] which I thought upon the most vendable sort, as minks and otters. We had better sell our cats for no profit, or some loss, as 2 marks per piece, than to refuse parcels because of some cats.

I desire thee refuse no reasonable offer but sell them at the 1st market, for we know not what another winter may bring. Better repent sold than kept, especially such perishable goods. . . .

London, the 14th, 8th mo., 1682

JOHN SPREAD

. . . The 2 hhds. of fish by [John] Foy and Jenners I received in due time and the silver according to advice, which I disposed of for Thomas Cooke's account and take very kindly thy inquiring after William Mumford. It was to serve a friend of mine at Worcester, but seeing he is such a cross fellow, I shall not trouble myself further about it. [This refers to the stonecutter that Claypoole had asked about on September 29 the previous year.]

By the *Priscilla*, John Place, master, I received 823½ oz. pieces of 8 and now have received yesterday a hhd. of fish by William Cundy [*Adventure*], which have opened and find the pieces of 8 and silver, and the bag of the master. I have not yet weighed them but do believe they are right, as the former were. I shall dispose of them for account of Thomas Cooke, as they were consigned. . . . I am glad thou hast sent silver and not sugar for Thomas Cooke's account, being much more profitable for him, though the commission is less for me. Pieces of 8 are worth 5s 3¾ d to 5s 4d per oz. if they be light, and most of them of the best sort. . . .

London, October 14th, 1682

LOVING FRIEND JOSEPH GROVE

. . . Thou advises of the sale of my mum at £3 17s 6d and that thou didst hope to send the produce thereof by Joseph Wasey [of the

Grayhound]. I hope thou wilt send it me in scraped ginger or cotton, for muscovado sugar will render but very poorly, especially pannels such as thou sent per Joseph Wasey. If it had been sold alone, would not have yielded 16s per cwt. I perceive thou hast sent 2 hhds. of the bottles to New England and had received some fish in return. I doubt it will render but a poor account.

I desire thee send me no more such muscovado sugar as the last; I had rather have any commodity or stay a year for returns. Thou thinks they are cheap, but they were dear enough for our market if they had cost but 7s per cwt. I am utterly discouraged from sending any more goods that may procure such returns; it is the way to bring a noble to 9d. [A noble was worth up to ten shillings; it was a small gold coin.]

I perceive we shall be greatly disappointed in our returns of our Carcavelos wine, which I did fear, by something I perceived here about ½ year after it had been gone away; viz., some bottles that were drawn out very fine had a great settling and came out in flecks and floated about the wine. I doubt it will prove all so, for I perceive it is not of so fixed a body as other wine, by losing its color. We find the way to have it drinkable is to keep the bottles all standing upright and pour it out gently, and so the settling stays behind. We drink ours so still, and it pleases some people well, it is sound and a durable wine. So I hope thou wilt dispose of it one way or another, either at a good price or a low price. If we can get 12s per doz., it is better than to keep them till they are spoiled, and I hope thou will get them returned from Jamaica or put them into other hands. . . .

Here enclosed I send thee our account in halves, the ½ proceed net being £21 15s I carry to thy account current. I desire an end of this account as soon as may be, because I do intend, if the Lord permit, to remove with my family to Pennsylvania in the spring of the year, the 1st or 2nd month, to remain there, and I shall be glad of a continuance of our correspondency there. I intend to write to thee again before I go.

Ralph Weeks has sent me some wretched sugar, so that I am imbursed and something over but not enough to pay his last bill for about £70, so would not accept it. I hear yet nothing from John Jones; he owes me on an old balance £3 15s 2d. I hope thou wilt get it me or place it to thy account, for I think thou writ formerly I might do so; which is all.

London, October the 14th, 1682

RALPH WEEKS

. . . I could not accept thy last bill by reason I have so little in cash towards it and no other effects, and I would not encumber myself at present by reason I am intending for Pennsylvania with my whole family in the spring of the year. [Nicholas] Churchwood [*John of London*] is not yet arrived but counted dangerous. If thou sends any more sugar, pray send better, for this is all trash thou hast sent hitherto and must needs turn to a bad account, which is a trouble to me. . . .

London, the 14th, October, 1682

THOMAS COOKE

. . . [I] have thine . . . by Edmund Yeoman, to whom I have delivered £630 bill, according to thy order, paid Robert Boyle, which has a fair receipt to it, with his own name to it and a witness, and I shall make what farther proof of the payment of the money may be requisite. I offered him £100 for thy account at 7% exchange, which I suppose he will accept of when he has occasion, but I drew lately for Cork at 6%, £100 at 21 days. Now since is come to hand the letter from Knight with the deed in it, which cost 5s postage, though he could have sent it by a friend; my man brought it from the post house. I shall get it to Yeoman as soon as I can, though I know not where he lodges.

I have received from John Spread for thy account bill of lading and invoice for pieces of 8 and 2 pigs silver, amounting to, in New England, £401 19s 9d and a bill of exchange on Richard, James, and Charles Pope of Bristol for £100, which is accepted, which is rated in the invoice at £125 1s. Some of the silver came in a hhd. [of] fish. I have it all home and shall sell it next week, which is all at present.

London, October the 17th, 1682

WILLIAM CHARE

. . . I hope thy next will advise that our furs are arrived and the greatest part sold. I must send away an account next post to Marcus von Middock of Bremen, who suffered my bill of £100 to be protested, through his pretenses of goods to come to my hands. I have accepted and paid his bills beyond effects for above £80 sterling and am doubtful [sure] that he will wrangle with me about the account I must send him, there being about £15 for interest at 6%, besides other articles, which he will take an occasion to quarrel at, if he intends not to pay me the balance. So that I doubt I must be forced to use the law at Bremen to recover my due, and in that case I have not a fit correspondent [at Bremen], for A[urend] Brummer is his cousin and I believe will not meddle.

So I desire thee to advise me to a man that may be proper in that case, and I will send my letter open to thee for thee to write under it. Besides, A. Brummer is not fit on this account—that a man cannot sometimes in 3 months get an answer from him. Also advise me what sort of justice one may hope for at Bremen. . . .

London, October 17th, 1682

Thomas Cooke

. . . I have sold the pieces of 8, being 1,048½ ozs. at 5s and 3⅛ d per oz., is £273 16s, and there was 40s English money which is placed to thy credit. The 2 wedges of silver I have caused to be assayed and shall have an account of them tomorrow night; they may come to about £40.

I received the deed as per advice, and according to thy desire have sent it to a scrivener of my acquaintance, and tomorrow he says he will have a rough draft to show to Robert Boyle, that the charge of engrossing may not be lost. I have almost perfected thy account to send it this night but am prevented by other extraordinary business, so cannot send it till next post. . . .

All deeds or legal contracts were "engrossed" or written out by specially trained men on fine parchment. Penn's charge for a deed of land in his colony was twelve shillings; these were fairly simple documents or indentures. Unfortunately, there is no hint as to what Cooke's deed was for; he had not bought Pennsylvania land or stock in the Free Society of Traders. A Robert Boyle, Irish scientist, was a friend of Penn.

SAMUEL CLARIDGE

... I want thy order to pay Philip Ford for the charge of the quit-rent deed, etc., and then I believe I may soon have it, and if I can get a book of the laws I may send thee one with the deed by this friend. I sent thy letter sealed and sent it to John Heywood but have yet no answer. The bills thou sent me on William Alloway for £100 and £35 I have sent for acceptance. It seems you are willing to allow me but 33s 4d for commission and postage, though I think I well deserve 1% for commission, for it is double the trouble as bills of exchange, for it is not ended yet and [I must] write to thee several times about it. But I shall acquiesce with what thou desires, which is all.

London, the 20th, 8th mo., 1682

MARCUS VON MIDDOCK & COMPANY

My last to Marcus von Middock was the 28th, 5th month. Since have received his dated 9th August, wherein he reflects upon me about the linen, then unsold, that I used no care in it but lost time by being abroad. I assure you it is not my fault or yours that [it] would not sell at a market price. And then when I had liberty to sell and was not limited to a price, I could not get any to buy them. You might well think, as I writ formerly, it was my interest to sell and not to keep them, for besides I have been so long out of my money and wanted it often, it has been prejudicial to me to have my warehouse so long taken up with such coarse goods and [I] have been necessitated often to hire room in other places not so convenient for my use. But if you call to mind the badness of your hammels and our market, you will no longer blame me. I would not really, for 10 times the commission, have the trouble and vexation again as I have had with them 3 packs. But now it is so far put to an end; they are sold and delivered as per the enclosed account.

But I have not received 1d of the money for the hempen [hammels] sold John Osgood & Company for £100. I would have allowed them but 2% for measure, which would serve for most of it, for I measured several pieces, but some pieces here and there one holding [were] short. They will have one % more or else have a sworn measurement, which would be worse. So I have placed the 1% to the account current, for the other account was made up before I heard their complaints.

The barrel of hogs' bristles I cannot sell; they are so exceeding bad. I have tried several chapmen, and there is none now will give me 5*d* per lb. for them. This day I was offered 4½ *d*, so I desire you to write to your correspondent here to receive them. It's possible he may sell them for more than I can. In the account current I have charged but 6% interest of money indisbursed, and I have 8% of others, so in that I have used you very kindly, and I think every other article will be found right, so for the balance thereof, which is £93 4*s* 8*d* due to me (besides the money for the linen, which is yet all to receive). . . . I understand that the 22 R[ix] D[ollars], 13 gros[chen] due to my account there, is paid to Aurend Brummer, which is well. So expecting to hear from you next post, I conclude.

London, October the 21st, 1682

FRANCIS AND GEORGE ROGERS

. . . I desire to know how you will have the deeds sent, whether by post or by sea. They will cost, I believe, 40*s* by post and may go as well by sea if there be no haste, by which way I shall send them if opportunity presents before I hear from you. S[amuel] Claridge had his sent by post.

I take very kindly your remitting any farther claim of the commission received of [in regard to] Clutterbuck; I doubt it would be a troublesome arbitration. It is like I may do you more service another way than that comes to. I have received of one of the insurers that writ £50 on the *Swallow* [for] Richard Gay, £39, and I do not doubt of two more, each £39, but one of them being dead may not come in yet this 2 or 3 months.

The other for the £250, [there] being four of them, joined with the attacher, as we believe, so I lately arrested them all four and we are now on a trial, which will come shortly. I am still told by counsel and others they must pay me the money at last, although they should have paid it first to him. . . . We have good news from Pennsylvania. Our friends all safe on shore. [The news came] by the *Amity*, by which John went.

The Amity, *Richard Dymond, master, which had left the Downs April 23, did not reach the new colony until August 3—a long voyage but with probable cargo stops in the West Indies. The eastbound crossing with the wind behind them was faster; some ships made it in four to six weeks. Several ships with Quaker colonists arrived before the* Amity *left the Delaware, but not the* Welcome *with Penn.*

London, the 23rd, October, 1682

FRANCIS AND GEORGE ROGERS

Here enclosed is your deeds for 5,000 acres land in Pennsylvania, 2 deeds for F[rancis] Rogers for 2,500 acres and a discharge for £50 paid for it, and for G[eorge] Rogers, 2,500 acres the like deeds and discharge. I have examined them all with mine, and they are exactly right. I have also sent 2 books of the Frame of our government. This vessel pretends to be gone tomorrow or next day. . . . Pray remember to write in your letters something of S[amuel] Fisher's books.

London, the 24th, 8th mo., 1682

ROBERT ROGERS

. . . I have made an end with Alderman Booth about the tobacco, which I wish I may hear no more of, for I have got better terms of him than he intended me. . . . [In this overoptimistic mood he sent on the account, £99 11*s* 6*d* to him, that is, Rogers, and £68 14*s* to Rogers' partner, Noblett Dunscombe.] I have enquired concerning insurance of several this day, and they say they will not take under 8% upon the vessel that sailed 14 days since, being as thou says from Cork to Barbados, the Leeward Islands and Jamaica, from thence to Madeira, and so to Barbados and the Leeward Islands and from thence to Ireland or England. But they will know what burthen the ship is of, which must be advised at all times in such cases.

Upon the other vessel, it's like 5% will be the lowest. When I have advice particularly and positive order I shall get it done as cheap as I can for thee. But it is always the advice to do when the ship is in port. They ask something the dearer now, because they fear a war with Angier [Algiers]. . . .

London, the 24th, 8th mo., 1682

THOMAS COOKE

. . . I have made up the account of sugar and fish and carried the net proceed of each cargo distinctly to thy account current, which

I have also perfected and send thee, and have carried the balance, being £418 12s 4d, to the credit of thy new account current. . . . I have made the most of the pieces of 8 and silver that could possibly be attained, and brought all to thy credit, and I endeavored this day to remit thee £200 or £300 and offered it at 7½%. . . . [Claypoole said he had to send to a man as far away as the Strand—about a mile and a half—but he would only give 7%.]

The next half-dozen letters were reports about bills of exchange with, however, a longer one to William Chare on the 31st. When Chare opened the fur parcels, two otters were missing. Claypoole suggested they be counted over more carefully; then, if they were still two short of the invoice, that Chare write in his own hand, stating this, and Claypoole would go to Thomas Glover and get him to "abate" 20 shillings for them. In any case, he asked that Chare sell them as soon as possible, for "we have great signs here of cold weather this winter."

London, the 7th, 9th mo., 1682

JOHN MASON

. . . If thou wilt send thy daughter to my house she shall be welcome, and we will be kind to her, but it must not be long, because I may probably let my house at London in 2 months' time. I have a house in the country and have had some years. It is an ill time of the year to send her to learn anything, for the days are short, the weather cold and the streets dirty.

The same depressing conditions no doubt existed at Exeter, where John Mason lived. But there is no hint as to whether the young woman ever came.
A ship was leaving for Hamburg, for he wrote Chare again the 10th, urging him to sell the furs "though our gain be little, rather than keep them another winter." He thought he could get three or four hundred minks; they would be 4s to 6s 6d apiece, or even 7s.

London, the 11th, 9th mo., 1682

THOMAS COOKE

. . . [I have] advised about the pieces of 8, which came to, freight and charges being deducted, a hundred 97 pounds [£197], 18s. . . . If thou wilt have a share of East Jersey, a 24th part, thou must be

[169]

resolute and positive, or else it will signify nothing, to be talking and treating one month after another. I have enquired [and] I can hear of but one that is to be sold, and the party asked £400 for it, besides the £50 that is to be put into stock. . . .

But Cooke would not invest. In a way it was Claypoole's fault, for he had written him before that he would try to get him a share under the current price.

To Marcus von Middock on the 14th he wrote again, complaining of the bad quality of his goods and saying he could not get the money from the dissatisfied customers. He also asked whether Aurend was "in health" and at Bremen, not knowing that Brummer's final illness was the reason he had not heard from him.

London, the 14th, 9th mo., 1682

Thomas Cooke

My last to thee was the 11th current, since have none from thee, nor should I have writ at this time but to send thee bill for £212 for thy proper account, drawn per Thomas Wilcox on Thomas Taverner [merchant of Limerick], payable to thyself at 21 days [usance] for which I paid him this day £200 and have placed to thy debit. The shares of East Jersey is upon the rising hand, and I am not sure I can purchase a 24th for £450. But if thou will give me order I will do for thee as well as I can.

A pleasant but formal note went to William Rogers on the 21st; Claypoole still wanted to know what to pay for the bottles of cider, as they were so small, and he added that the bill for 120 milreis on Richard Gay had been protested.

He wrote to Robert Rogers saying he had the insurance on the Providence *and the* Arabella *for £400 each, and "as to Richard Gay, I refer thee to George Rogers, who can inform thee." Gay was hiding in Ireland. He wrote Thomas Cooke that he had got a good policy to insure John Spread personally against capture by the Turks, at 2% by good men. So the Boston merchant was on his way to Ireland.*

He wrote Claridge that Gay had gone to Cork, and then he wrote to Gay himself, enclosing the letter in one to the Rogers brothers, asking them to deliver it.

The new clerk with the large slanting handwriting, who did not believe in unnecessary work, summarized the next few letters. Then Haistwell took over the copying, and he faithfully put in every word. The next

(24th, 9th month) went to William Chare and said: "I would have bought some minks and woodchucks, but that there is no certainty of any ships going [to Germany] this winter." He reported in detail on those checks; having been washed, they were thin and the color altered. It was no neglect on his part, for immediately after that accident he had sent the bale to the "whitesters"; they were properly dried and calendered, after which he kept them well covered in his warehouse. However, they were not selling. What Claypoole did not say was that in a small place, such as the City part of London, the story of the horse and cart and bales of linen getting soaked in the river was being laughed about in every tavern.

He was in difficulties with another German correspondent.

London, the 28th, 9th mo., 1682

MARCUS VON MIDDOCK & COMPANY

. . . As for my account, it is very moderate, and I think you cannot justly object against it, by balance whereof is due to me £93 4s 8d. . . . [You] are like to put me to the extremity of prosecuting you at law, which I would not do if you would be persuaded to do the thing that is just. I have sent to William Chare the copy of the account I sent you, and I intend next post to send a copy to A. Brummer, and am willing to refer any difference to them two, or if you like not that, you may add another or two more to them.

I know my cause is right and just; however, I do not desire to judge for myself, but will refer it to honest men, which I think is very fair, and if you will not do that, it's a sign you do not intend honestly and will occasion me to take a journey to Bremen in the winter, to prosecute you for my just due . . . it will neither be for your reputation nor peace of conscience, to persist in this wrong. . . .

As for my selling the hammels at 3½d, I had kept them long enough in hopes of getting [3]¾d and did use the utmost of my endeavor to advance them, as if they had been my own. But they were exceeding bad and did not deserve the name of hammels. . . . [Claypoole wrote much more to this effect and also assured Middock he had charged most moderately for interest and warehouse room; none of which soothed Middock.]

Claypoole had drawn on them a bill "payable at double usance" or twice the period of time allowed for the payment of bills to foreign countries, to be paid through Edward Haistwell. It was not accepted.

[171]

On *December 1* he wrote *William Chare that he was getting money back from Glover and Gawthorn for some otters and other furs that had proved unsatisfactory.* "I am invited to a parcel of minks and woodchucks alone," he wrote, "which I intend to go to see, and if they are good and reasonable, and any vessel going for Hamburg, I may buy them." *He added that if he could find one hundred choice otters, he would buy them, too.*

December 5 he mentioned the first sign of a depression in a letter to Robert Avery, "for now is a great want of money, and it's hard to get any in."

To Chare on the 8th he wrote that Turner's bill for £100 was protested, and "he is now certainly gone off." *But ships were readying for Hamburg and he was trying to buy more minks, otters, and woodchucks.*

To Alloway on the 12th he wrote that money was scarce. "Here some great goldsmiths and other tradesmen broke, and several merchants. . . . I have escaped all that have failed this year."

The depression was his main topic throughout December. He had, however, got the insurance for John Spread's freedom in case of capture, though several small English and Irish vessels had been taken by the Turks.

By the middle of the month there was the news that the great firm of Bolitho & Company had gone under, and more merchants and goldsmiths in London had failed.

However, Claypoole continued to do what he could to settle Richard Gay's affairs, so on the 19th of December he wrote the Rogers brothers that he needed a new power of attorney "for that he sent from Bristol was a sorry blotted thing." "It's like I may stay here till the 2nd month [April]," *he admitted,* "but next week I may recommend to you an excellent correspondent." *He repeated the number of merchants and goldsmiths that had failed,* "and more is expected, but through the good providence of God I have escaped them all."

London, the 29th, Xber, 1682

WILLIAM CHARE

. . . As to the difference between us, I am willing to refer it to the 2 names thou mentions, [Nathaniel] Cambridge and [Francis] Stratford, though I know neither of them. And shall write to them next week but this night I have not time. In the interim, let them not be influenced, but let thy demands and my answer be communicated together, for I intend to send it open to thee.

Turner's blaming my man for the linens falling into the Thames is like the rest of his lies, for there never could be any pretense or fault in him, for there was a bale of Holland likewise in the cart, and the horse ran violently back over the campshot [the barricade] and the man with him, and the man was underneath, almost drowned, and the horse I think did never well recover. For I think it is a cruel thing to prosecute the poor man that 'scaped with his life so narrow-ly. . . .

I took a view last week of the otters, minks, and woodchucks I mentioned, intending to buy them, but finding the otters very slight and the minks but indifferent, I would not bid money for them. The same person has a great quantity of raccoons, foxes, and cats, which will be sent to your market in [the] spring and be sold cheaper than last year. So I desire thee if possible to dispose of ours this winter, that I may have the account cleared by the end of the 1st month called March, about which time I hope to be ready to embark for Pennsylvania with my whole family. . . . [He goes into details here about the coming arbitration and about the "diaper" material and checks that he still held.]

As to the wharfinger, I have long since debated the matter with him, and though I was advised and did think the loss might be fixed on him, yet considering he had a campshot, which the cart ran over, I believe he will thereby be cleared. . . .

I have constituted here in my stead and sealed writings with John Bawden and John Gardner, merchants of great eminence in this city, both for estate, honesty, and experience in trade. John Bawden I believe is the greatest dealer to the West Indies, of any man in Eng-land, his commissions being computed for above £1,000 per annum from Barbados. I have let my house to his partner John Gardner, so these two I recommend my correspondents in all places, and do be-lieve they will have their business managed with great safety and honesty. So if thou wilt correspond with them when I am gone, it may be well, but while I stay, which may be above 3 months, I would not have thee begin with another.

My servant Edward Haistwell is not willing to go to Pennsyl-vania, so I think he will have a room and some conveniency for trade in my house, and apply himself chiefly to the mum trade, wherein it's like I may be concerned myself. He has now two year and ½ to serve and is very honest and capable of business. . . .

Claypoole also mentioned his reluctance to journey to Bremen in the winter, so he was sending a power of attorney to clear accounts with Middock and John Brummer, who would "wrong" him of £55. Still trying to clear up bills and debts, he wrote to Cork.

London, December 30th, 1682

JOHN HAMMOND

. . . According to thy order I readily paid John Osgood £100 for thy account and would have paid him the rest, but that I would first agree with thee what the balance is. So herewith I have sent thy account, by balance of which is due to thee £38 17s 4d, for which, if thou chargest a bill upon me to him it shall be punctually paid.

The tenor of the bill may be thus: "Cork, the —, the — month, 1682. At 21 days sight, pay this my only bill unto John Osgood, thirty-eight pounds, seventeen shillings and four pence, being the balance of account due to me, and this with his receipt shall be a discharge in full of all accounts, from thy loving friend, J— H—."
. . . [Claypoole continued about his new correspondents, whom John Osgood also knew, and said he would give them a reference.] But while I am here, I desire thee to make use of me as formerly, and I shall be willing to serve, who am, with true love to thee and thy wife.

London, December 30th, 1682

ROBERT ROGERS

. . . Enclosed I send thee copies of the two policies on which have gotten £800 subscribed for thy account. The one comes to, with charges, £19 6s and the other £31 1s 5d, which is £50 7s 5d placed to thy debit. I am settling my affairs here to embark with my whole family for Pennsylvania about 3 months hence. So I have constituted in my stead here and sealed writings with John Bawden and John Gardner whom I recommend. . . . They are merchants of great eminency and experience in trade of most kinds, especially John Bawden, who is an elderly man of as great estate and repute as few beyond him in this city. We have been near neighbors these many years, so I know him well and can recommend him sincerely to thee as a man to be confided in, in every respect, and do believe thy business may be managed by them with great care and safety. To John Gardner, who is a young man, and his partner, also related to him, I have let my house. . . . [Claypoole seems to have changed his opinion of Bawden since last June 27.]

London, the 30th, 10th mo., 1682

THOMAS COOKE

. . . Here has been little business these idle days, so as yet cannot get a bill for Dublin to my mind, but next week am promised one, which shall send to S[amuel] Claridge for thy account. Herewith I send thee copy of a bond and of warrant of attorney for a judgment against James Barry, which if thou wilt accept of, let me have thy answer per first [post] and that there be no time lost. Then I must give up the bills and protests and discharge the security for the £65.

But if thou wilt not accept of this, let me know per first, that I may deal with him according to his deserts. Have had a great deal of trouble in hunting him from one lodging to another, for he keeps very private, and I could never yet speak with him but under a promise to let him go and come free. I entered an action long since in thy name and had 3 baylys [bailiffs] to a tavern in King Street, where he was at dinner with many blades [slang of the period for the gay and rakish gentlemen, who of course carried swords]. They [the bailiffs] were afraid of their lives, else they might have taken him. One of them got away his sword, but he made an escape to the rest of his company, and then there was no venturing on him. I do not question but I can get him, having found his haunts, but I would have thee consider whether it is not better to take bond and judgment than lay him in gaol.

Walter Benthall is not yet come, nor do I hear from Samuel Carpenter. . . .

Both these men were devout Quakers, both West Indies merchants; Carpenter was already planning to live in Pennsylvania. At this point the clerk copying the letter added a note of his own, "the same about John Bawden, etc., as to Robert Rogers," and so ended the letter sensibly without unnecessary work.

[175]

London, the 30th, 10th mo., 1682

FRANCIS AND GEORGE ROGERS

. . . [Claypoole had received £77 and later £19 on that insurance; he was doubtful if he would ever get the full amount.] I desire you draw no more upon me yet, unless you send effects, for I would not be straitened for money near the time of my going away. Have writ this day to William End and directed my letter to your house, which I desire you to open and read and deliver to him yourselves. It is chiefly about Miles Forster, who is kept a prisoner on their account and may be utterly ruined if they have not some compassion on him. So I desire you to deliver the letter and intercede for him and let me have his answer. I believe what he [Forster] writes is true in every particular. They must pay 4d postage, 6d to Dublin. . . .

I desire you to send me per first opportunity John's bed and other things if worth redeeming. However, his bed, etc., it will serve on shipboard. . . .

London, the 30th, 10th mo., 1682

WILLIAM END

. . . I have been still in expectation to hear from thee, that thou hadst got the money from Wheedon and Gamble, and seeing Wheedon is at liberty methinks something might be done in it, which I desire thee to advise me of. The other side [of the paper] is from Miles Forster, who is [in] a condition to be pitied. Though he has been much to blame and has deserved a prison, yet with justice we must have some mercy; he has given thee an account of his condition which I believe really is true, and I am sorry that I have been an instrument, through your order, to keep him thus long in prison, and now desire your answer if I may not let the suit fall, he paying the charges. For the longer you keep him, the farther you are from your money, but if you give him his liberty, it's possible he may in time recover and pay you. . . .

So ended the year as we know it, with the most compassionate letter that Claypoole ever wrote. The young man was let out of the debtors' jail, for, shortly after, Miles Forster turned up in East New Jersey. He mar-

ried the daughter of the governor, *Gawen Lawrie. The New York Quaker records give her name, Rebecca, and no date, but a son died in 1689. Miles became one of New Jersey's prominent men.*

As for the bed and bedding which his son John had left with the Rogerses and which James asked for so often and so patiently, he never got it, nor, apparently, did the Rogers brothers ever bother to answer his requests.

The first weeks of the 11th month, or January, 1682/83, must have been unusually busy, for except to William Bolitho of Exeter, of a distinguished merchant family, several important letters were written but not copied into the book: on the 5th, "To William Penn, a long letter," and the same day, "To Dr. More, a large letter." On January 9 there was another note "To Edward Cole, a short letter, and sent these 3 by Singleton, master of the ——— in a letter under cover to himself" [Singleton].

Claypoole's clerk did not know the name of Singleton's ship, as a blank was left for it. It was the Thomas & Anne, *which left for New York and Pennsylvania about mid-January.*

At last he caught up with that gay young blade, James Barry.

London, the 9th, 11th mo., 1682/83

THOMAS COOKE

. . . James Barry has signed and delivered before three sufficient witnesses a bond for £200 bearing date the 28th past, the condition of which is to pay unto thee at the Town Hall in Cork £45 2s the 25th, 1st month next, and £68 4s the 1st, 3rd month next, and has given a warrant of attorney to pass a judgment to thee at thy suit for £200, and has paid me 5 guineas is £5 0s 6d for exchange and charges past, which have brought to thy credit, which is the best security I can get. And indeed I think it may very well satisfy thee. . . . Have received the pieces of 8 according to bills of lading, for thy account, 1,299 ozs., and 376 ozs. for his account, and have enquired among the goldsmiths and find that the most they will yield is 5s 2¼ d, at which rate I think to sell them tomorrow or next day or at ¼ d [a farthing] more if I can get it.

If John Spread be come, remember me kindly to him; shall take care of his 7 hhds. sugar and sell it tomorrow . . . could not get a bill to my mind for Dublin or Cork this day; there are bills offered at 10% which I am not willing to take, for these are hazardous times. . . .

[177]

I should be glad to hear that thou dost intend hereafter to correspond with John Bawden and John Gardner; thy signifying so much to them might be a real kindness to me, which, with my love to thee, is all at present.

Abel Ram had been doing business in Ireland for James's brother Wingfield and recently had collected some money for him. As captain of a troop of horse under Cromwell, Wingfield had been given land; the money collected could have been for the sale of this. The Calendar of State Papers for Ireland for 1662 contains a petition of some of these landowners, signed by Wingfield, the petition saying cautiously that some of these people had always been loyal to the Crown—though fighting for Cromwell.

London, the 9th, 11th mo., 1682/83

DEAR BROTHER WINGFIELD CLAYPOOLE

The above written from Abel Ram I received last week, so I have missed one post sending it to thee. If he got in the money 3 months since, thou mightst have had it returned for 5%, and now the exchange is at 10 [%] and may be worse more likely than better. I believe I could draw for 8% and that is the lowest. But I know where to have 10 and more if I would take bills. . . . I desire thee remember what I spoke to thee of, about a joiner or carpenter or cooper for Pennsylvania, or a plowman or gardener or any that have skill in husbandry. I do hope still, before I go away, I shall have time to come with my wife to Northampton, to see my sister [Dorothy] Holled. Mine and my wife's true love to her and also to thyself. . . .

London, the 9th, 11th mo., 1682/83

ROBERT TURNER

I received yesterday thine 29th past. As to our intended voyage for Pennsylvania, we hope to be ready to embark about the end of the 1st month [March] and are looking out for a good vessel to carry us. I am in treaty with one Jeffries, master of a ship of 500 ton, which will require 2 months' time to get ready in. He has used the Virginia trade and may be very fit for us, both ship and master, if we can but procure company and goods enough to make a bargain with

[178]

him, to engage him into Delaware River directly [not to go to the West Indies or other ports on the way], which we suppose about 80 passengers and 50 ton of goods may do. She is by report, for I have not yet seen her, a very brave ship, as not many merchant ships in England exceeds her.

So if thou knowest of any friends in Ireland that have a purpose of going to Pennsylvania or New Jersey and will take this opportunity, it may be a great accommodation to them as well as to us. If thou hears of any, I desire thee write to me about it.

As for any news for Pennsylvania, we have of late none but good. There had been 21 sail ships arrived last summer in Delaware [this was before he had Penn's December 29th letter mentioning 23 altogether], and the country is very well liked for pleasantness by the people. William Penn was well, and things was like to be settled to content, and [he] was received with a great deal of love and respect and had held a court in Pennsylvania and was gone to hold another at New Castle. And there also the people readily subjected to him, and there was like to be a good understanding and a fair settlement of the bounds between Baltimore and him.

I suppose thou heard long since of 31 Friends that died in William Penn's ship of the smallpox. But as for other reports, which we believe are lies, it is in vain to mention them. We are in daily expectation of another ship from New York, which will bring us more ample account of all things, which I may advise thee of. In the meantime I desire to hear from thee, when and how thou intends to go, and any other advice that thou thinks may be serviceable. With my true love to thee, I am.

Exchange for Dublin, 8 to 10%.

London, the 11th, 11th mo., 1682/83

FRIEND EDWARD COLE

I writ to thee the 9th and mentioned something of a servant, which I have now agreed with and bound for 8 years. His name is Philip Brooks, as per the enclosed indenture, which I send thee, as also the bill of lading from the master and an invoice of his things, which I desire thee to take care of and see that he has them all. I have also sent 2 pieces of coarse linen, containing 60 and 59 each, is 59½ [average] ells, or 75 yards, which may be sold to buy provision if there be need. I hope it will yield 6d per yard, but sell it as well as thou canst. [Claypoole put the linen on board without paying customs; it is not in the 1683 port books. Perhaps he had it passed as young Philip's personal property!]

If thou hast not employment for him, let him work for some other body for wages, for I would not have him idle, and keep him in subjection and good order. I have committed the care of him and his chest to Thomas Singleton, master of the ship, and given him an account what there is in it, that while he is on shipboard he may look a little after him, and see that he doth not make away his things [sell the new clothing Claypoole had bought for him]. I send the less now because I hope to be with you within 3 months after this ship's arrival. But if I had had more time, I would have sent some other things to sell. However, I hope thou wilt make reasonable shift with this and what was sent before, till we come.

As I said before, I hope there will be a little house built for us, if it be but like a barn, and if possible, let there be a cellar made, to keep some wine and other liquors cool in, that I intend to take with me, for it's like we shall come there in very hot weather. And if there could be some fruit trees set at the right season it might be well, and if thou shouldst want a supply on these occasions to the value of £5 or £6 sterling, John Goodson, I suppose, will supply thee. I say five or six pounds sterling, but I hope there will be no need.

If thou shouldst meet with any extraordinary trouble or be wronged or abused by any, address [thyself] to the governor in my name, or in his absence to Dr. More or to Thomas Holme or Ralph Withers—but we hear that Ralph Withers is dead; if living, remember my dear love to him and also to Thomas Holme. I have sent with the boy more things than he needs, but let him wear his old things out first, and upon those days he does not work, his new things.

Friends are under great suffering for truth in many places, but the Lord preserves us through His power, by which He has made us willing to suffer for His name, and His reward of peace and joy and satisfaction is sure to all the faithful. So, friend, my desire is for thee as for myself that we may be kept in the blessed truth which sanctifies the heart, that we may serve the Lord with faithfulness in our generation and bring forth fruits of righteousness to His praise, that our whole conversation may be coupled with fear, so as this new plantation, as it comes to be peopled, may be as a garden of the Lord, and from thence the truth may spread to other colonies, yea, even among the Indians, that His name and truth may be honored. And then we shall inherit the blessing, and His salvation will be as walls and bulwarks unto us. So to the Lord I commit thee, who is able to keep us and will keep and preserve all that trust in Him, and abide faithful to what He has made manifest. With my love to thee in the truth, I rest.

London, the 12th, 11th mo., 1682/83

WILLIAM CHARE

. . . I intended this night to have given instructions for the ending of our business but was prevented by other business, nor could I get time since to write to Mark Middock. He has given fresh orders to his correspondents here, Carletons, to pay me £47 10s, which is about £45 less than my due, and they pretended to pay me last week, and now they say they have not received Middock's money yet but will pay me next week. So it is altogether uncertain.

I herewith send thee the account current, fairly writ and the errors mended that was in the last, by balance of which was due to me the 24th, 9th month [November], £292 13s 5d. . . . [Matthew Carleton's business was in Fenchurch Street.]

London, January the 13th, 1682/83

THOMAS COOKE

. . . I hope thou wilt accept of the security I offered thee from Barry, for better is not to be had, and indeed I think it is safe. I am offered 2 sufficient men's bond for 40s [£40?] to secure the payment of his bond when due. His credit is gone, [so] that he cannot go on wasting his estate as he has done, and I am satisfied by what I have heard that as yet his estate is not mortgaged, so pray let me have thy answer that I may send the bond and judgment to have it entered forthwith.

I have sold thy pieces of 8, being 1,299 and ½ ozs. at 5s 2¼ d; £337 1s 2d, and have paid 1% freight. John Spread's were 376 ozs. at same price, £97 10s 6d. And have met with a bill to my mind, which

I am very glad of, and send it thee here enclosed. It is drawn by Thomas Hart, payable at 30 days sight to thyself, by [on?] Richard Pierce and Company of Limerick, £250 at 10%.

I entreat thee in thy next to advise John Bawden and John Gardner that thou dost intend to correspond with them when I am gone, and that thou wilt order thy correspondents in the West Indies to send thy effects to them. And this cannot be a prejudice but an advantage to thee, and it will be really a great kindness to me and make some business I have with them more easy. And I desire thee to engage John Spread to do the like. I do assure thee I have aimed at my correspondents' benefit in this matter, for I could have had a far greater advantage to myself in recommending my business to a person that thou knowest, who has a partner also, but upon diligent search I did not find it so safe, so I would not have thee be inveigled by him, lest thou repent it hereafter....

London, the 15th, 11th mo., 1682/83

WILLIAM POPPLE AND ROBERT STEWART

... I take very kindly your advice about the vine plants and your willingness to accommodate me therein, but the season of the year was not suitable. But now I hope it may be very seasonable. So I desire you to send me as many as can be packed in one hhd., with earth to preserve them. I hope there may be 1,000 pieces, by what I hear, and also I desire one peck of grape seed. And pray advise me how long they may probably keep to grow again, for the ship I intend to send them by will hardly sail from hence till the end of the next month, and it may be two months before she arrive in Pennsylvania. So that if they will not in probability grow if they be not set till 3rd month, May, it will be in vain to send them at present.

However, I desire the seed, for I believe that will keep all the year and a peck of chestnuts, and if it were not for troubling you too much, I would desire a tun of white wine and a tun of claret to carry with us when we go to Pennsylvania. But pray let it be good wine, and I shall take it as a great kindness and shall be ready at all times to serve you.

We intend to be ready to go on shipboard about 1st, 2nd month called April. We have had letters from William Penn there that all things were like to be well settled in the country, and there was 21 sail of ships arrived that last summer with passengers. I intend to write to thee, W[illiam] P[opple], when I come there and shall be glad to hear from thee, for I shall still remember thee as my good friend. I sent thee a brave book this summer called *Caballa Denudata*, but thou dost not mention it, so I doubt it is not come to hand. . . . My love to you and Mary Popple, is all at present from your loving friend. . . .

What shall be done with W. P.'s box of old books ? [Young William Popple had visited Claypoole earlier.]

The Caballa Denudata *consisted of two volumes on Hebrew theology and metaphysics, published in 1677. William Popple, a scholar and friend of John Locke, had been educated by the poet Andrew Marvell, his uncle. Later he or his son became secretary to the Board of Trade in London.*

London, the 16th, 11th mo., 1682/83

DEAR BROTHER EDWARD CLAYPOOLE

. . . [The letter began with an account of the sales of sugar and of Edward's balance of £466 12s 4d; then he praised Bawden and Gardner. Claypoole admitted that he had "some consideration for 3 year."] But I have not closed with them only for my own advantage, for I could have had far more profitable terms from others. But these men I am sure are more safe for my correspondents to deal with, and as for experience in the Barbados trade . . . I believe there is no man in England beyond them, and their reputation and estates are accounted equal to the best aldermen in London. . . .

I suppose Dr. Harding has advised thee to deal with Thomas Hinchman, who is his friend. [James Harding, physician, had £50 in the Free Society; the shipmaster was John Harding. Hinchman was a merchant in Aldersgate Street.] But if thou does, I am sure thy business will be neglected and thy sugars ill sold, and possibly a bad debt, for he dwells in the country and has only a lodging in London and is seldom seen at the Exchange. And I do assure thee, if I was in thy stead, I would rather give John Bawden and partner 5% than give him 2½%. So if thou hast begun with T. H. or promised him before my letter comes to hand, I desire thee to clear with him as soon as thou canst and go on with them.

And as for the balance of thy account I shall readily pay thy bills or to whom thou wilt order it only one hundred pounds. I entreat thee let me have in my hands till I come to Pennsylvania. . . . the reason that I desire this kindness of thee is that I cannot get in my estate from other parts, which yet is in safe hands, viz., I have near £1,000 in Germany, most in commodities unsold, and some in Ireland and many debts here in England and elsewhere. . . . I think thou wilt be in no danger of losing anything by me whether I live or die, for I leave concerns here that I hope in 2 or 3 years' time will bring me in £500, and I have £200 stock in the Pennsylvania Society, and 50,000 acres [he meant 5,000] of land there and £100 per annum as treasurer to the Society for 7 years. And William Penn [being] my singular friend, whatever profitable employment I may be fit for, I know I shall have it as soon as any man. I intend to take a considerable adventure with me, I believe to the value of £700 or £800, and do not intend to owe any man in England £10 when I go away, and then I am like to have as good correspondents as any man in Pennsylvania. . . .

I have sent thee as a token of my love by this vessel, the *Orange Tree*, John Hull, master, a large Cheshire cheese sewed in canvas and directed to thyself, which I have committed to the care of Charles Wager, whose father and mother are my especial friends. Here have come letters from William Penn above a month since that he was well in health and was settling the country, and they had begun to build a city which they call Philadelphia, and there had been that summer 21 sail ships arrived there with passengers. I sent 2 servants, an elderly man, a brickmaker, and a boy of 14 years old, and I have, to go with me, 4 or 5 servants more, and as for the Negro man and woman and boy and girl, if they are not sent, I desire they may be sent by the first opportunity. And pray, brother, send such, if thou canst, as may be likely to prove good natured and tractable.

We have not had a line from John since his arrival in Pennsylvania, but lately I saw a letter from Richard Dymond at B.B. [Barbados] that seemed to be of John's writing, but we know not certainly. . . . My brother Claypoole has got a considerable place in the Lombard [Street] office, so that I am now in hopes of getting my money of him before I go away. His place is worth some hundreds per annum, and they are like to begin in a few weeks. He owes me near £300, part being on a bond, but some part he will not acknowledge.

I have an horse about 15 hands high, an able, stout horse that paces exceeding well and easy, and has all his goings very sure-footed and good quality. I have rode him both single and often double these 2 years and ½ past and never had a fall. He cost me £17 12s 6d, and I have been offered many times 20 guineas for him. He comes 9 years. I have a purpose to send him to thee that thou mayst keep him for thy own use at a market price, or else sell him for the most thou canst get. But he has got a great cold at grass, and a cough which I cannot get him cured of, and if it be not dangerous, his dying at sea upon account of his cold, I [would] conclude to send him.

If thou art acquainted with Sir Richard Dutton, I desire thee speak to him to pay the £5 to Joseph Grove, else it will be so much lost to me. . . .

London, the 16th, 11th mo., 1682/83

DEAR BROTHER WINGFIELD CLAYPOOLE

. . . I perceive thou hast an evil jealousy in thy mind, that I had advice of Abel Ram's receiving the £100 before [thou] went hence, and that I concealed it through some ill design. What that design was I know not. Thou shouldst have told me thy mind plainly. As to the time of thy going hence, I know not when it was, but Abel Ram's letter to me which gave me the first advice of that money was dated the 19th December and came to this post office, as by their seal may appear, the 3rd [January]. . . . And I was at Kingston 4 or 5 days or else thou hadst had an account of it sooner. And this is the very truth of the matter.

I would not have thee be so earnest about the £80, as if thou thought I would go away in thy debt, for though I cannot promise it thee this month with conveniency, yet be assured thou shalt have it ere it be long, for I design to be clear of all debts in England before I go away.

Remember a servant for Pennsylvania. With love to thyself and sister and cousin I rest.

Thine to me cost 4d and to A. R. 6d.

A letter to Abel Ram was copied the same date, mentioning two bills for £571 and £700 each and enclosing a letter that Wingfield had sent

Claypoole to send on to Ram. He mentioned in the letter that Wingfield said he was going to Ireland shortly. William Alloway's letter of the same date, the 16th, expressed great praise for Bawden and Gardner.

London, the 16th, 11th mo., 1682/83

ROBERT ROGERS

... [Claypoole asked Rogers to let him know when he had written to Bawden and Gardner and said he still expected to leave for Pennsylvania in April.] [I] shall be glad to correspond with thee there, but at present I know not what trade we shall have. If thou wilt buy 50,000 [5,000] acres of land there, which cost £100, or ½ that quantity, advise me thereof and it shall be done. And if thou wilt send over a trusty servant, it [the land] may be improved and I will see about it when I come there, and advise thee the needful concerning it. The last news we had from William Penn was that he was well, and all things like to be settled for content. There arrived 21 sail ships and passengers the last summer.

Exchange for Dublin and Cork, 8 to 10%.

London, the 17th, 11th mo., 1682/83

SAMUEL CARPENTER

I have not written to thee lately so have several of thine to answer. ... I understand thy purpose is for Pennsylvania. I wish thee all happiness and prosperity in thy undertakings and do hope I shall see thee there in a few months, for I do intend, if the Lord permits, to remove thither in the spring about the beginning of the 2nd month with my whole family, and am very desirous that our friendship may continue, and that we may have dealing and concern together. ... [He added that he had sealed writings with two merchants in the city whom he was sure Carpenter had heard of, and he signed himself his "real, loving friend."]

The friendship, unfortunately, did not last. Two years later Carpenter brought an action in a Philadelphia court against Claypoole and the Free Society of Traders.

The Barbados mail took another letter, this time to Joseph Grove. Claypoole said he heard that Grove had recently been married and also had been ill. He was busy settling accounts; he wanted Grove to collect from Sir Richard Dutton and to settle his own account.

To Ralph Weeks he wrote apologizing for not accepting a bill, which he would have done if he had been staying in England.

To William Rogers he wrote about insurance and added an excuse for brevity, "I am not well, so must be shorter than I would." This may have been another attack of the stone, for the letters were brief and to the point for some days.

London, the 23rd, 11th mo., 1682/83

RICHARD GAY

... [I have] done what was in my power to recover the money of the insurers; I have at length made a full conclusion. . . . It cost great charge and trouble to bring it so far, but we see that the lawyers at last would get all if we went on, and we should have nothing to divide. There is only now £39 due by the executors of William Hinton, which I have hope will prove good, but he has not been dead near 1 year yet. . . . What I recover from Hinton must be carried to F[rancis] and G[eorge] Rogers' account.

I assure thee I have had a great deal of trouble about it and would not have the like again for £50. So I think I deserve a beaver hat as thou promised me, besides my ordinary commission. So I have placed £3 to account for it.

I have received the letter of attorney, which is well, and have sent it to the court to be there laid up. It seems John Earle has done unkindly by thee and he did a little uncivilly by me, for he sent a bayly [bailiff] to me when I was at a friend's house at dinner, as if he would arrest me. . . . I am tomorrow to treat with a ship for Pennsylvania; we intend to be ready in 3 months. I shall be glad of thy company if all things concur to thy mind.

Claypoole wrote to the Rogers brothers at the same time, saying, "we are agreeing for a ship to carry us to Pennsylvania and to be ready in the 2nd month, but we expect there may be near 200 of us. There is one ship gone away thither last week." That ship was Singleton's Thomas & Anne. As for the number of passengers on the new Concord, he was far too optimistic. At one time it seemed as if he would have only a third that number, and possibly the long delay they had in getting off was due to a lull in emigration.

[187]

A letter went to Benjamin Furly, Penn's friend and his agent in Holland, explaining that Claypoole was going to Pennsylvania, where he would be willing to serve Furly or any of his friends. As to his business in London, which had been considerable "through the blessing of God", he was leaving it with Bawden and Gardner, whom he recommended. He added that they often shipped to Holland, especially Rotterdam.

London, the 24th, 11th mo., 1682/83

DANIEL LODGE & COMPANY

I had occasion to trouble you this last summer and to put you to a little charge of postage for advice about a ship with tobacco from Antego [Antigua], which Alderman Rogers of Cork designed for Amsterdam, and so should have been consigned to you for sale, I having before recommended you to him for correspondents there. The said ship by his order came hither, and I disposed of the tobacco, supposing this to be the best market.

However, your charge and trouble may not be in vain, for another time it's probable both he and others of my correspondents may deal with you for your advantage. I wish I had known in time of your corresponding with C[harles] Turner, I would have given you a friendly caution that you should not have been concerned with him. He [Turner] would have done the like by William Chare of Hamburg, but my advice prevented him there. [After this cold comfort Claypoole added that he was going to Pennsylvania and praised his successors, who "send ships often to Holland, especially to Amsterdam."]

London, 30th, 11th mo., 1682/83

THOMAS COOKE

. . . There is no getting any insurance done at reasonable rates when the ship has been so long from port. But being she is arrived at the Canaries, I do not question but to get it perfected tomorrow. As for James Barry's estate, which thou says is so encumbered, I am very well assured from good men that there is no judgment or encumbrances upon it, but his father would have people believe so, that he may have neither credit nor money and so be forced to go for Ireland, which he cannot well be blamed for, by reason his son leads so bad a life here. . . .

No doubt Claypoole felt some sympathy for this parent, thinking of his own trials with his son John.

To Thomas Hart, who had written for one barrel of mum, he replied: "I would have the old score cleared first. . . . The gauge of a barrel [of] mum is about 50 wine gallons, some a gallon or two less and some a gallon or two more, so that at 6d per quart, makes out £5 [per barrel]."

London, 6th, 12th mo., 1682/83

SAMUEL CLARIDGE

. . . The £1 (commission) thou says is too much for the extraordinary trouble in the East Jersey business. Thou says Anthony Sharp wonders at it and that he and thee would do twice as much for me for ½ the money. It is soon said. But you know not what trouble I had and hazard also, for I was fain to go beyond the bounds of your order, or I believe you had been to seek your bargain at this day. I assure thee I had a great deal of trouble in it and would not do the like again for twice the commission. Yet I may serve thee or Anthony Sharp, or any other friend in another way, as far, I believe, you would me, for love and not money. . . .

London, the 6th, 12th mo., 1682/83

ROBERT TURNER

. . . As for the time that we purpose to go from hence, I suppose it will be in the 2nd month, but whether the middle or latter end I know not. We are all inclined to go in this vessel now put up; she is a brave ship of 500 tons burden, and 26 guns, called the *Concord*, the master, William Jeffries, who has used long the Virginia trade and is well acquainted with that voyage. We are to give 40s per ton for dry goods, and 25s for liquors, and to pay full £5 per head for all above 12 years of age, and all under 12, 50s, and sucking children free. But we have not yet signed [the] charter party so are neither of us engaged. But if thou sends any goods, thy order shall be observed in what ship they shall be sent. [As Turner was in Dublin, this would mean shipping goods from London in partnership with one of his correspondents there.]

Last night Guli Penn had a letter from her husband, dated 16th, 10th month [December], in Maryland, where he was treating with

Baltimore about the bounds [the southern boundary of Pennsylvania] in which they went on very amicably and like to have a fair conclusion. He was very well and had not been sick at all so far as we know [to combat the rumors that Penn had died, or turned Catholic, and that a ship full of Quakers had foundered]. . . .

They had a General Assembly and the foreigners naturalized, and New Castle added to Pennsylvania, and had many blessed meetings to the great satisfaction of Friends and others, which, with my true love to thee, is all at present.

The same Irish mail took a letter to Thomas Cooke, who had objected to anyone else's handling young Barry's bills, though Barry had bound himself legally to pay. "I am glad to hear that John Spread is arrived; I have writ him a few lines underneath. I saved the [in margin: about] £15 for insurance on that ship . . . so I hope thou wilt allow me to put 20s to [my] account." And he added the good news about Penn.

The "underneath" message to Spread, safely arrived from Boston, was written on the same paper, making the two letters one, hence requiring only sixpence postage. Claypoole repeated what he had got for the pieces of 8, from letters written last October.

London, the 6th, 12th mo., 1682/83

WILLIAM CHARE

. . . I have it still under consideration whether to go to Hamburg and Bremen this winter, and therefore I have not yet given up to N[athaniel] C[ambridge] and F[rancis] S[tratford] my objections to thy demand. [See his letter of the 29th, 10th month.] But if I resolve not in 14 days to begin my journey I will then without farther delay write to them. As for the damage on the checks, if the buyer had been honest there would have been nothing on that kind, for I made a positive bargain with him. . . . I have been endeavoring by all I can by brokers and others to dispose of the copper [plates] but cannot sell any yet. I would take £5 8s for the thick and £5 18s for the thin, ready money, but they have been used to buy copper at 6 months, and to have the thick plates warranted they will endure milling. . . . A brazier told me yesterday he could buy thick plates at £5 6s, which is a miserable price. . . . As to thy order about buying some otters and minks, when our New York ship arrives, I shall do my endeavor to effect it, which [ship] is expected every day. . . .

NATHANIEL CAMBRIDGE AND FRANCIS STRATFORD

Friends though unknown, I kindly salute you. I say unknown because I never had an opportunity to converse with you either by word or writing. But through the good report that you have had these many years, I conclude you to be my friends and men of understanding and honesty, which has induced me to beg the favor of you, to consider and determine a difference that has happened between my friend William Chare and myself. It was my desire to have it determined here, by reason I knew none at Hamburg, and I thought would have been upon more equal terms, he having many intimate friends here, besides his own brother a counselor. And I have also pleaded with him the hard circumstances I should be under to refer a difference to his intimates, he being present to plead for himself, and I through my absence not capable to give answer, and the persons altogether to me unknown. But he would not comply with me, and I am for peace. . . .

With this tactful, if lengthy, introduction, Claypoole settled down to a history of the dispute, running over several pages, going back nearly ten years and to the period when Chare's brother had been alive and in charge of the business. Most of the sums involved were petty and have appeared in Claypoole's letters. The most interesting thing about the dispute is the fact that they were trading in furs with places as far away as Archangel and Danzig. Claypoole asked the arbitrators to hurry their decision, as he was going to Pennsylvania, and added that he was still good friends with Chare.

London, the 9th, 12th mo., 1682/83

WILLIAM CHARE

. . . [Claypoole reported that he had written Cambridge and Stratford, sending the letter unopened for Chare to read (in which he certainly showed his Quaker trustfulness). At the same time, he wanted their accounts brought up to date and asked what he might expect from goods that were in Danzig, Stockholm, and Copenhagen, mostly furs. He also wanted the 90 bags of black ginger sold for whatever the market would bring. He did not understand why Chare had to bring in a broker to sell their furs; this meant paying an extra commission.] If thou couldst send a good fisherman that know [how] to catch and cure sturgeon, or had a general skill in fishing, he should have very good terms from me, such as may satisfy any reasonable man, for in Delaware River there is a vast quantity of sturgeon, so that they leap into the boats. And there is also many whales and abundance of other sorts of great and small fish. This week we have received letters from thence to our great satisfaction.

I have sent a letter of attorney to John Cassawe of Bremen to receive my corn of the widow Brummer, being 10 lasts of wheat and 10 last of rye [bought for him in the summer of 1681]. . . . I desire thee to receive of Christian Pitch 11s 8d for postage of letters and 20s for my soliciting his business with Van Baselar and place it to my credit. Here is a New York ship come, so I shall endeavor to get some minks and otters, according to thy desire.

In a letter to John Cassawe, of the 9th, 12th month, Claypoole complained that the mum which he had just received was "slight" and not to be compared with what Aurend Brummer had sent. In connection with his dispute with Von Middock, he intended sending copies of their letters to Cassawe but wrote, "[I] cannot do it tonight, for I am not very well. . . . I am very sorry that my good friend Aurend Brummer is dead."

London, the 13th, 12th mo., 1682/83

SAMUEL CLARIDGE

. . . Thou hast charged me 4s too much for commission. Thou never mentions Samuel Fisher's books I sent thee so long since to sell for me. I hope they are sold for 15s per book, for so F. Rogers has sold 5 of them at Cork. Thou objects against the interest I charge thee, though it is a little and ought to have been more, which I shall also examine again and charge what is due, for I have been out £200 at a time, and seeing thou art so strict to charge 12%, I may very well charge 8%. As for £1 commission for extraordinary trouble on the East Jersey purchase, I am sure I deserved it, and am not willing to abate it. . . . [But Claypoole was not as acrimonious as he sounded, for he signed himself "thy loving friend." He often began a letter in a bad temper, worked off his annoyance as he wrote, and ended in a conciliatory mood.]

The same day he wrote Abel Ram asking for enough business so he could have at least £5 commission to make up for some past losses in

Ram's affairs. He would be "very willing to serve thee or any friend of thine in Pennsylvania; we have very good news from thence of William Penn being in health and the rest of our friends, and all things like to go well, near 30 sail ships arrived there this last year."

This last statement is interesting. Penn in letters written December 29, which would not have arrived in London yet, and in letters the following summer said there were twenty-three ships, sometimes adding "with passengers." Or was this Claypoole's habit of slight exaggeration? As to their entire number Penn was always vague. He once wrote "forty trading vessels" and at another time, "fifty ships, great and small." These would include small coastal and Barbados ships.

London, the 15th, 12th mo., 1682/83

THOMAS HART

I received thine 12th ditto with £4 15s which is in full of all accounts, and I will now send thee a barrel of mum, according to thy desire, but that I intend to leave England in a little time, but that I must have present money for what I sell, that I may take what I can with me. So I desire thee not to take it ill, for this is the only reason. But if thou wilt send by the wagoner £3 4½s, I will send thee a very good barrel of mum, or 2 barrels for £2 9s [each]. I assure thee it is right new Brunswick mum. . . .

It is pleasant to find that Claypoole was paid some of his bills, even if they were the small ones. John Mason in Exeter finally paid his £39 and was immediately offered more mum for £3 3s a barrel, "free of all charges, paying me present money" or cash.

London, the 16th, 12th mo., 1682/83

DEAR BROTHER [EDWARD CLAYPOOLE]

. . . [A note said the letter went on the 20th by the *Mary & Elizabeth*, John Gadsden, master, and began about some corrected bills. Edward now had over £476 credit with his brother. The letter also included another power of attorney, witnessed by Gadsden and a Joseph Wood.] My horse I do intend to send thee unless I can dispose of him here very well to content. . . . As for the Negroes I advised for, I am still of the same mind and desire they may be sent by the 1st opportunity to Philadelphia, consigned as advised.

[193]

We are to be ready at Gravesend to sail, if wind and weather permits, the 30th, 2nd month called April, so that through the help of the Lord we may hope to be in Pennsylvania before mid-summer, for Captain Arnold, by whom went the president of our Society and servants, arrived there in 29 days, and another great ship about the same time in less than 5 weeks. [No such time was made by any London to Pennsylvania ship after the *Jeffrey*, but it could have been a Maryland or New York ship.] We have good news from all, and a great commendation of the country, so that we may hope for and expect a great deal of comfort and content in transplanting, and our Company concerns go on well and may come to be a very profitable undertaking.

They send by our ship workmen of several sorts to set up a glass house for window glass, bottles, etc., and we hope to have a iron work. If thou hast a mind to have a share in the stock, £50 or £100 or a quantity of land, 1,000, 2—3 or 5,000 acres, I desire thee write to me about it; 100 acres cost 40s, and so 50,000 [5,000] cost £100. Here is a vindication of William Penn to prevent lying reports.

With my true love to thyself and my sister and daughters, I rest, thy very loving brother.

Claypoole had the Vindication of William Penn *right off the press. Philip Ford signed his pamphlet the 12th of February to combat rumors that Penn had died—and as a Papist at that! Claypoole wrote the 16th, but his letter did not go until the 20th, so there was just time to enclose the newly printed pamphlet. The printer, Benjamin Clark, marked it 1683, as it was so near the beginning of the new year, as reckoned in the seventeenth century.*

An interesting point in the letter is Claypoole's mention of sending workmen of several sorts by the Company's ship—the Jeffrey—*to set up a glass house. It was thought that Pennsylvania did not begin making glass until much later. Joshua Tittery, a glass maker indentured to the Society, did not arrive until August 1683. The Bristol Port Book for 1683 has an item (unpublished) dated July 6, showing that William Penn was sending "18 hhds. of earth for making glass" to go on the* Unicorn, *Thomas Cooper, master.*

Always a worrier, and not feeling well at the moment, Claypoole wrote Chare on the 20th that he had some doubts about Cambridge and Stratford. He hoped they were honest and would do him justice even though they were friends of Chare. He begged him to get rid of the ginger and furs so he could have the money by April. "There is a New York ship arrived in the Downs. . . . I shall endeavor to get the quantity thou advised for of otters, 300, minks, 600, sables, 600," and he again recommended John and Joseph Moore, well-known traders, and the Quaker merchant Thomas Barker.

To John Brummer he wrote that he had had some purpose in going to Bremen that winter, "but it is a long journey," and he added an apologetic "I intended to write Dutch [German] but could not go on." The same day he wrote John Cassawe, another Bremen merchant, and added, "Excuse my writing English, for I cannot express myself in Dutch and I believe thou mayst easily get this and the other letters interpreted."

London, the 20th, 12th mo., 1682/83

AUREND BRUMMER'S WIDOW

. . . Some weeks since I heard the news of thy husband's being dead, which I was very sorry to hear, with whom I had corresponded and accounted many years. I believe his weakness did hinder him from writing to his correspondents sometimes what was necessary, for I had not a letter from him, I think, in 6 months. . . .

They had still not arranged for their passage to the new world, for on the 27th Claypoole wrote to Thomas Cooke in Dublin, "I doubt we shall not get away before the 3rd month."

Still simplifying his business, he sent back the unsold linen to Edmund Travis by the Manchester carrier. "I have let my wife have 3 pieces, which I have rated at 8d per ell, but it is dear." The number of yards, or ells, in a piece varied according to the type of material but was certainly ten or more yards. Mrs. Claypoole was stocking up for a life in the wilderness, and Claypoole was giving Travis more than the expected retail rate.

That business depression continued, for Abel Ram was told on March 10 that "other great goldsmiths failed, and more expected, so that we know not where it will end."

London, the 10th, 1st mo., 1682/83

THOMAS COOKE

. . . I have been in the country this week to dispose of my house and some things there, which is wholly done, and all my family removed to London. . . . This afternoon I saw thy wife, and my wife and I desired her company tomorrow to our house, but she was before engaged. But I hope we shall have an opportunity to manifest our love and respect to her. . . . If he [John Spread, still in Dublin] is going to Pennsylvania, I hope to see him there in summer, for we are preparing to go. . . . Paul Lumbard is broke, and one Duncombe, a great goldsmith, and several others and more expected. . . .

Charles Duncombe and his partner Richard Kent were indeed "great goldsmiths"; their offices were in the famous Grasshopper Inn, in Lombard Street. Paul Lumbard is not listed in the 1677 directory.

Another bit of unfinished business was the sale of the books he had sent Claridge. He worded his inquiry to him another way: "I desire thee to enquire for a box marked J C at the Custom House, where is 10 books of Samuel Fisher's Works, and pray sell them for what thou canst get, or barter them. Francis Rogers sold 5 of them I sent to him."

London, the 13th, 1st mo., 1682/83

BENJAMIN FURLY

My last to thee was the 24th, 11th month, to recommend for correspondents here John Bawden and John Gardner, who is the same that John Osgood's brother [made] thee acquainted with, and it was partly through his means that I let my house to them. They are great dealers to the West Indies, especially Barbados and Virginia. I should have answered thy letter before this time but have had divers hindrances both in city and country, and I was still in expectation that I might give thee account of our agreement with a vessel, which hath been, through the means of others that were wavering in their minds, detained from day to day and week to week, that to this day we had not concluded, and so we have lost time.

The ship is called the *Concord*; the master is William Jeffries, about 500 ton or more, 26 guns, 40 men, to be ready to sail from Gravesend the 16th, 3rd month next, upon some considerable penalty which we reckon will be about £10 a day. The master is a very kind, civil man, and hath been 7 or 8 times in that coast so knows it well, and the ship is a brave, stout, strong vessel, convenient for passengers. The ship is the best that sails to the West Indies. He is to carry no more than 180, which may be done with ease. She is 130 feet long between decks and 32 feet broad, and they will build, for every considerable family, a room whereby they shall be private with their beds, etc.

For the victualing we shall choose the butcher, baker, and brewer [to supply the ship] and many other conveniences and accommodations that will take up too much time to relate, and for the guns, which may be in our way, he has promised to stow about ⅓ part of them in the hold. The price is £5 per head for every person above 12 years of age, and 50s for all under, except infants that suck and are under a year old; they pay nothing. Dry goods pays 40s per ton freight, liquors about 24s per ton, and under this price neither owners nor master can afford to carry either people or goods unless it were for Virginia, Barbados, or some other places where they may be sure of lading [a cargo for the return voyage].

So if any of thy friends will go in this ship, I desire thee to give them timely notice, that they may be here by the 7th or 8th of the 3rd month. But if they do intend to go, they must give timely order, else they may be disappointed, for as soon as the number is made up, there can be no more admitted, for 180 is the utmost and they can take in no more than 160 unless we see it convenient.

As for goods proper to carry thither, I know not what to advise, for we want letters from particular persons. But butter and cheese may do well, and apparel of all sorts to serve 2 or 3 years, iron work for building of houses, and tools for workmen of all sorts, and some pieces of 8, and English money, or [Rix] dollars, cordage, nets for fish, and guns for fowl and wild beast. As for servants, any that are able and industrious may do well, and 4 years' service is usually required for their passage, apparel, etc.

But carpenters, joiners, masons, coopers, smiths, bricklayers are most to be desired and, according to their deserts, may have better terms, as a sum of money when they are out of their time, or a salary yearly, or to serve but 2 or 3 years according as a man can agree with them. As for contracting with families, we have no rule or method in that, nor know I how to advise about it. It would be tedious to write that which we might discourse if we were together.

As for thine and the Frankfords' land to be set out upon a navigable river, that is only in the power of the governor to do and not so far in his power as to prejudice others, or take away their lots. If thou or any others will give me instructions, I shall serve you so far as I am capable. As for your lots in Philadelphia, you being the first purchasers, there is no question but you will have 100 acres, for every 5,000 allotted there. . . .

George Keith is yet in prison, Van Helmont is now at my house, and George Fox, who is in health. Both their loves is to thee and thy wife. Guli Penn is safe delivered of a daughter, and it's like will be ready to go for Pennsylvania in the 7th or 8th month, which with mine and my wife's dear love to thee and thy wife is all at present.

Here is great persecution in most places in England. At London we are kept out of our meetings and several Friends carried to prison, and their goods [di]strained in divers places. But truth prospers, and the Lord is with us.

Give me order about sending thy quitrent deed.

Furly had bought off part of the quitrent, reducing the payments to 5s a year; the practice was soon to be discontinued. Claypoole gave Furly bad advice about the "Frankfords." They were not strictly First Purchasers, their deeds being signed after Penn sailed and officially closed the First Purchaser books. However, at Pastorius' insistence Penn took from his own land to give them city lots and liberty land.

Keith was the man who less than ten years later in Philadelphia split the Quaker ranks wide open, taking away more than a thousand people for his own interpretation of the Bible. At this moment, he had succeeded Christopher Taylor as head of the school at Edmonton.

Francis van Helmont, nobleman, scholar, and Quaker convert, lived much of the time in England, usually at the home of Viscountess Conway. A mystic, he believed in the transmigration of souls; possibly his influence caused Keith to defect from the strict Quaker interpretation of the Bible.

Almost nothing is known of the child of Penn mentioned in this letter, who must have died shortly after the March visit of the Claypooles, Fox, and Philip Ford's wife. Guli Penn wrote Margaret Fox that the baby lived three weeks and that she was ill for some time after.

London, the 13th, 1st mo., 1682/83

JOHN GRATTON, *Prisoner at Derby*, Dear Friend

To whom is my love and fellowship in the truth. There was a Friend who dwells near Derby that was at my house when thou went last from London, that thou recommended to me for advice about his going to Pennsylvania, and we liked each other so well that we soon agreed, and I promised to write him word when I had bargained with a vessel to carry us, which was not till this day. And now we are agreed on all points, and the day prefixed to be ready to sail from Gravesend the 15th or 16th 3rd month next, so that all the passengers must be there on board, or they may be left behind, after they have paid half their passage, viz., 50s per head at least a month before the day. Which I desire thee to acquaint the Friend, Hugh Masland, that he and his wife may be here by the 14th or 15th of the 3rd month, for I have positively engaged for their passage with the rest of my family, so I hope they are not wavering, but fixed to what we agreed.

I intend to write to him in a week or two but cannot at present for want of time. This I write to thee, that if there be any other Friends or others have a mind to go about that time from hence, thou mayst inform them of this conveniency. It is accounted the best vessel that sails to the West Indies; the master is a civil, fair conditioned man that has gone 7 or 8 times to Virginia. He is to carry us to Philadelphia at £5 per passenger and 40s per ton goods, and next week begins to take in goods. I should write more fully but am straitened for time, so must take another opportunity and conclude at present.

John Gratton was a "traveling minister." His home was in Derbyshire, and in 1680 he was imprisoned in the town of Derby. Some histories say that he was not released until 1685 or 1686, but Claypoole's letter shows that he was in London in 1681 or 1682, though in jail again afterward. Hugh Masland, sometimes spelled Marsland, and his wife came over as indentured servants to the Claypooles.

The same day, Claypoole wrote the Bristol merchant James Freeman explaining the virtues of the Concord *and its captain. It should have occurred to him that Bristol Friends went from their own port. However, his idea was to spread the word that an extra safe and comfortable ship was about to leave. "A better conveniency we could hardly have in all respects if we should stay 7 year for it," he put in the Freeman letter.*

London, the 13th, 1st mo., 1682/83

WILLIAM CHARE

. . . I sent per Wakeling [the *Merchant's Delight*] a barrel of pippins directed to thee. There is 1,000 very good ones, ½ which pray accept of, and if Francis Stratford and Nathaniel Cambridge will accept of the other, I desire thee send them from me. I hope they have ended our difference before this time. The damage of the checks cannot be above £4, for I have received the rest, but I expect it will not be above 20s and that it will be ended in 2 or three days. . . . [Claypoole had sold some of the copper plates and found it very strange that Chare had been told these sold for a higher price than Claypoole could get. He concluded the mischief-maker was Charles Turner. He reported again that Holt promised to pay that £5 in a week, and he said that now it was known that he was going to Pennsylvania, many merchants were shy about taking his bills.] I have been viewing several parcels of furs. . . . They ask 12s for the best otters, or 10s runnings, 6s woodchucks, 4s minks, if all good, and 2s martens.

Letters were brief during this period; probably Claypoole was not feeling well. George Fox was staying with him, and they intended going to see Penn's wife in Sussex.

However, he wrote again to Chare that he expected to be gone the middle of May unless "hindered for want of my effects from Hamburg and Bremen." He was promised some furs by Glover and Gawthorn, and the order was for 300 otters, 600 minks, 600 martens, 40 or 50 woodchucks, and 20 or 30 black bears. This order would amount to nearly £400.

To Cassawe he complained about the evils of Von Middock, went back over his troubles selling German linen, and then recommended Edward Haistwell as London correspondent, who would be specializing in the handling of mum.

London, the 17th, 1st mo., 1682/83

FRANCIS AND GEORGE ROGERS

. . . I have accounted with Philip Ford for £18 10s for the quitrent deeds, which I may send when you give [me] order . . . and for the books as many as are sold, and for those that are unsold, to clear the account I am willing to take 12s per piece. . . . [Then follows a long description of the *Concord*.] So if you know of any that would go about that time that have not a conveniency from Ireland, wish them hither. Or if in any business I can serve you there, you may freely make use of me.

But I hear you have sold your land. But now it is risen so that

William Penn sells no more than 3,000 acres for £100. Besides William Penn may take it a little unkindly that you would not hold so small a concern with him in his country. If Edmund Yeoman be arrived at Cork, I question not but you have received your deeds. Sir Thomas Clutterbuck has been dead above this month, so I suppose you will not be molested if you have seized the ship.

I do not doubt but I shall get the £39 due by the executors of William Hinton upon the policy on the *Swallow* frigate in a month. . . . I desire that John's sea bed and things may be sent. . . .

Pray let me have an answer to this in a little time, and what William End says about M[iles] Forster. . . .

Claypoole wrote Cooke, "Thy wife is well this day," so she was still visiting in London, and he wrote Robert Rogers in Ireland about his wonderful ship, the Concord. *But the Irish sailed from Cork, Dublin, or Belfast, many on Liverpool ships, which stopped at Irish ports. Claypoole's friend Robert Turner of Dublin was preparing to sail, but he, his daughter, his seventeen servants, his friend Joseph Fisher, and the latter's family and servants took almost the entire space of the small 90-ton* Lyon of Liverpool, John Crompton, master.

George Fox had preached at the two chief Meetings in London on the 16th and 17th, and on the 19th he was at Guildford in Surrey. James and Helena Claypoole were certainly with him, having left London the day before. On the 20th they arrived at Penn's home, Warminghurst, seven miles back from the coast, in the South Downs. The spring rains had made the roads so bad—and they were never very good—that Fox reported in his Short Journal *they had to go ten miles out of their way because of this, which would make the distance nearly sixty miles. They traveled by coach with Bridget Ford. They stayed at Warminghurst until the 26th, and it was on the 25th that Fox laid his hands upon Claypoole and eased the pain of the stone; in fact, he was cured of this painful trouble, for according to Fox it "came away from him like dirt."*

Claypoole does not mention this in the letter he wrote Penn reporting on the visit.

London, the 1st, 2nd mo., 1683

Dear William Penn

In the pure heavenly love by which we are brought nigh unto the Lord and unto one another, I salute thee, feeling as I have done, often times since thou went hence, the streams thereof flowing to our mutual comfort.

I writ to thee at large the 5th, 11th month [January, by the *Thomas & Anne*, a letter unfortunately not copied into the letter book], by Thomas Singleton, who had a good wind for many days, so that we hope he might arrive with you above a month since.

I had the sight of two letters from thee, one to G[eorge] F[ox] and one to A[lexander] P[arker] and G[eorge] W[hitehead], which were very acceptable to us, after the many wicked lying reports that were spread about concerning thee. And indeed it was very comfortable [comforting] to us to hear and see of the goodness of the Lord to you, and how eminently He did appear to your refreshment, and how His wisdom and authority was with thee and other Friends. So that the spirits of people, both high and low, were bowed, and truth shined over all and the name of the Lord was magnified. To Him be the praises forever who fits His people for His service and honoreth those that honor Him, and He will still keep you and prosper your ways, and increase His love and life and power and wisdom among you, as you keep low [humble] in His counsel, and have an eye to His glory above and beyond all.

I know the Lord never did forsake such nor ever will but attends them with His presence and carries them through all difficulties; but if we look out and have an eye to self and take [away] any part of God's honor, He will suffer us to be abased. Oh, I have found it great hindrance and hurt, when I have had precious gifts and openings, and an utterance has been given for the service of the Lord, looking a little at self, I have been shut up [shut away] and sorrow has come over me, and I have travailed in spirit and cried to the Lord many a time, that that might be removed out of the way that would exalt self and thus hinder the work of the Lord, and truly my fervent desire still is that I may be kept in the simplicity, in tenderness, in fear and true humility, and be nothing but what the Lord will, that I may be as low as the dust of the earth as to His truth and service, and always empty unless the Lord fills me.

I know it is always best with us when we are kept low, for the Lord beautifies the meek with salvation, and He teaches the humble His ways, and the high and lofty One that inhabits eternity and dwells in the highest heavens, He dwells also in the humble and contrite heart. And the beauty of humility shines most and is most amiable in persons that are set in high places, and this is a defense upon our glory which can never be stained while we keep here. So my prayers to the Lord is that thou and I and all God's people may be preserved in this tender, humble, contrite state, that we may go on in the work and service of the Lord to His praise and glory and finish our testimony with joy, keeping always the assurance of an immortal crown of life that is laid up for us and for all the true Israel of God.

Two days since I received thine to me and my wife, dated 29th, 10th month [December], which was a great refreshment to us. And I take it very kindly that in the midst of such great concerns, thou wouldst remember us and write to us two sides [of a sheet of paper] with thy own hand, for I believe thou hast but little time to spare and many people to write to. Truly I value thy love and do hope I shall never lose that place I have in thine, and the hearts of Friends, for it's part of my best treasure, and I prize it beyond all outward things.

The 20th inst., my wife and I, with G[eorge] F[ox] and Bridget Ford, came to thy house at Warminghurst [like Penn, he spelled it Worminghurst, as he heard it pronounced in the hard Sussex dialect], where we were very kindly entertained by thy dear wife, and stayed there till the 26th, then came away. And that morning she and thy 4 children were in good health. [Claypoole had told Furly of the birth of Guli's baby March 13. Letitia, William, and Springett Penn were living at Warminghurst; other children who had died in infancy were buried at Jordans in Buckinghamshire. But this was a long journey from Sussex, and Guli was not well. This unnamed child died shortly after this visit, and its burial place is not known. There is a legend in that part of Sussex that a child of Penn's was buried in the tiny graveyard belonging to the Blue Idol Meeting. Old graves are not marked, and the Quaker records do not mention such a burial.] We had a comfortable time of it with George; I believe I shall never forget it. The benefit of his society is highly to be valued, that innocent, pure, heavenly, seasoning [seasoned] savory life that appears always in him is as a continual Meeting.

Thou and the Friends in those parts are much engaged to him for his fatherly care for your good and the good of the country, and [he] is so glad when he meets with anything of good advice that may be beneficial, either inwardly or outwardly. We left him at

John Rous's at Kingston, where he is, I suppose, at this time. [Margaret, wife of John Rous, was the eldest daughter of Margaret Fell, hence Fox's stepdaughter. According to Fox's *Short Journal*, they stopped along the way at Henry Gill's, near Godalming, Surrey, and on the 28th they had a large meeting at the widow Smith's, 15 miles from Kingston. So the Claypooles would not be back in their London house before the 29th or 30th.]

Our Meetings are kept in the street still [the civil authorities had locked the doors of all Meeting Houses and put men on guard to keep the members out; the Quakers stood outside in the street, holding their silent Meeting], and almost every day the informers and constables are at Friends' houses to strain [distrain, a good seventeenth-century racket, seizing and selling their goods as "punishment"]. But I shall say the less because William Gibson goes in this vessel (F. Richardson, master) and can give thee a more full account.

I have not had one letter from Pennsylvania but thine. I wonder that neither my son John nor Edward Cole, my servant, nor Thomas Holme, John Goodson, R[alph] Withers, Dr. More, would not write me one line. Yet I cannot tell what to think unless some letters be miscarried or gone far about. Thou says thou hast written to P[hilip] Ford about the Society, but he tells me little but that the Charter was not confirmed by the Assembly and that the president [More] wanted assistants to carry on the affairs of the Company, so that we are like to suffer, both in our stock and reputation. When it comes [out] among the people, I am afraid they will say they are all cheated, for the Charter or Patent which thou signed was a great inducement to many to subscribe, and to others to pay in their money that had subscribed. And we did not doubt but, according to our desire and thy promise, the first Assembly would confirm the Charter and choose assistants to manage the business.

As to the president, he has no power but by a committee or court of assistants, and he and the other officers must see that their orders be performed. But if you leave him alone and will not afford him help, he may well be disgusted and let the Company's concerns go to ruin, and that will greatly redound to the dishonor of truth and the reputation of Friends, both as men and Christians (thee as well as others) and be a great hurt to the country. So, dear William, I entreat thee do not slight it, but get all things done in relation to the Company, to answer our engagements and the people's expectations.

If the Charter be uneasy, let it be mended; if it cannot be mended, lay it aside and make another, for a Charter there must be, or the Company cannot subsist. And then as to assistants, if some refuse, others may be chosen, and if not so many as the articles express, yet some there ought to be that may have the power and carry on the business to the people's satisfaction.

I know it not, but I doubt there is some feud which the height of the president possibly might occasion. [Either Claypoole felt that some stockholders might resent the importance of Nicholas More, or else that temperamental character was already showing signs of the arrogance that was later to ruin him.] But thou knowest that it is meekness must overcome haughtiness and love must overcome enmity. He is a man may be won and governed in love, but if he would not be persuaded, but be perverse and stubborn to the prejudice of the Society, he may, by our first constitution and agreement, be laid aside and another chosen in his room. If R[alph] Withers would not act in my stead, he should not have taken it upon him, and then we should have taken another [deputy treasurer]. I think it is very unkindly done, and I know not how he can answer it, but I do not conclude it to be so till I hear farther.

I am still preparing to get away, and many have been my exercises and troubles with unreasonable men, but I have ended most of them. The greatest bar in my way at present is about £700 I have at Bremen and Hamburg, most of it in goods unsold, and my correspondent at Bremen lately dead, and another there has played the knave with me [Von Middock] so but for that I would have been ready at this time. But I cannot well discharge all concerns here to go away with a good repute unless I have at least ½ [of] that home, which I am now in good hopes of, in 2 or 3 weeks, having sent a letter of attorney, etc.

So I have agreed with one William Jeffries, master of the *Concord*, a ship of 500 ton, a brave, strong, good ship every way, and the master an experienced man that has been 7 or 8 times at Virginia. He is to be ready to set sail from Gravesend the 16th next month.

I am glad to hear our son John is employed in surveying, and take very kindly thy counseling of him. I hope he will reform and be a comfort to us at last. I and my wife and 7 children are all in good health and very well satisfied in our intended voyage, still believing that the Lord will bless us and carry us through, to our joy and comfort. With mine and my wife's dear and sincere love to thee, I rest, thy friend and brother in the blessed truth.

My dear love to C[hristopher] Taylor and his wife, J[ames] Harrison, R[alph] Withers, etc. Sir T[homas] Clutterbuck is dead.

I have had several letters lately from dear Robert Lodge. In one dated the 5th, 12th month [February], he writes that his wife was deceased, and that the priest was so envious that he had indicted him and some other Friends at the sessions for the burial. And the 21st, 1st month [March], he writes that he would gladly come to see us before we go away but has not freedom to stir much from home, being in daily expectation to be taken to prison. He desires me in that letter to mind his dear love to thee. J. C.

Penn signed the Free Society of Traders charter March 24, 1682. The first Assembly, which met in December, debated as to its power briefly, but if any conclusion was reached, it was not recorded in the minutes.

William Gibson, preacher, haberdasher of London, purchaser of 500 acres from Penn, was the Cromwell soldier who went to a Quaker Meeting to scoff and remained to pray. It was perhaps his son William who was on the ship; the elder Gibson died in 1684 in London. Robert Lodge of Yorkshire, preacher, butcher by trade, and friend of Fox, was a frequent martyr for his faith.

The ship taking this letter, the Endeavour *of London, Francis Richardson, master, was loading only for New York and East Jersey, according to the London Port Books. However, it did stop briefly at Plymouth, where the Quaker preacher Roger Longworth boarded it, and probably went on to Philadelphia.*

London, the 3rd, 2nd mo., 1683

WILLIAM CHARE

. . . Pray get the arbitrators to end our difference as soon as possible. . . . Money is exceeding scarce now at London. I have not known the like these many years. . . . I desire thee again let the furs and ginger be sold at price current that I may raise some money from them to answer some concerns here before I go, or else I must put off my intended voyage for some time longer, which may be greatly to my prejudice, and must lease my house here before the next month is out, for I am very much wanted in Pennsylvania, as William Penn writes me. . . .

Claypoole wrote Cooke that his pipes of wine were not yet sold, as Cooke's wife did not want to take less than £30 per pipe, which he knew he would never get. He wrote Spread, at the time in Teneriffe, that he was soon leaving for Pennsylvania, where he hoped they would become better acquainted.

He wrote the Rogers brothers that he was about to arrest William Hinton's executors for the £39 still owing, and he was unable to resist a little dig at them for having sold their Pennsylvania holdings. He had a letter from Penn "wherein he writes much of the praise of the country, what precious Meetings, that land was risen double the price."

An interesting thing about the letters at this time is the arrival of a new clerk, who ruled lines in pencil and wrote along them, forming his letters almost like printing.

Preparations for the new life were taking most of Claypoole's time, and he was trying to simplify his affairs. It did not help when Cassawe sent him more than 40 barrels of mum, which had not been ordered, but which were good-naturedly accepted.

London, the 7th, 2nd mo., 1683

SAMUEL CLARIDGE

. . . I desire thee to remember the books of Samuel Fisher's that was lodged in the Custom House, for I would not lose them. For thy trouble thou mayst charge what thou pleasest to account. I hope they may yield me 15s per book, as Francis Rogers sold [them]. But sell them for what thou canst get for above 10s per piece. . . .

London, the 7th, 2nd mo., 1683

THOMAS DENNISON

. . . I did not refuse acceptance to thy bill payable to Mary Watkinson, for I was not at home, and my servant only told the person he had no order to accept it and desired him to call again when I was at home. He said he would protest it [the bill of exchange] and without any provocation called him quaking dog. And this day [the same person] came to my house to know when I would pay the bill. I told him when it was due. So he said my man had affronted him, which I had not heard of before. Whereupon I called my man, and before he would hear him speak he called him sirrah [a terrible insult] and held up his cane, pretending to break his head.

So I told him he was uncivil and abusive . . . and that I would not let him come within my doors again. So he went to the door and called me to come to fight with him, having a sword by his side. So he said he would return the bill and went away in a great huff. . . .

Meantime, he had news of the arrival shortly of the great German leader Francis Daniel Pastorius, founder of Germantown and forerunner of the emigrants from Frankfort and Crefeld, who was anxious to reach Philadelphia and settle with Penn the bounds of their property. Claypoole expected him to go on the Concord *and welcomed him to London.*

London, the 14th, 2nd mo., 1683

DEAR FRIEND WILLIAM AND ELIZABETH HARD

Since we saw you last, our proceedings have been a little obstructed by reason of another ship taken on for Pennsylvania that has gotten away some of our passengers, so that we are forced to put off the day for our sailing from Gravesend to 31st, 3rd month, upon which we are fixed, and I do not see anything likely to hinder us but that we shall then be ready to sail, so you may order your business accordingly and come to London about 29th or 30th next month.

If you will lay out 20, 30, or 40s [surely £ is meant] for me in anythings that you think good, that may be reasonably bought and useful or salable, I shall take it kindly and pay the money to whom thou wilt, now or when you come hither. If there be any Friends or others, thereaway, that do intend for Pennsylvania or New Jersey, they may be informed of this conveniency that if they should wait years for one, they cannot have a better.

And William, I desire thee, if thou canst hear of a carpenter, bricklayer, or joiner that will go over as a servant, let me know of it. Such may have as good terms from me as from any. With mine and my wife's dear love to you both and also to your father [-in-law] William Bayles, I rest.

The Hards had a 70-foot-wide lot on Third Street. William evidently died shortly after their arrival, for in 1684 the lot was recorded as the widow Hard's. A William Hard, probably a son, became a Keithian and died in 1697, but Elizabeth lived to the age of 90; her death is recorded in 1744.

London, the 14th, 2nd mo., 1683

HUGH MASLAND

I received thine dated the 26th past which signifies that you were preparing to be ready to come hither by the middle next month, which was answerable to what I writ thee; that the 15th or 16th was the day agreed upon. But now, since for some reasons which could not be avoided, we have put it off till the 31st, and then to be ready to sail from Gravesend, so if you are here the 29th or 30th, 3rd month, it may be well. . . . As for your confidence in us I know your expectations will be answered in our kindness and honesty towards you. . . .

Cheese cloths may be very proper to carry, or anything either of household goods, tools, or apparel, except wooden ware, that are cumbersome. . . . If thou couldst meet with a carpenter or joiner that would go, I should be glad of one. Direct thy letter only to me, Merchant in London.

London, the 14th, 2nd mo., 1683

THOMAS COOKE

. . . [I] have this day paid thy wife £30, which was all she desired at present, and I told her she might have £150 more when she pleased, which I suppose she will have occasion for in a few days. [The following letter to End and Savery was enclosed, with a request for its delivery, saving Claypoole a few pennies postage.]

London, the 14th, 2nd mo., 1683

WILLIAM END AND DANIEL SAVERY

. . . I have done what I could with Miles Forster to procure a sum of money for you, and held him in suspense till this day, and if [he] be not out [of prison] the 16th, another action is liked to be laid upon him, will keep him in long. So seeing I could not persuade his friends to anymore, I have taken a note from his mother for £15 which he promises to pay in a week or two, and I ordered the attorney to take a judgment of him for £235 or £240 and so let him go.

I have had a great deal of trouble about this business, but if William

[209]

End will be so kind to me now, to get me in the debt of £18 of G[eorge] Gamble, I shall account it requital enough. . . .

Against Claypoole's petty faults must be set a generous action like this. His only reason for this trouble and expense was that he liked the young man and thought his imprisonment unjust. In 1688 End and Savery appointed an attorney in America to collect for them; the amount by then was £500. Forster paid and got his release in 1693, by which time he had become a rich New York merchant.

William Chare also seemed about to take on another London representative and asked about a Philip French; Claypoole's only recommendation (April 17) was that he "lives the next house but one to mine." The 1677 directory places his house at the corner of Bush Lane and Scots Yard.

Throughout this month and part of the next there were many letters, usually brief, showing how hurried and harried Claypoole was. The widow Brummer had to be soothed: she was cross because the ropes and wrappings of goods previously sent had not been returned, and Claypoole allowed her ten shillings on the account, explaining that these wrappings were generally rotten when the goods arrived.

He was £400 "out of cash" for Chare and £370 for Ram. To Ram he wrote that he had gone to the Temple [outside the walls of the City] to collect Ram's bill but was put off with the usual vague promises.

He discovered some logwood which had been lying around for years to the Rogerses' account and wrote William in Bristol on April 26 that he was sending it to him, having heard it would fetch a good price there. "Thou mayst now be the better able to compass because it is a time of leisure both as to the fruit and cider trade."

He wrote Masland on May 1 that they now expected to go the end of the month, what "they call Whitsun Week." He wrote Ram again, reminding him that the blank paper enclosing his letter cost an extra sixpence.

London, the 5th, 3rd mo., 1683

THOMAS COOKE

. . . I paid thy wife when she was here £150, to her content, I think, but I could not show her respect as I would have done, by reason of many troubles that encountered me at that time. One thing was being tried at the Sessions for a riot, for being at a Meeting, and [I] had like to have been sent to Newgate, which hindered me many days in my business, and I was hurried from one magistrate to another by a warrant and constable. . . . I cannot get a chapman for the Canary though I would be glad now to take £27 per pipe for it. . . .

This was the incident described by Joseph Besse in his monumental work on the sufferings of the Quakers. Besse, however, said that Claypoole went to jail.

He wrote to Ram again on May 12: "I must be packing up my goods to go, but it will now be the middle next month before the ship will be ready."

London, the 12th of May, 1683

FRANCIS AND GEORGE ROGERS

I am now to answer yours of the 31st, 1st month, and 24th, 2nd month. You have been often jealous of me without any cause, and so you are still, that you should think that if you had accepted my bill, Philip Ford or myself would impose upon you to pay £18 for quit-rent without order. We soon found the mistake, so P. Ford allowed it me again. But if he had not, I should rather have taken it for myself, than have put it upon you when there is no occasion for it. . . . [Claypoole then wrote that the insurers were trying to compound the £39 for £20.] He [one of the insurers] is the harder to deal with because he is one of the king's servants and cannot be arrested without leave. I believe I might get £30 of him but am not willing to abate so much without your consent. . . .

London, the 15th, 3rd mo., 1683

DEAR FRIEND BENJAMIN FURLY

. . . [Claypoole had letters from Furly, with some enclosed for Francis Daniel Pastorius] which I have delivered, and two bills of exchange, for £100 each for account of the said Pastorius. . . . I shall assist him in buying such goods as may be most proper to carry with us [him], which we shall have now time to do, for the day we have fixed on to be at Gravesend is the 20th of the next month, and then any passengers that will go may be entertained on board at the ship's cost. But till the 30th no demurrage to be paid. So it will be yet about 6 weeks before we leave England, which thou mayst advise the Frankfords [the Germans who were to go on the *Concord*] that

[211]

they may be ready against the time, and I shall, if thou wilt give me orders, engage for them, that so others may not take up the room, for we intend he shall carry but 120 or 130, though we yielded to more formerly. If I do engage, it is requisite I should have half the passage, which is 50s per man, remitted me, and that being paid, the master is obliged under a penalty not to sail without them till the day limited, which is to be the 30th, 4th month [June], and then those that are not ready may be left behind and must lose their ½ freight, which is reasonable, for the master must lay in a store answerable to his numbers and must at the day be ready. And then to stay for a few, with 40 seamen on board and it may be 100 passengers, would be a great prejudice to the owners, so is provided against in our charter party [agreement with the ship's owners].

Pastorius and his friend talk of going in another ship, which will be, or pretends to be, gone next week. But then we cannot have time to provide goods. I shall leave them to their freedom, but ours is a far braver vessel and I believe above twice as big.

There are divers acts of Parliament in the Book of Rates, that shows what goods are prohibited. And then as to the ship's sailing from one place to another, the Act of Navigation shows everything plainly, which I suppose thou hast. But as to edge tools, which is wrought iron, all wrought iron is prohibited [unless it paid customs duties]. The ships that touch [here] have to pay ½ custom upon the plantation voyages, must land all their goods to have them searched, and if they [the customs men] find a false entry, probably may open every pack and fatt and take the contents. This they are liable to, but I believe they [the exporters] find generally more favor by feeing the officers.

No English ship can [sail] to any of the English plantations but [only] from our king's dominions. Neither can they sail from the plantations but to the king's dominions; otherwise foreigners would get the trade and make them [it] of no value to England. Those of New England have traded to Spain, it's like, and to other places, for which they are called to account and in danger of losing their patent. As for ships from hence to Pennsylvania, there is but 2 at present; one pretends to be gone the next week, and then our ship the next month, and not another till about the end of the 6th or beginning of the 7th month.

Pastorius has had but £20 of the £100 received and that was to buy him clothes and necessaries. I intend to write to thee once a week how we proceed, that the friends may not want advice, that intend to go. With my love in the truth is all at present.

The ship "pretending" to be gone next week was the America, with Joseph Wasey, previously master of the Grayhound. It did not, however, get away from Gravesend until about June 4, and it arrived at Philadelphia August 20.

To Chare on the 16th Claypoole wrote that his servant, Haistwell, had got a partner, that Claypoole had "nothing to do with his trade," and that they had decided to accept the mum that was not ordered. Wistfully he added that he wished he had that wheat of his back in England; it would yield above 70 rix-dollars a last.

London, the 18th, May, 1683

BENJAMIN FURLY, Dear Friend

. . . If the Frankfords do intend to go in our ship, they must be at Gravesend by that time [the 30th]. They need not come to London but stay there and save charges. There they must enquire for the *Concord*, William Jeffries, master, for Pennsylvania. And if I be not there, they must write to me per first [post] directed to Scotch Yard by London Stone.

There is not that advantage by pieces of 8 as thou thinks, for [only] the light pieces are esteemed here and will yield 4⅓s to 4s 5d per piece and much more by the ounce than the heavy pieces will yield. If Peter Boss comes to me for 20 pieces of 8, I shall provide him. All foreign coins, both gold and silver, may be imported and exported free.

I have been assisting Pastorius in getting his goods ashore and buying commodities of several sorts and shall be further helpful to him, but he takes Colans [Collins?] chiefly for his adviser. He intends to go in Joseph Wasey who possibly may be yet 8 days before he sails from Gravesend. There is several people come this day to town, and G[eorge] Wertmueller, who is to serve Pastorius. If I must engage for the Frankfords that they may be sure of passage in our ship, I must have positive order from thee for how many, and 50s per man to pay to the master that he may buy provisions. For he will lay in store for no more than those that are sure to him. . . .

[213]

Still trying to end his affairs, he wrote Chare that he had no account from those arbitrators, and he asked him to speak to Christian Pitch, who owed him £1 11s 8d. An interesting sidelight on land prices in Pennsylvania is given in the next letter, after considerable talk about bills of exchange.

London, May the 19th, 1683

ABEL RAM

... If thou or any friend of thine will be concerned in our country of Pennsylvania to buy 1,000, 2,000, or 5,000 acres of land, let me know it. I can pleasure them beyond another by means of one that would sell 4,000 acres for £100 sterling, or 1,000 for £25, whereas it is risen to 3,000 acres for £100. And if I can do thee any service while I stay here, or when there, thou mayst freely command me who am.

Undoubtedly Claypoole was trying to unload—at a profit—the second 5,000 acres, which he had felt obliged to buy and which at the moment he could not afford. The Minutes of the Board of Property for Philadelphia show that he did manage to dispose of 2,000 before he sailed.

On the 25th he wrote again to William Chare, enclosing a letter from Bawden and Gardner in a different and more modern style. It was copied into the book by his clerk.

London, 25 May, 1683

MR. WILLIAM CHARE

Sir:

We have bought of Mr. James Claypoole his half of the furs in your hands, whereof you sent us a memorandum, viz., 3,188 raccoons, 942 foxes, 468 cats, 86 wolves, and 11 sables, which accordingly be pleased to transfer to our account. Also we have agreed that the £200 drawn by said Mr. Claypoole upon you 20th April last at 34s 11d to Michael Heush be also transferred or placed upon our account, and further we refer you to what we shall write you more largely this night, and so rest.

Your affectionate friends and servants,
John Bawden and John Gardner

Claypoole's business must by now almost have ceased. He wrote William Hard and Hugh Masland not to come until the end of June.

London, the 5th, June, 1683

Dear Friend Benjamin Furly

... I understand the people from Crefeld have agreed to go in our ship, and so [they] have 287 R[ix] D[ollars] to remit thee for ½ their freight, which with 78 R.D. in thy hands for 6 persons makes 365 R.D. for ½ passage of 33 persons at 50s per person, which is much about the same sum. And I being upon enquiry fully satisfied that Thomas Lurting will not venture to go for them, nor can any ship be procured that is fit for that voyage to fetch them, I have therefore, according to thy order, secured passage for them (to wit, the 33 persons named in thy letter) in the *Concord*, William Jeffries, master, for Pennsylvania ... and have signed and sealed charter party whereby I am engaged to pay for the said persons 50s per person, for everyone that is wanting upon the 6th July, which is the day limited for sailing from Gravesend, if wind and weather permits, upon the penalty of £500.

And if I stay the ship upon my concerns, I must pay the ship £5 per day for every day after the 6th, 5th month [July]. But he [Jeffries] is obliged to be at Gravesend and to receive all passengers on board and entertain them at the ship's charge upon the 30th inst., and then to sail by the 1st opportunity if we are all ready. Otherways to stay till the 6th next month and no longer.

And for all other accommodations, for cabins, provisions, and landing us at Philadelphia and waiting there 10 days at the least upon us [to give them a chance to find sleeping quarters and to land their goods], it is all inserted with all large extent as can be desired, and the people may be sure of kind and honest dealing, both from me and the master, [he] being, as I advised formerly, a very fair-conditioned man. And for room and air [the ship is] far beyond what may be had in a little ship, for he is limited to carry but 140 at most and has room enough for 150.

But he is not to stay beyond the day for one person, but to sail if with 60. So now I having engaged [passage] by thy order, I desire thee not to fail, but send me the money, and let the friends get here in good time to take up their goods and ship them again, and buy such necessaries as they want, which will take up 6 or 8 days' time. So before the last day of this month they ought to be here.

I have been helpful to Pastorius according to thine and his desire

[215]

and have paid him the £200, and he is gone we suppose this day from Gravesend....

Thomas Lurting was the shipmaster famous for escaping from the Turks without firing a shot. He sailed that year to Maryland. It was lucky for Claypoole that he could not take the German families, for he, Claypoole, was having trouble getting a full shipload for the Concord.

London, June 5, 1683

JOHN CASSAWE

... Thou must do me the kindness to sell the wheat and pay thyself out of it and send me an account as soon as possible, for I shall not stay here above 4 or 5 weeks, and then I shall not come again in less than 2 year, and then I hope I shall visit my friends in Hamburg. ... [Referring to his unsold wheat] at present it is worth 80 R[ix] D[ollars] per last, and it may happen that if wet weather continues 14 days to be worth 200 R. D....

London, June 9th, 1683

THOMAS COOKE

... [I] have at last sold it [the wine] for £48, the two pipes, and the ullage for something less, to John Grassingham at 4 months.... John Bawden and John Gardner, to whom I have paid today for thy account £157 16s, which I now received for 604 ozs. pieces of 8, at 5s 2¾d per oz., deducting 2¼s for brass, which came from Edward Shippen of Boston.... We have pitched upon 6th July to sail from Gravesend....

London, the 12th, June, 1683

WILLIAM END

... I have berated with Miles Forster, seeing I could bring him to no better terms than to pay £15 and to give bond for the rest at several payments, and I promise to withdraw the action. But he has not been with me in many weeks, nor know I where to find him. He has paid £4 19s 6d and promises the rest but cannot get money.

If I cannot get it before I go, which I hope will be by the middle next month, I will then leave it with John Bawden and John Gardner. . . .

London, June 15th, 1683

BENJAMIN FURLY

. . . I have according to thy order, of which I advised in my last, agreed positively with Captain Jeffries, master of the *Concord*, for the passage of the 33 Dutchmen, and I must pay him now quickly 50s for each person. And if they come not against the time agreed upon, which is the 6th next month, to be ready to sail from Gravesend, they may be left behind and the master will not pay back any of the money. But it's probable we may stay till the 10th, but I would have them be here by the 30th inst., that there may be time to take up and ship their goods and buy some necessaries that they will want. I was something inclined to draw the money on thee this day for their ½ freight, but being well assured thou wouldst not make me engage and then leave me, I rest satisfied, expecting to hear from thee in a few days.

I sent thee 2 letters from D. Pastorius. They were favored with a good wind and stayed but little in the Downs. We have no news, and being in haste I conclude.

London, June 19th, 1683

DEAR FRIEND BENJAMIN FURLY

[I] have thine dated the 18th and 20th, 6th month, with one enclosed for Pastorius which I shall carry with me, and according to thy order shall receive the deeds of Peter Langly and get them registered in Pennsylvania, and shall, according to this lease and release from Jacob Taylor [Telner, Penn's agent and a leader among the Dutch Quakers] to take up the said land of Pastorius on thy account, and for what further I shall do for thee I shall expect advice. I am glad to hear the Crefeld Friends are coming. If they be here at London by the last day of this month, it may be in good time, for I believe we shall not sail from Gravesend till near the middle next month.

I desire that the money for ½ their passage may be remitted forth-

with, that I may be so far secured in my engagement, which would
be an ease to my mind, for till that is done I count not myself absolutely safe, for he[re] is many lying reports and striving by masters
[of] ships to get passengers, that possibly their minds may some of
them change when they come here, and then I must come upon thee
for damage which would be a great trouble to me, for I know what
thou doest is to serve them and the country. . . . Here are various reports of scarcity in Pennsylvania and William Penn is coming home.
But is all invented. I assure thee, we have no bad news nor any discouragement, but all well so far as we hear. . . .

London, June 19th, 1683

WILLIAM END

. . . The other day I met with Miles Forster, who promised me the
rest of the money, but as yet I only received £4 19s 6d. . . . He
promises to get 4 bonds for £240, viz., £60 payable in 2 year, and
£60 in one year more, and £60 another year, and £60 the 5th year. I
could not persuade him to better terms, but I intend he shall pay the
attorney before I go away, which may be about 3 weeks hence. I
intend to send thee a perfect account.

We have hitherto no news but good from Pennsylvania. . . . Great
persecution is here both in city and country.

*A somewhat pathetic note was in a letter to Samuel Claridge: "[I] have
nothing to demand of thee but the proceed of 10 Samuel Fisher's books
sent thee to sell for my account."*

London, July the 3rd, 1683

BENJAMIN FURLY

I hope thou are come safe home before this time, which I should
be glad to hear before I go away, which now is like to be longer than
we expected, by reason of the Crefeld Friends not coming. We are
fain to loiter and keep the ship at Blackwall [down river from the
city but not as far as Gravesend] upon one pretense or another, for
when she comes to Gravesend the owners will not suffer her to stay
many days. And indeed it would trouble me very much to go away
without them, besides the great loss it will be to them, for the master

will abate nothing of the ½ freight. But I hope they will be here in a few days.

I believe we shall not be ready to sail from Gravesend till the end of the next week. . . .

The letter ended with a note that either a Dutch firm or Jacob Telner had £20 to send to Cornelius Bom, who became Philadelphia's first baker and who had sailed in the America *with Pastorius and his Swiss friend Wertmueller. Claypoole was to buy pieces of 8 to carry to Bom, otherwise Haistwell would exchange the money and send it next month by Captain Arnold in the* Jeffrey.

On July 10 Claypoole sent the last letters to go from England. One was an apology to Ralph Weeks, whose bill he had refused, asking him to draw it on him in Pennsylvania. He understood ships went frequently between there and Barbados.

London, July 10th, 1683

DEAR BROTHER EDWARD CLAYPOOLE

It grieves me to think what I must write to thee, but I cannot help it, for so it is that I have been, and am still, so disappointed of money and cheated by many that are indebted to me that I am not able to buy those things thou writ for, which indeed I am ashamed of. But necessity must plead my cause, and I hope thou wilt bear with me till I come to Pennsylvania, and then, through the Lord's assistance, I doubt not but I shall make thee full satisfaction.

My trouble is so great that it has almost overwhelmed me, and I am so ill that I am scarce able to write. I have left a letter of attorney with Bawden and Gardner to receive my effects from Bremen and Hamburg. In Germany at Bremen I have £100 [worth of] quarters of wheat and £55 owing me by 2 Dutchmen, and at Hamburg some debts for goods sold [for] which, as it comes in in time, they shall send thee goods. But I cannot depend upon it but do reckon to make thee satisfaction from Pennsylvania.

I could be glad [if] thou wouldst take 2 or 3,000 acres of land at price current. I am forced to leave some debts here unpaid, which I am ashamed of but cannot help it, and if some people were not kind and favorable I could not go away. My brother [John] Claypoole is very unkind. He owes me above £300 and will not pay me 1d, and brother Wingfield, to whom I owed but £50, vowed he would arrest me at Exchange awhile since, though I suffered more by him than that comes to. So I was forced to pay to keep myself from a prison and disgrace.

I am going away this week in the *Concord*, William Jeffries, master, and have left insurance here for £200. We have been lately exercised with many troubles; 2 of our children have been sick of the smallpox, nigh unto death, but through mercy they are recovered. I have sent thee three pair of agate-hafted knives, 1 pair for thyself, 1 pair for my sister [his sister-in-law], and 1 pair for your eldest daughter. I would not have my sister nor any others know that I go away thus in thy debt. Which with mine and my wife's true love to thee and wife and children is all.

I do again recommend to thee for correspondents John Bawden and John Gardner, who I believe would be to [thee] as great advantage and safety as any in England.

Sent from Gravesend by [James]Manbey [the *Arabella.*]

London, July 10th, 1683

FRANCIS AND GEORGE ROGERS

I have at last with much trouble got 30 guineas for the subscription of William Hinton['s estate?] on the policy for Richard Gay, of which I paid 1 guinea to the man that procured it, and that was all I could get without a suit of law. . . . I am threatened by [Robert] Hubbold, that attached me for £1,000 for R. Gay, and I know not but they may arrest me before I go, which would be a great disappointment to me. . . . I have left 10 books of Samuel Fisher's works to be sent to you to sell, and the rest I shall pay you in Pennsylvania, or you may draw it upon me if you have an opportunity.

We have had great trouble in moving and making up accounts with all people and have been cheated by divers of some hundreds, and considerable effects lies out still at Bremen and Hamburg, that I count it great mercy that I am able to get away at all, and now at last if I am preserved from these attackers on R. Gay's account, I shall account it a great deliverance. So pray do not take it ill nor disparage me about it, that I leave part of your £31 to pay. I may be capable to serve you in Pennsylvania, which, if you have occasion, I shall do very heartily. And if you will buy any land, let me transact it for you. I know I can do it with William Penn to as good advantage as anyone. . . .

We hear a good report of our son John from Pennsylvania, where he is employed in surveying.

On July 10 also he wrote to William End, saying he was £4 out of cash for him but adding that he expected to get £10 more from Miles Forster. With that and some other small bills, he looked for £18 or more credit with them, which they were to credit the Rogers brothers. But young Miles Forster, like Clutterbuck, was quick to promise and slow to deliver. According to the final settling of the debt, in 1693, Claypoole had only another £5 from him.

He wound up his affairs with Cassawe in Bremen asking him to remit to Bawden and Gardner the money from the wheat when it was sold, Von Middock's £50, and some money due from Brummer. He would, he added, be glad to hear from him when he was settled in Pennsylvania.

To William Chare he wrote the same day, putting him in charge of collecting other money owed him at Hamburg and telling him to forward it to Bawden and Gardner. "Christian Pitch doth very unkindly by me to say he had given Theodore Jacobson order to pay me the £1 11s 8d due to me, and has not done it, so I desire thee receive the money and remit it with the rest due to me."

London, July 10th, 1683

DEAR FRIEND BENJAMIN FURLY

. . . It troubles me much that the Friends from Crefeld are not yet come, and the wind being still contrary I doubt [am sure] we shall go away without them. The ship went to Gravesend the 7th and intends for the Downs the 17th, and then to be gone with the first fair wind. We have loitered several days on their account and shall do still, which may be £50 damage to the ship, but we cannot blame them. But if it were the will of the Lord, I should be heartily glad they might come before we go, for it troubles me to think what a great disappointment it will be to the poor Friends, besides the loss of their money, which I have paid to the master long since. [The Crefelders left Rotterdam July 24.]

This stay of the ship is by consent on both sides, but if I detain him beyond the time agreed upon, I must pay £5 per diem demurrage. I send my son again this day to Gravesend to see for them. We go all this week. I have acquainted [Arent] Sonmans with what thou writes.

There is another great ship, near 500 ton, bound for Pennsylvania, which Friends have agreed for, and is to be ready the next month. Her name is the *Jeffrey*, Thomas Arnold, master.

If the wind should be westerly when we come into the Downs, we must stay, and if it be possible, I will get him stay 2 days for them with a fair wind, but I cannot promise it. I may write again from Gravesend.

We have many convenient cabins made and private rooms for families, and 14 excellent oxen killed and 30 ton beer and abundance of bread and water, so that we are victualed for 120 people, and may want ½ them for what I see yet, which is a great disappointment to the master and owners.

However, the thirteen Crefelder families arrived in time: Abraham, Derick, and Herman op den Graeff, Thones Kunders, Reynier or Reinert Teissen, Willem Streypers, Jan Lensen, Peter Keurlis, Jan Siemes, Johannes Blijkers, Abraham Tunes, Jan Luykens, and Lenart Arents. In his account of those on the Concord, *Claypoole wrote, after the name Arents, "Leonard Teissen his brother," noting that he was a freeman. But Claypoole used the old form of the possessive case for Leonard [or Reinert?]. Teissen's brother evidently came as a servant and therefore would not be named, but he had since acquired his freedom.*

Sonmans (Sonnemans), wealthy Holland merchant, shortly went to Scotland and while riding with Robert Barclay was shot by a highwayman. Elizabeth Bennett is mentioned in the "Partial List" of people who came to Philadelphia as being on the Concord, *and Claypoole brought over the Maslands as servants, Sisilla Wooley, and his carpenter's son, Edward Cole, Jr., as well as a fifth servant, not named. William and Elizabeth Hard came then, but the elder Bennetts sailed on the* Jeffrey.

There were to be more delays and anxieties, but at last they got off, and one hopes that Claypoole was rested and relaxed by the comfortable voyage. The letter book still had many blank pages and so was taken along; impressions of the new city went into it, as usual combined with business details.

Philadelphia, 2nd, 10th mo., 1683

DEAR BROTHER EDWARD CLAYPOOLE

My last to thee was the 10th, 5th month, which I sent from Gravesend by Captain Manbey [the *Arabella*], with 6 agate knives, which

I hope are come safe to hand. If I can, I will upon this sheet send thee copy of the said letter.

As to our voyage from England to this place, we went on board the *Concord* at Gravesend the 24th, 5th month, and after we lost sight of England, which was in about 3 weeks' time, we were 49 days before we saw land in America, and the 1st, 8th month [October], some of us went ashore in Pennsylvania. The blessing of the Lord did attend us so that we had a very comfortable passage and had our health all the way.

We came to this city the 8th or 10th, 8th month, where I found my servant had builded me a house like a barn, without a chimney, 40 foot long and 20 broad with a good dry cellar under it, which proved an extraordinary conveniency for securing our goods and lodging my family, although it stood me in very dear. For he had run me up for diet and work near £60 sterling, which I am paying as money comes in for goods. To this I built a kitchen of 20 foot square where I am to have a double chimney, which I hope will be up in 8 or 12 days.

I writ to thee to send me 4 blacks, viz., a man, a woman, a boy, a girl, but being I was so disappointed in England as not to send thee those goods thou wrote for, I could not expect thou wouldst send them. If they had been sent, I should have taken it very kindly and have balanced account with thee in some reasonable time. Now my desire is that if thou dost not send them all, however, to send me a boy between 12 and 20 years, and, if thou wilt, send some rum and molasses which are now in great demand, 5s per gallon and 2s per gallon. I will dispose of it for thee and send the produce either in bills for England or silver or oil, or some other way which yet we know not. Thou must send also a ton of sugar, 2 hhds. thirds and 2 hhds. fourths, and ½ ton of ginger, 5 cwt. scraped, and 5 cwt. scalded, and I shall, if thou wilt, be ½ concerned.

My lot in this place proves to be especially [good] for trade, one of the [best] in the city, and though I employ my time in serving the Society, being treasurer, for which I have £100 sterling, yet my wife and children with my direction shall manage the business as well as if I did it myself, and I will be accountable for all. So I desire thee, let us have a little trade together, and as I writ formerly, if thou wilt take for thyself, or for any other, 1,000 or 2,000 acres of land in this country, the sooner the better. For people come in so fast that it is like to be much dearer in a little time. It's judged about 1,000 people came in 6 weeks, so that it is already worth double what it was, 1,000 acres being now at £40 sterling.

Samuel Carpenter is next but one to me and is likely to get a great estate quickly. William Frampton is on the other side of me, building a great brewhouse. If I had time and could write for cold, having no chimney, I would have filled some sheets of paper in giving thee account of the country and our settlement, trade, and laws, etc., but now I must be excused till another time, only this in short, I do believe it will prove a very healthy country, and that great improvements may be made in a few years by industry and skill.

I have sent thee by this vessel, the *Comfort*, George Thorpe, master, 12 [18] beaver hats which I brought from England, 12 black and 6 white. No. [6] is 8 [hats] at 50s per piece, No. 7 is 4 at 55s, and the 6 white beavers are £3 per piece, which are the price they are sold at London for, though they cost me something less buying a great parcel. I desire thee to sell them amongst thy acquaintance as well as thou canst, either for more or less, as also a fatt of French barley containing, net, 450 lbs. at 4d is £7 10s, and the hats comes to £49, which in all [is] £56 10s.

I hope thou hast received £80 of William Lewger for my account, and something of Joseph Grove, to whom remember my love and tell him I could not now write to him, and also to Ralph Weeks, and tell him that I shall again write effectually for my correspondents at London to pay his bill for £42. I was strongly disappointed or I should not have disappointed him, but it was chiefly his fault, for I never received a word of advice of his bill to this day, so I could not accept it.

Ordinary muscovado sugar is sold here at 40s per cwt. our money, which is 6s for a piece of 8, or 15d for an English shilling, the difference being 25%. I have other goods which I would send if I had time to pack them, or that I knew that they were fit for your market. Pray advise per first [post] if horse harness may do well, and I have some silver-hafted knives and agate knives, which I would send upon advice from thee. Or I could load a vessel with pipe staves and timber.

I could not get 1d of brother Claypoole at parting towards the money he owed me, and my brother Norton is not able at present to pay me anything. I have trusted him with above £30 more since I came, so that now he owes me above £200. He is in a thriving way, and the governor has given him a place that may be worth to him £40 or £50 per annum. He does intend to sell his land and houses where he lives and come to dwell at this town, and then he will pay me, he says, what he owes me.

Advise what commodity whale oil may be with you, for we have 24 men fishing in the Bay that are like to make a good voyage. Here is a great deal of silver in our river, that was taken at the wreck, which may be purchased at reasonable rate with goods, as rum, molasses, and sugar. I have a great deal more to write, but time fails, for the boat is going quickly, so must conclude.

Thy assured loving brother.

Let me know of the receipt of this [letter] per first. Here is one enclosed from brother Norton.

Samuel Carpenter had a 200-foot lot on the Delaware Front St., just north of what is now Walnut; Claypoole was on the south corner of Front and Walnut. Frampton's wide lot was on the west side of Second St. between Walnut and Spruce. To Claypoole's long letter was added an invoice and a postscript.

Invoice of a box of hats and a barrel of French barley shipped in the *Comfort*, George Thorpe, master, for Barbados and consigned to my brother Edward Claypoole for my proper account, marked as per margin, and 13 knives

JC	No. 1 A barrel containing 450 lb. net of French barley at 4*d*	£ 7	10*s*	0
	No. 2 A box cont. 18 beaver hats			
	No. 6 is 8 black beaver hats, 50*s*	£20	0	0
	No. 7 is 4 black beavers at 55*s*	11	0	0
	No. 8 is 6 white beavers at 60*s*	18	0	0
		£49	0	0
	For the box & canvas & cord		3*s*	0
	12 silver-hafted knives & one odd blade at	8	10*s*	0
	Sum	£65	3*s*	0

My wife has advised me to send thee my silver-hafted knives which I have added to the invoice, so it is now £65 3*s*. I de to sell them; if not, thou mayst keep them thyself at £9.

by one of my neighbors last week £12 for them, or money which is near £10 sterling. So I hope they will yield £10, but sell them as well as thou canst. I have sewed them in canvas and directed to thyself and delivered them to the master.

Particular account as follows; they are warranted sterling silver upon the goldsmith's word.

23 ozs. 8d weight silver, which I can affirm to be right weight, at 5s 2d	£6	1s	0
12 hafts, the workmanship at 3s	1	16s	0
13 blades, 12 in the hafts & putting in cost me		13s	0
Sum	£8	10s	0

Claypoole was confused about the ships, though correct about the captain. George Thorpe had the Endeavour, *which had recently arrived with passengers from Liverpool. It then went on to Barbados, where the Colonial Office records show its arrival in January with Claypoole's barley and hats, and its master's name, George Thorpe. Whoever kept the registrar-general's records when the* Endeavour's *passengers registered made yet another mistake, putting her down as the* Endeavour *of London—a mistake explained perhaps when Claypoole said his son John was writing for the register! The London* Endeavour *was captained by Francis Richardson.*

The Comfort *was a Bristol ship; its master was John Read. Incidentally, Claypoole may have bought those hats in Philadelphia; a Simon Bow had sent three dozen "felts" the previous January on the* Thomas & Anne. *No hats are listed in the port books for Claypoole on the* Concord.

Philadelphia, the 23rd, 11th mo., 1683/84

FRANCIS AND GEORGE ROGERS

The 19th ditto I received yours by way of Maryland, dated 18th, 7ber [September], which was an answer to mine dated 10th, 5th month, which is very uncharitable and is uncivil, and you must needs have been filled with pride and enmity or you could not have vented yourselves so opprobriously. Methinks you might have queried with me first and have had my answer before you had judged me so scornfully, especially considering the matter was so small and did not ~~~ all concern your reputation but your purse only, viz., £30 3s 6d ~~~ for you a little before I came away from London, of which ~~~ 8, I may say justly about £20, these several years, being due to me by George Gamble whose estate George Rogers received to pay his debts withal, the right of which debts appears by the account sent Thomas Wheedon, and again to William End. [Claypoole had been begging End to collect money owed by Wheedon and Gamble for more than a year. Wheedon apparently had been in prison but was released by December 1682, as Claypoole mentioned in his letter of December 30.]

Then for the ten books of S[amuel] F[isher], which I left ready bound with Edward Haistwell to send you per first [ship], I concluded you might easily sell them as you had done the other 10 books, and that they would produce, free of all charges, £7, then there would not be much due to you, in justice and equity not above £3. And the reason I calculate it thus at this time is because I perceive by what you write that you would not pay to William End (to whom I had given a letter of attorney) any part of Gamble's debt. So I have ordered Edward Haistwell to pay him the £7 17s 6d, and that debt of George Gamble's I leave wholly in your hands. So that you would have lost but about £3 by me if we had been all drowned, and that would not have been lost wholly, for you have my son John's bed pillow, bed clothes, and other things that he brought from sea with him, which you pretended for a year and more to send me and never did.

Besides this, I writ you that you might draw the balance upon me in Pennsylvania, which, if you had done, I would have paid your bill, although it had been for £20 more. Also I told you that if you had occasion for money in Pennsylvania, either for land or otherways, I would be willing to transact for you and disburse for you, and the time may come when you may [have] occasion for my friendship, as much as you despise me and scorn me now.

Now farther in answer to the particulars of your letter, as follows: first you charge me with a design to prevent you for drawing a bill upon me by ordering my letter not to be sent till I was gone. I assure you that was not the reason of my keeping that letter and not sending it away per first post, but this was the reason: I was often threatened by Robert Hubbold, who had attached me for £1,000 for Richard Gay's account, and did expect every day a summons to give answer and security to the court. Even at Gravesend, where we stayed till 25, 5th month, I accounted myself in danger, and at Deal also, so that if I had been served with a summons before I had got away, I must have gone back and have lost my passage in that ship.

And then that £30 must have been expended, as occasion had offered, to defend myself by law, which you know is chargeable in England. If you had given me that £30 for procuring the rest [of Gay's debts and the insurance], you had been but grateful, for it was with the hazard of my life and estate that I got it for you, for sometimes the trouble and perplexity of it was so great that it made me sick, and many a sorrowful, care-full hour I had about it, both with the assurers and attachers, and I would have given sometimes £100 of my own money to have been clear of it.

You may find upon your account current that I gave you credit in one sum for that assurance money, £145 7s 11d, which I could have wiped you of every penny and have gained half to myself, or it may be £100 of it, and you should never have known it, if I would have complied with some of the attachers and have let them condemn it. And then I should have been such an one and [as] you represent me to be. But I was conscientiously honest and drove it as far for your interest as I could possibly have done for my own, and you have ill rewarded me.

But I can commit my cause to the Lord, who knows the secrets of all hearts, and that I never designed to cheat you but to pay you and all men what I owe them to 1d. But I assure you I never had a great estate as some did suppose, although my charge was very considerable, and I lived still pretty plentifully, hoping still it would be better, and at last near the time of my coming away I was wronged by several to my loss and hindrance, some hundreds of pounds, especially Robert Stepney, who did most treacherously and wickedly by me, the day before I came from London.

And when I came to Gravesend, if a friend had not helped me, I must have sold some of my goods to provide some necessaries I wanted. So you may see I was not very high, yet not so low spirited and shabby as to intend to cheat you of 1d.

As for my sending no bill on William End, if there was none, which I cannot tell, it was merely forgotten and not purposely omitted. However, I wrote effectually to William End the 10th, 5th month, that he should pay you £10 2s 6d for my account, which I believe he would inform you of the first opportunity.

As for your complaining of me and exposing me as a cheat, and of sneaking, low-spirited, shabby tricks, I value it not, for I have done nothing by you but what is excusable in the sight of God and man. And you cannot expose me to root me out of the hearts of the faithful friends of truth, but you may expose yourselves and manifest your pride and enmity, especially Francis Rogers, for whom I am really troubled that he should be so captivated and in bondage to the spirit of his brother George for outward advantage and conveniency in trade. I must confess when first I read your letter it was a temptation to me, and passion was rising in my mind, and an indignation against you. But then sinking down to the word of God's patience, I was preserved in humility and tenderness, and now I am over it in my spirit and can say the Lord forgive you, especially Francis, who in his circumstances is most to blame [Francis being a recognized minister].

What, could you not remember some kindness that I have done you formerly, how I have been out of cash to serve your occasions above £2,100 at a time, and how I took up your protested bills on Clutterbuck for £1,000 in a few days? And I never wronged you in all the course of our dealing of 1d. So pray reflect upon yourselves that you have been too severe and unkind.

I have stated the account here underneath, as I am willing to make it up with you. And if you can make it appear that I have done you any wrong, I shall readily make you satisfaction. And so I conclude.

Your friend J. C.

Claypoole added to this a copy of the account, going back five years to a bill the Rogerses had not collected from an Irish firm, and which they could have collected from the estate of the recently deceased George Gamble, George Rogers being an executor.

1678

6th mo.	Francis & George Rogers, Dr.			
To balance of Gamble & Wheedon's account then due to me		£17	15s	0
To postage letters since			8s	0
To interest for 5½ years @ 8%		7	19s	0
This to be paid in London		£26	2s	0
To balance of this account to be paid them by Edward Haistwell		£ 5	10s	0
		£31		

1683

5th mo.　　　　　　Francis & George Rogers, Cr.

Per balance of account then due
　　　to them　　　　　　　　　　　　£30　　3s　6d
Per interest of 7 months @ 8%　　　　1　　8s　6d
　　　　　　　　　　　　　　　　　　　‾‾‾‾‾‾‾‾‾‾‾‾‾
　　　　　　　　　　　　　Sum　£31　12s　0

　　　Per J. C. errors excepted.
Philadelphia the 24th, 11th mo., 1683/84

I shall give order to Edward Haistwell to pay you the £5 10s, if
the books be not sent, but if they be I must desire you to sell them
and pay yourselves, and the overplus send me in beef when any ship
comes from Cork hither. I hope, Francis Rogers, thou wilt not think
much to sell 10 books for me, which cost me above £30 printing for
the service of truth.
　　　　　　　　　　　　　　　　　　　　　　　J. C.

You must sent a general release when E. H. pays you the £5 10s.
And pray send my son John's bed and other things hither.

Sent by Jasper [Farmer], going to Maryland and so to Cork.

Since the aforegoing, I met with the conveniency of Thomas
Holme's bill for six pounds which I was very glad of, and I send it
you here enclosed, for I had rather pay you 20s too much than 5s
too little. It is the first bill for six pounds payable at 20 days to yourselves or order in Dublin, the value of me. So now if you have received the books, I must desire you to sell them, and the proceed,
which I hope will be about £7, send me hither in some provision as
above. [A second or duplicate bill would be sent by another ship.]

　　　　　　　　　　　　　　　I am, Your friend J. C.

　　　　　　　　　　Philadelphia, the 1st, 12th mo., 1683/84

WILLIAM END AND DANIEL SAVERY

My 2 last to William End was the 19th, 4th month, and 10th, 5th
month, from London, since have none from you. I perceive by a
letter to me lately from Francis and George Rogers that they will
not pay you any part of that money due to me by Gamble and
˙ eedon, so I have ordered them to keep it all in their own hands
　　　made up accounts with them accordingly. So to answer the
　　　　　to you for money received of Miles Forster, I send you

enclosed Thomas Holme's bill on John Tottenham for £8, payable to yourselves or order in Cork, at 20 days' sight, the value of myself, which will balance accounts between us. Here is a letter of advice with the bill, which also mentions a bill of £6 sent Francis and George Rogers.

Miles Forster is arrived in East Jersey and is there secretary, which is a very proper and profitable place for him, so it's probable now he will pay you those bonds sooner than the times expressed, for I think he is an honest, ingenuous [ingenious?], diligent man.

We are all in health and like the place very well. With my true love to you both, I rest.

Philadelphia, the 1st, 12th mo., 1683/84

Thomas Cooke

My last to thee was the 30th, 4th month, from London, wherein I advised that I had paid the balance of thy account, being £51 14s to John Bawden and John Gardner, since have none from thee. We sailed from Gravesend about the 25, 5th month, and were seven weeks between sight of England and America, and we have all had our health indifferent well and like the place and country, and the blessing of the Lord is our portion, and His presence and love and life we enjoy to our great comfort and satisfaction.

I should have written to thee and other Friends long before this time, but first for above a month, which took up most of the 9th month, we were getting our goods on shore and settling them. And then the 10th and 11th month [December and January] have been so cold that we could seldom write. And the Society's business hath taken up so much of my time, besides the great uncertainty in such opportunities as we had for sending, so that all things considered, I may be very well excused.

I might give thee a large account of the country and divers matters relating thereunto, but thou may have it by word of mouth with more satisfaction from Jasper Farmer, by whom I send this. Only as to provision, till we can raise some of our own, they are and will be dear, viz., pork and beef, salt or fresh, 3d per lb. which is ⅕ value of English money, viz., 15d is an English shilling [instead of 12], and a piece of 8, which cost there 4-5s, goes here for 6s. Butter and cheese by retail, 7½d, by wholesale, 6d at least. I believe Irish beef and pork will yield currently 40s per barrel in quantities. So if thou or any other have a mind to send a small vessel, from 50 to 100 ton with provision hither, [it] may doubtless turn to a very good account. Thou may consign to me if thou pleases. I shall do as well as I can for thee, and for returns for the proceed we have timber and pipe staves.

But the principal thing is pigs of fine silver, which we purchase under 5s per oz. sterling, and sometimes bills of exchange present. I am now sending for London a bill of exchange for a good sum, and near 400 oz. of fine silver. Besides, we shall have tobacco to send, and the goods of the southern plantations, as sugar, cotton, indigo, and ginger, etc., for here are 2 if not 3 ships going to those parts at this time. And there is a sloop with a great many men lies below in the river, bound to fetch silver from the wreck. So that I hope we shall have a trade in a few years, as well as our neighbors as New England, Virginia, Maryland, etc.

We have corn plentiful in the country, though it is now dear here because the river hath been long frozen. Indian corn 3s, wheat 5s, rye 4s per bushel. English goods we sell generally for almost double money, which is 60 to 70% advance. Irish frieze and stockings is a good commodity.

It is now very cold and time is short through multiplicity of other business, so for further advice I must refer, and at present conclude.

Philadelphia, the 1st, 12th mo., 1683/84

ROBERT ROGERS

I intended to write to thee and some other Friends soon after my arrival in America, which was the 1st day of the 8th month, but had not an opportunity for sending and have had a great deal of trouble in settling my goods and family, and for two months together it hath been so cold I could seldom write. I might give thee a large account of the country and trade and matters relating thereunto, but thou may have it with more satisfaction from Jasper Farmer, by whom I send this. Only as to provision, till we can raise some of our own, etc., as mentioned to Thomas Cooke verbatim.

Jasper Farmer had purchased 5,000 acres from Penn and arrived early to have some of it laid out. He returned to Ireland, collected his family and that of his son, and sailed on the Bristol Merchant *in the fall of*

1685—a party of fourteen and nineteen servants. But Jasper and his son Jasper died on the voyage over.

Philadelphia, the 13th, 12th mo., 1683/84

EDWARD HAISTWELL

I have not written to thee since I came hither, nor to anyone in England, having met with many exercises and hindrances, so I have before me to answer, thine 31st, 5th month, 16th, 6th month, and 1st, 8th month. As to Sir St. John Broderick who I perceive complains against me, I shall write him a letter in a little time by another messenger that is to go hence for Maryland and so for England, which may satisfy him, at least vindicate my reputation from his slanders.

Enclosed I send a 1st bill drawn by our governor William Penn upon John Danvas of Corsham [Wiltshire] for £30 sterling payable to George Foreman at 10 days' sight, and by him endorsed to me, and by me to thee, which is to be paid at Philip Ford's. I desire thee receive the said £30 for my account as soon as thou canst, and pay to Thomas Hart £15, and take a receipt in full, I say £15, and pay John Heywood 5s provided he will give a receipt in full. I thought I had ordered it so from Deal. The rest of the £30 and what other money thou hast of mine in thy hands, pay to Edward Mann in part.

I have 4 small wedges of fine silver, near 400 ozs. which I keep for an opportunity to send for England, and have had some of it near 3 months. Also have some beavers, raccoons, musquashes [muskrats] and buck skins to send per first [ship], which shall be for Ralph Weeks in full, Alexander Parker, and Edward Mann. And if I can get another great wedge of silver which I have been treating for, I shall send it to thee and give order for goods to be sent me.

Here is tobacco, skins, silver, pipe staves, and timber, to be had for returns for England, and whale oil and bone. Our fishermen have taken 4 or 5 whales already in the Bay and are like to continue fishing till the end of the next month which will be the best time, and there is hopes of getting a great many.

If thou sends pieces of 8, may be a very good commodity, and I can return thee fine silver, which we buy here for a piece of 8 and 4d sterling per oz., and may be worth in England from 5s 6d to 5s 9d per oz. There is a vessel going out of the river that has lain here all this winter, with about 100 men bound for the wreck to fetch silver, from whence we have had a great quantity. There may be expectation of bringing £20,000 or £30,000 worth.

I had a very abusive letter from Francis and George Rogers, to which I have sent them an answer directly for Ireland, and a bill of exchange for the balance of their account, drawn by Thomas Holme, so thou must not send the books if not already sent. But if so, have ordered them to return me the proceed in some provisions. I have assigned them the whole money of Gamble and Wheedon; have sent William End and Daniel Savery a bill also, to balance their account. I am to have something from Samuel Claridge, which when thou writes to him, put him in mind of it, and further I have no account depending with anyone in Ireland.

Remember mine and my wife's dear love to G[eorge] F[ox], A[lexander] P[arker] and wife [Prudence], G[eorge] W[hitehead] and wife [Anne]; must write to them all and to many other friends, as to Thomas Hart, John Osgood, Philip Ford, William Sherlow, John Sweetapple, John Bawden, Edward Mann, Thomas Glover, John Wallis, William Puvrier, J[ames] Hall, R[ichard] Gawthorn, to whom remember me particularly, and to our maids and Kingston friends, John Rous and wife [George Fox's stepdaughter and her husband].

Have sent considerable effects to my brother Edward at Barbados and shall send more when opportunity presents. . . . My time is expired so must conclude, though have many things to write.

Thy loving friend.

Direct and seal the enclosed.

The next letter, to Christopher Taylor, ex-schoolmaster and an old friend of both Penn and Claypoole, is interesting because it is James's first attempt to secure a position he very much desired and one which he held at the end of his life. The post of registrar-general was a lucrative one, but the post of deputy, which was little more than a clerk, was not.

Philadelphia, 12th, 12th mo., 1683/84

DEAR FRIEND CHRISTOPHER TAYLOR

Concerning my deputation from thee to serve in the register office, etc., I have considered that it will not be for the credit of the governor [Penn] nor neither of us for me to act as a deputy in that which is but the business of one man. Neither is there any need of a deputy, but by reason of thy removing from hence where the office must be kept. And this way of getting grants for offices and putting in deputies for a share of the gain may be an ill precedent and made use of to the people's wrong in times to come, which we must be careful of for truth's honor and our own. And further I believe the governor would not have conferred that office upon thee had he expected thou wouldst have removed from hence. So this I have to propose, that thou consent, in answer to this, to let me (if the governor please to grant it) have a patent for the office in my own name, and I will sign and seal to thee any obligation that is proper, to pay to thee the ⅓ part of the profit of the said office, which, with my true love to thee and thy wife.

I desire thee let the bearer, Isaac Pearson, the governor's smith, have as many coals as the shallop will carry, without measuring, and for what is or will be farther measured, I hope thou wilt keep some small account, and I shall serve thee in a greater matter. Let the coals now to be sent be out of the first heap if there be enough.

I do not propose to have a patent for the office for any advantage or profit beyond what I [would] have in being thy deputy, for I desire but ⅔ as above but [only] to prevent reflections which has been grossly given already in public. Neither do I insist upon it to have the office myself, but leave it to thee to settle any other in it if thou please. For as a deputy I am not, will not serve.

Philadelphia, 24th, 12th mo., 1683/84

Dear Friend Gawen Lawrie

I was very glad to hear of thy safe arrival in East Jersey and should have written to thee by William Haige [Lawrie's son-in-law], but about the time of his going hence I had business in hand that required necessity of dispatch, and sometimes it falls out so here that one has not an hour to spare in several days. But I hope when this summer and the next winter is past, we shall have more rest and quietness.

I long to see thee and to have some discourse with thee, which to attain I must break through difficulties and lay aside my business, and

I think it will not be many weeks first, the weather being also encouraging. I have often thought it would have been as a blessing and comfort to us, if it had been the will of the Lord to have cast our lots near together in this part of the world, that we might have enjoyed the benefit of thy good society and counsel here, as we have in our native country, which has been an advantage to us both inwardly and outwardly. However, I hope we shall still live in that blessed union and fellowship of the gospel and heavenly love, that we may be always ready and willing to lend a helping hand in time of need.

Since we came from England as well as before, the Lord our God has been with us and blessed us and preserved us through many trials and dangers. We had a comfortable passage, and the presence of the Lord was with us and we were kept in the savor of life, so that our conversation was such as becomes the gospel and answered the witness of God in all people. After we lost sight of England, that day 7 weeks, we got sight of American land, and the 1st, 8th month (which was the month I was born in just 49 year), I went ashore in Pennsylvania. About the 10th we came to this place staying on board 7 or 8 days to get our goods out of the ship.

We had before we came here the carcass of a house finished, 40 foot long and 20 broad, with a cellar, and we have added 20 foot to it and have been from that day to this fitting it to dwell in. My lot proves to be one of the best in the town, having 102 foot to the river and 396 long, and about 1¼ acre in the High Street [Market St.]. There is a swamp runs by the side of my lot [by the Dock Creek] that with a small charge might be made navigable and a brave harbor for sloops and small ships.

Here are divers ways to improve a stock of £1,000 or £2,000 to very great advantage. But I am not for striving or making haste to be rich, but my intent and desire is to go on quietly and moderately and to have a regard to the Lord in all my ways and proceedings; and principally and above all to seek the kingdom of God and the righteousness thereof, that His plantation work may go on as well as ours, that righteousness may run down like a stream, and peace and truth may kiss each other, that we may grow as trees of righteousness, the planting of the Lord, and bring forth fruit to His praise.

We have had our share of trials and troubles here, but the Lord has been with us and comforted us with His presence and life and power, and the joy of His salvation, so that our consolation has abounded and far exceeded our troubles, so that we have no cause to repent our coming hither but to bless the Lord for His lending hand and counsel. We have here very precious heavenly Meetings, and many Friends have a blessed living testimony, and we are united in sincere love, so that we have the mark upon us of the disciples of Christ Jesus.

William Penn, our governor, has been exceeding kind and is so still to me and my family as if we were his nearest relations. And I hope his love will continue and I know it will, as we abide in Christ Jesus, the heavenly vine, the root of life from whom we receive nourishment, for that is the spring and fountain of the everlasting love and fellowship. Truly he [Penn] is very precious in his testimony and conversation, and we may be sure he takes counsel of the Lord, for there is much of the wisdom that is from above manifest in his conduct and management of affairs here, by which he is made a fit instrument in the hand of the Lord for the work and service he is called to, and I wish with all my heart that all the governors upon the earth were such as he is.

I have heard that thou art chosen by the Proprietors and come over to be governor of East Jersey, which is well and may be a blessing both to thee and the people if thou stands in God's counsel and acts in His wisdom. Otherwise high places are slippery, and more snares attends him that governs than him that suffers. So my dear friend, my desire is that thou mayst walk in wisdom's path and wait at the posts of her gates, that she may fill thy treasury. And then thou wilt be the people's treasure and have their hearts, and then it will be easy to govern and righteousness will establish your government. I know thou art grave and solid and wise and patient, having a command of thy own spirit and many other qualifications and endowments fit for a governor. Yet all will not do without the pure wisdom that is from above and a meek and a quiet spirit which is of great price with the Lord, for the meek He guides in judgment and He teaches the humble His ways.

I have lately seen a letter or a copy of one in thy name, disowning Samuel Jennings and charging him with breaking his allegiance to the king and betraying his trust with Edward Byllinge, and acting contrary to the principles of truth, and comparing him to plotters and subverters of government, etc., ordering the said charge to be published, which I did admire at and was much grieved to see, and could wish it had been deferred till thou and he had discoursed together. And that had been gospel order, and it's possible he might have given thee such satisfaction as to have prevented this public disowning, or thou mightst have convinced him of his error (if he be wrong) and brought him to repentance, and so have saved him. Which is better than to destroy, as Christ Jesus came not to destroy men's lives but to save them.

For my part when I think of it, I am grieved and dread the consequence of it how the enemies of truth and of the prosperity of these new plantations will open their mouths against us and say, "What! are these Quakers? Now they are tried with government, they rise up against one another to destroy one another." For it seems as if thou wouldst induce the people to disown his [Jennings'] power as being illegal and expose him to the severity of the law as a traitor against the king, and to be disowned by Friends as a treacherous person that acts against the principles of truth, and all this from reports and seeing the acts of their Assembly, without speaking with him or writing to him.

For my part, except I had seen it, I could not have believed that a man of thy wisdom and moderation, that knows the practice and order of the gospel in such cases, should give such a rash judgment. But I am afraid thou hast adhered to the counsel of some that are rotten-hearted and would lead thee into the snares of death, as they have done their own souls. Yet I am in hopes that when this business comes to be debated before solid, weighty Friends, and either thee or he is sensible of your error, there will be a condescending, and the breach healed and not made wider. For I would not have the hand of the Lord go against either of you, for I love you both, and my desire to the Lord is that you may be preserved and be a blessing to the people over whom you govern.

I and my wife and 8 children are all at this place in good health and so have been mostly since we came. John, my eldest, writes for the register, James is bookkeeper to the Society. So with mine and my wife's dear love in the truth to thee, I rest

Thy endeared friend.

Samuel Jennings, the former governor of New Jersey, believed elective power was for the people, all the people, as stated in the original

Concessions and Agreements *written to induce immigration. Lawrie would have put government into the hands of the big landowners and officeholders appointed by the king, or a powerful group in England. It was a bitter dispute that went on for years.*

Jennings, Thomas Budd of New Jersey, and a friend were on their way through Philadelphia to Maryland to take ship for England and to argue the case before George Fox, Edward Byllinge, and a group of powerful Friends. Lawrie apparently stated his case in a tactless letter, for that October Penn wrote from Sussex: "G. Lowry has writt a most wicked letter about West Jersey business against me, what shall I say of such men [?] I leave them to the just Judge and pray they may repent" (letter in the Huntington Library).

Philadelphia, the 4th, 2nd mo., 1684

EDWARD HAISTWELL

My last to thee was the 13th, 12th month, whereof enclosed is copy. Then sent a bill for £30; this is the 2nd bill [a duplicate of the first]. I have through multiplicity of business and being absent from home lost some opportunities of sending my silver and skins, but now I hope I shall get them away by Thomas Budd and some other Friends who are to come here from Burlington to go for Maryland and so by shipping for London.

Just now is come to hand thine of 11th, 9th month, per Captain [John] Purvis [master, *Duke of York*] and one for James. I observe thou hadst received £4 18s debenture money of the wine, which is well, and paid the cheesemonger, etc. I wish thou hadst paid John Heywood 5s, which is all I owe him, for he writes peevishly about it. But I remember very well that [I] offered him the money divers times if he would take what was due to him, which he refused, and in his letter he writes as if I was run away in his debt. So pay him 5s and take his receipt in full, and I have done with him.

I have been three weeks from home, about 150 miles, of where they take the whales. They took 2 while I was there. They had killed about 12 in all and lost 3 of them, and they intend to stay till the end of this month and may expect to get 5 or 6 more. They fish for the Society but must be paid the market price for ⅔ of the oil and bone, besides some other charges we are at, so that we are like to get no great matter by it this time. This is the first year of their fish-

[239]

ing, and they were not provided with necessaries in time, else they might have made £100 each man, here being great plenty of whales and very easy to take them.

Here is also abundance of sturgeon and other fish. Many things I should write largely of but have not time nor opportunity, being perplexed with the Society's business far beyond what ever I expected, or would have undertook if I had known it, for 3 times my salary. I hope it will be better quickly, for the president [Nicholas More] has laid down his place, and we are to have a general court this month. I cannot write to the committee or council there [in London] till our affairs [are] in better order, and I have more leisure.

The 29th, 5th mo., 1684

Since the above written, which I missed the opportunity of sending, I have received thine of the 2nd, 1st month, the chief import of which is an account of the wonderful frost, etc., and great persecution throughout England, which we are sorry to hear, but satisfied in this, that the Lord will preserve in the time of trial all that trust in Him, and reward them many fold for all their sufferings, that are faithful to Him.

As for Sir St. John Broderick defaming of me, which I perceive he has done to Friends and others, pray tell him I take it very unkindly and did not expect it from him. He might consider how I accommodated him with great sums of money by exchange, £400 or £500 at a time when none else would, to his great conveniency and my hazard, for if he had died in the interim I believe I had lost it every penny. And then his not paying the bills in divers months after they were due, whereby I lost the profit of one return by exchange if not two, which might have been double what I charge him for interest. It is true Francis and George Rogers winked at it to keep in his favor or for some private advantage, but there is no reason or equity that I should lose it. Then for the £20 I charged him with in a former account—but in the first account I gave his sons, it was omitted by reason the goldsmith paid it, and I had not accounted with the goldsmith and had paid divers sums without receipts—that £20 being omitted he denied it and I could not prove it, so I said little of it, and rather than I would have gone to law with him, I would have lost it. But I believe in my conscience he had it, and it is plain the goldsmith chargeth me with it. And of this there is £14 3s 8d due to me, which it is like he will never pay.

As for the £40 he says was charged in a former [bill], if he can make that appear, I will pay him £60 for it. But I have examined the account and find most certainly that it is not charged twice. Satisfy G[eorge] F[ox] and J[ohn] O[sgood] and other Friends in this case, where he has scandalized me.

Enclosed I send thee an invoice of 4 hhds. and 1 bale furs, and 330¼ ozs. silver, which together amounts to £172 6s 4d and the £30 bill of exchange makes £202 6s 4d, whereof I desire thee to pay Thomas Hart £15, Ralph Weeks £42, provided I may have a discharge in full, Alexander Parker £50, Thomas Glover £53, and take up my bond and send it me canceled, and the rest to Edward Mann, which I hope may be £40.

The silver comes to me a great deal finer than sterling, therefore I ⸺ it at 5½s per oz. and hope it may yield more, but sell it as well ⸺ canst, as also the skins and furs, and pay John Heywood 5s ⸺ e no money else to any in England, but to John Osgood ⸺ Sherlow, which I shall take care to pay in a little time, ⸺ o Edward Mann.

⸺ trust most what we sell, and people will not pay ⸺ Society's treasurer [Ralph Withers], before I ⸺ d sold almost all their goods for great profit ⸺ nding out to this day. So that we have ⸺ w must sue people at law or be ⸺ going and are setting up a saw the first good opportunity 3 firkins of the best-keeping butter and 5 cwt. of Cheshire cheese and 2 firkins soap. Or if the cheesemonger in Whitechapel, or Thomas Cooper, will send me a ton or two of cheese and 10 or 12 firkins of butter, I shall make him returns in a little time to his content; or if anyone will send any commodities that may be proper, as linen, serges, crepe, and Bengal [piece goods from India], and other slight stuffs. But send no shoes, gloves, stockings, nor hats, nor wine of any sort. But if thou wilt send 10 or 20 barrels mum, iron bound, may turn well to account.

For my part, I am so weary of the Society's business that I will get clear as soon as I can, and then I shall be more capable to serve myself and others. Deliver the enclosed. I should write to divers and will if I have time. If not, thou must excuse me to them. I have above £800 owing me in America, but it comes in very slowly.

Tell John Turner [and] John Sweetapple about their land, that they can have no benefit of it till they either come or send, or others that have bought land. Send no window glass nor iron is much wanted, and nails very much, viz., *6d*, *8d* ton of each sort would quickly sell, I conclude.

The ironmonger that lives by John Corke would ton of sorted pots and have trusted me for the re do it, let me have a ton per first and 20 small ¼ cwt. to 5 cwt., and 1 or two for 10 cwt. And 2 or 3 doz. brass cocks of several s

Tell Richard Gawthorn I take how to digest it, that which

MASTERS AND THEIR SHIPS MENTIONED BY CLAYPOOLE

[*From the London Port Books, chiefly E 190/99/1 (1681), E 190/109/1 (1682), and E 190/115/1 (1683); and Colonial Office Records, CO/33/13 and CO/33/14 and the appropriate folios bound up in these volumes, at the Public Record Office, London. Nearly all of these ships sailed from London.*]

Alcock, Maskolin, *Increase*, to Ireland, also Barbados.

Archer, Valentine, *Unity*, to Germany, 1681 (shipwrecked?).

Arnold, Thomas, *Jeffrey* or *Geoffrey*, 500 tons, to Pennsylvania, 1682; before that, the *Thomas & Anne*.

Aubenny, Thomas, *Experiment*, 180 tons, 22 guns, to Barbados.

Bagg, Roger, *Bachelor*, 170 tons, to West Indies.

Ball, Joseph and James, *Hope*, 200 tons, 21 guns, to New England and Barbados.

Barrett, Thomas, *Horne* or *Herne*, to New England and New York.

Beeding, William, *Friendship*, also the *Mary*, formerly the *Conclusion*, all to Barbados.

Bendix, Paul, *Love*, to Germany; later the *Neptune*.

Bennett, Elisha, *Elizabeth & Mary*, 60 tons, 5 guns, to New York and New Jersey (Perth Amboy).

Blowers, Humphrey, *William & John*, to the Canary Islands.

Bruce, Thomas, *Dove*, usually to Germany.

Churchwood, Nicholas, *John of London*, 75 tons, to Barbados, 1681.

Clark, Benjamin, *Speedwell*, to Bruges; later to West Indies.

Clark, Peter, *Society*, to New England.

Cock, Allan, *Experiment*; alternate captain with Aubenny or perhaps of another ship of the same name.

Cooper, Thomas, *Unicorn*, 300 tons, Bristol to Virginia and Pennsylvania.

Crompton, John, *Lyon of Liverpool*, 90 tons.

Crop, James, *Biscay Merchant*, to West Indies.

Cundy, William, *Adventure*, to New England.

Cutter, William, *Phoenix*, to Hamburg, 1681, 1682.

Daniel, Edward, *Biscay Merchant*; possibly alternated with Crop.

Davies, Robert, *Elizabeth*, to Ireland; the usual captain was Thomas Gouldney.

Dietien (Detjen, Datyne), Daniel, *St. Peter*, to Germany.

Dymond (Diamond), Richard, *Amity*, 240 tons, 12 guns, to Barbados and Pennsylvania; there were several *Amity*'s.

East, William, *Hester & Hannah*, to Pennsylvania, 1682; in 1684 he had the *Gulielma*.

Edwards, David, *Thomas & Susan*, to New York and New England.

Edwards, Thomas, *Supply*, to New York and New England.

Elsers, Herman, *Clarke*, to Germany, 1681.

Emberley, William, *Prosperous*, 70 tons; sometimes quoted as 100 tons, 4 guns; to Barbados.

Foy, John, *Dolphin*, to New England and New York.

Gadsden, Thomas and John, *Elizabeth & Mary* (or *Mary & Elizabeth*), to West Indies and Virginia.

Gouldney, Thomas, *Elizabeth*, to Cork and Dublin.

Greenway, Robert, *Welcome*, 284 tons, to Pennsylvania and Barbados; previously Greenway had the *Bachelor's Delight*.

Groome (Groom), Samuel, Jr., *Globe*, to New York and Virginia, 1682.

Grove, Benjamin, *Amity*; he died in 1680 or 1681.

Harding, John, *Carolina*, 200 tons, to Barbados.

Hill, John, *James & Mary*, to Barbados.

Hindmer, William, *Loving Friend*, 160 tons, 8 guns, to Hamburg.

Howard, Christopher, *Deborah*, to Dublin.

Hudson, Emmanuel, *Patience*, 150 tons, 20 guns, to Barbados.

Hudson, Thomas, *Elizabeth Ann & Catherine*, 250 tons, to Barbados and Pennsylvania, formerly master of the *Patience*.

Hull (Hall), John, *Orange Tree*, 200 tons, to Barbados.

Hume, Edward, *Mary*, to Hamburg, also Bordeaux.

Jeffries (Jeffreys), William, *Concord*, 450 or 500 tons, 40 guns, to Pennsylvania, 1683.

Jewell, John, *Expedition*, 100 tons, to Barbados.

Leffield (Sheffield?), John, *Guannabow*, 350 tons, 20 guns, to West Indies.

Lock, Thomas, *Samuel*, to Lisbon, 1683.

Lurting, Thomas, *Owner's Adventure*, Ireland to New Jersey, 1681.

Manbey (Manby), James, *Arabella*, 80 tons, 4 guns, to Barbados.

Newham, Christopher, *Employment*, 150 tons, to Barbados.

Place, John, *Priscilla*, alternated with Cundy, to New England and Barbados.

Purvis, George and John, *Baltimore* and *Duke of York*, usually to Virginia.

Rawlings, John, *Lark*, to Hamburg.

Read, John, *Comfort*, of Bristol, 200 tons, to Pennsylvania.

Richardson, Francis, *Endeavour*, of London, 120 tons, to New York; confused with the Liverpool *Endeavour*, George Thorpe, master.

Index

Scot, Edmund or Edward, *Hare*, to Barbados, later the *Adventure*.

Scotting, Robert, *Katherine*, usually quoted as 170 tons, 14 guns, 18 men, to Barbados.

Sheffield, John. See Leffield

Simpson, Thomas, *Swallow*, to Hamburg, Norway, and Bordeaux. The frigate *Swallow*, probable master Robert Griffith, 300 tons, 30 guns, went to Lisbon.

Singleton, Thomas, *Thomas & Anne*, to Pennsylvania, New Jersey, and New York, 1682, 1683.

Smith, Henry, *John & Sarah*, 100 tons, to Pennsylvania, 1682.

Stepney, Robert, *Endeavour*; alternate captain with Richardson or of another ship called *Endeavour*.

Strong, William, *Broderick*, to Ireland and the Canaries.

Strutt, John and James, (old) *Concord*, 200 tons, 12 guns, to Barbados.

Summers, Thomas, *Blessing*, to Ireland; later the *Betty*.

Tendall, John, *John's Endeavour*, to Exeter.

Thorpe, George, *Endeavour*, 60 tons, often confused with the *Endeavour* of London; Thorpe brought West Country people to Philadelphia from Liverpool.

Thorpe, Henry, *Anne & Ellen*, coastal ship to Liverpool.

Vogelsang, Wilkin, *Vogelsang*, to Germany; called the *Singing Bird* in the port books.

Wakeling, William, *Merchant's Delight*, to Hamburg.

Wasey, Joseph, *Grayhound*, 150 tons, to Barbados and New Jersey; in the summer of 1683, Wasey changed to the 200-ton *America*.

Witheridge, John or George, *Pelican*, 150 tons, to Barbados.

Young, John or James, *John's Goodwill*, to Amsterdam.

Heush, Michael, 214
Heywood, Anthony, 63
Heywood, John, 66, 149, 166, 233, 241
Hicks, Thomas, 36, 37
Hill, John, 161
Hinchman, Thomas, 78, 183
Hindmer, William, 135, 137, 140, 145
Hinton, William, 187, 201, 207, 220
Hirst, John, 41
Historical Society of Pennsylvania, 3, 23
Hodges, William, 52
Hodgson, John, 46, 99, 107, 114; letter to, 87
Holcombe, Richard, letter to, 29
Holled, Mrs. Jeremiah. *See* Claypoole, Dorothy
Holme, Thomas, 8, 100-101, 104, 107, 109, 118, 151, 153, 180, 204, 230, 231, 234
Holt, Edmund, 28, 64, 84, 89, 132, 200
Hope, 27, 109
Horne (or *Herne*), 117
Howard, Christopher, 96
Howard, Lord William, 39
Howell, William, 61
Hubbold, Robert, 147, 220, 227
Hudson, Emmanuel, 48, 119
Hudson, Thomas, 46, 48, 49, 50, 59, 140
Hull, John, 49, 59, 126, 136, 139, 155, 184
Hume, Edward, 90, 108

Increase, 33, 35, 102, 136

Jacobson, Theodore, 28, 86, 96, 221
James, Ann, 6
James & Mary, 161
Jarvis, Thomas, 63
Jeffrey, 13n, 140, 150, 154, 194, 219, 222
Jeffries, William, 12, 17, 178, 189, 196, 205, 213, 215, 217, 220
Jennings, Samuel, 237, 238, 239
Jersey, East, 141, 143, 144, 146, 148, 149, 150, 157, 158, 170, 192, 206, 231, 235, 237. *See also* New Jersey
Jersey, West, 239. *See also* Jersey, East, *and* New Jersey
Jewell, John, 119
John & Sarah, 67
John of London, 164
John's Endeavour, 116
John's Goodwill, 48
Jones, Charles, Jr., 70, 71, 72
Jones, Griffith, 19, 118
Jones, John, 79, 163
Jones, Theodore, 142

Katherine, 40, 139
Keating, John, 124

Keith, George, 15, 123-124, 198
Kent, Richard, 196
Keurlis, Peter, 222
King, Walter, 118
Kunders, Thones, 222

Langly, Peter, 217
Lark, 32
Lathum, John, 145
Lawrie, Gawen, 75, 81, 84, 177, 239; letter to, 235-238
Leffield (Sheffield?), John, 99
Lensen, Jan, 222
Lewger, William, 41, 59, 78, 109, 127, 155, 156, 224
Lloyd, Thomas, 20
Lock, Thomas, 122
Locke, John, 183
Loddington, William, 107, 108
Lodge, Daniel, 121, 129
Lodge, Daniel, & Company, letters to, 137, 188
Lodge, Robert, 34, 35, 206
Lodge family, 122
Londonderry, fourth Earl of. *See* Ridgeway, Robert
London Stone, 5, 53, 95, 213
Love, 111
Loveday, John, 154, 155
Loveday, Thomas, 155; letter to, 154
Loveday, William, 154, 155
Loving Friend, 137, 140
Lumbard, Paul, 196
Lurting, Thomas, 52, 215, 216
Luykens, Jan, 222
Lyon of Liverpool, 13n, 108, 201

Manbey, James, 220, 222
Mann, Edward, 233, 234, 241
Markwerk, 32
Marriott, Robert, 49
Marshall, Charles, letter to, 91
Martin, Isaac, 118
Martin, Joseph, 118
Marvell, Andrew, 183
Mary, 90, 108
Mary & Elizabeth, 193. *See also* Elizabeth & Mary
Masland, Hugh, 199, 210, 214, 222; letter to, 209
Mason, John, 64, 116, 193; letters to, 88-89, 169
Matson, Margaret, 14
Mauks (or Macks), Hans Christopher, 35, 59, 82, 96, 103, 125, 132, 137, 155, 159; letter to, 108
Mead, William, 74